Shakespeare, Sex and the Print Revolution

Shakespeare, Sex and the Print Revolution

GORDON WILLIAMS

ATHLONE

London & Atlantic Highlands, NJ

First published 1996 by
THE ATHLONE PRESS LTD
1 Park Drive, London NW11 7SG
and 165 First Avenue,
Atlantic Highlands, NJ 07716

British Library Cataloguing in Publication Data
*A catalogue record for this book is available
from the British Library*

ISBN 0 485 11495 X hb
0 485 12121 2 pb

Library of Congress Cataloging-in-Publication Data
Williams, Gordon, 1935–
    Shakespeare, sex, and the print revolution / Gordon Williams.
        p. cm.
    Includes bibliographical references (p.) and index.
    ISBN 0-485-11495-X (hb). -- ISBN 0-485-12121-2 (pb)
    1. Shakespeare, William, 1564–1616--Criticism, Textual. 2.
Erotic literature--Publishing--England--History--17th century.
3. Erotic literature--Censorship--England--History--17th century.
4. Shakespeare, William, 1564–1616--Stage history--To 1625.
5. Erotic literature, English--Criticism, Textual. 6. Shakespeare, William, 1564–1616--Publishers. 7. Shakespeare, William,
1564–1616--Censorship.
8. Printing--England--History--17th century.
9. Theater--England--History--17th century. 10. Sex in the
theater. 11. Sex in literature. I. Title.
PR3071.W49   1996
822.3'3--dc20   95-31871
                                                                  CIP

Typeset by
Bibloset

Printed and bound in Great Britain by
the University Press, Cambridge

To Rose and Katrine

Contents

Preface

This examination of sex in Shakespeare results in part from a long-standing interest in early modern sexual usage which has already spawned *A Dictionary of Sexual Language and Imagery in Shakespearean and Stuart Literature* (Athlone, 1994). But the present book has also grown out of my experience of teaching a Renaissance component in a Literature in History course at the University of Wales, Lampeter. This course has been very much concerned with the relationship between late Elizabethan literature and the large movements of political and cultural change which had been taking place during the previous hundred years. A momentous factor in this change is print, which transformed the sixteenth century just as the silicon chip has transformed the late twentieth. The one prompted the diffusion of literacy and the modern notion of authorship: the other has produced a computer literacy which offers a challenge to that notion.

However, the theatre occupies an anomalous position since its scripts are not in the first place literature. Though there is a dialectical relationship between the content of printed and staged works in the reign of Elizabeth, the latter are not designed for reading; yet paradoxically our knowledge of Elizabethan plays depends almost entirely on printed texts. Shakespeare himself, who presents a striking example since his modern reputation is so bound up with the circumstance of print, has left little evidence beyond what was posthumously preserved through the agency of the press.

Although my concern is not primarily bibliographical, that Shakespeare's theatrical scripts have been mediated through printed versions of varying reliability means that recognizing the nature of the text under scrutiny has been a necessary starting point. That I have reached a finishing point is in no small measure due to my wife, with whom I have engaged in critical dialogue throughout the period of writing.

A NOTE ON THE TEXT REFERENCES
Works cited in abbreviated form in the text may be found in the Select Bibliography.

Introduction

Our immediate concern, the sexual element in Shakespeare's work and its negotiations with power, is one tense with oppositions. It is a tension largely induced by one of the most momentous circumstances of the sixteenth century. For, like everything else in the period, Shakespeare's work owes much of its shape to the fact that this was the first century of popular print.

In arguing for the continuity between late medieval popular drama and the Elizabethan stage, Robert Weimann takes the view that the miracle play's 'channels were not primarily verbal'.[1] That probably remains true for the theatre in Shakespeare's day, which plainly asserted its vitality in various complex ways; but there is no denying the importance of the linguistic component. Shakespeare himself provides ample demonstration, not least in his deployment of sexual expression. It may be asked whether print actually boosted the extent of sexual vocabulary or merely made it more visible. But given the general language explosion – in the sixteenth century the language almost doubled itself from foreign sources – it is reasonable to suppose that the sexual vocabulary grew in line with the rest. One voice to be raised which had been muted for centuries was that of pagan enthusiasm, a glorying in the sensual life. A whole new world of sexuality was explored in language lifted from the geographers or other sources embodying a suitably awakened sense of wonder or excitement. And in this post–print conflation less approving notes were also to be heard.

But language is first of all oral, and to emphasize the importance of print for Shakespeare's theatre is not to underplay the significance of the oral tradition. Rather, it is to recognize the theatre's occupancy of a rich border country where the two cultures met. It has been established that even the rituals of informal punishment and pleasure which D.E. Underdown dubs 'street theatre' were clearly marked by growing literacy (a process intimately involved with an advancing print culture). He observes a correspondence between the degree of elaboration reached by these rituals and the literacy level of the participants.[2] Hence the development of a highly sophisticated formal theatre at the centre where print culture had taken most vigorous hold is hardly surprising; for the Elizabethan theatre is an obvious, if indirect, beneficiary of that culture. Its rapid development in the late years of the reign parallels that of woodcut in South Germany following the advent of print. There too, the medium was not new; but it was the energy released by the printing press which so dramatically expanded its scope and sophistication. By the start of the sixteenth century, it was exhibiting a vernacular vigour remarkably similar to that which transformed the Elizabethan theatre later on. And in both cases the medium was non–literary, one which was accessible to literate and non–literate alike.

That Shakespeare's art is for the most part non–literary (i.e. theatrical) makes no difference: Elizabethan theatrical writing is everywhere complicated and compromised by the impact of print on oral culture. The contradictory and dialectical nature of his drama is part of that ferment of debate released through the agency of print when it broke Roman Catholic monopoly of thought. No better paradigm offers than the theatre script, meeting ground for written and oral languages, though the status of the Shakespearean script is further complicated by its elevation into literary text. Having been granted an existence apart from the ephemeral production, it could be at once retrieved for popular art and positioned within the new élitism of print. The professionalizing of the theatre was itself a consequence of print, and so of course were the proliferating controls of censorship. Shakespeare's activity is split by the ideological demands of the state and the subversive nature of poetry; but he is also Janus embodiment of that historical shift from fluidity to fixation which was taking place during his career.

Part I addresses some of these factors. It begins by considering Shakespeare's reputation and specifically the seventeenth–century impact of his erotic imagery and stage bawdry. There follow chapters on the internal constraints and the external pressures which helped to shape his work. The former means essentially the author–company relationship which operated in the Elizabethan theatre. That relationship involves notably controversial questions of rewriting and improvisation, both particularly germane to a consideration of sexual usage. The most immediate external factor was censorship, its encroachments on sexual expression being an index to the kinds of restriction placed on ideas. The best evidence of how censorship contoured sexual use is non–Shakespearean; but it can still provide valuable insight into the limits within which he worked, and the kind of script–modifications likely to be enforced. Scrutiny of some of Shakespeare's sexual language is designed not only to illustrate patterns of evasion but to open up an issue which is explored further in Parts II and III. Thus he is caught up in the great expansion of language; and the sexual vocabulary, like other linguistic areas, was absorbing many new terms from a variety of sources. New words entail fresh ways of seeing the activity to which they are applied. Caught up in shifting perceptions is the activity of writing itself; Part I concludes with a look at this, together with some of the strategies which it fostered. The new availability of information made possible by print focused anxiety in the old terms of forbidden knowledge. So weighty was the symbolism that merely to open a new book might imply mystery, danger, even sexual discovery. Nor was it only the reader who was implicated in a quasi–sexual activity; a theatrical opening night could be sexual revelation in a world of abruptly self–conscious voyeurs.

Texts receive more sustained discussion in Parts II and III; Part II looks at works rooted in a long–established literary culture, while Part III groups together plays addressing socio–domestic issues. The former allows Shakespeare to gratify a taste for settings in the ancient Mediterranean world which spanned his writing career. Sometimes he plays against the expectations of educated readers; at other times he is mediating between a print culture and a substantially illiterate audience. But whichever direction he takes, these classical settings provide some of Shakespeare's major sexual figures, figures established as archetypes over the centuries but which were now powerfully, in some respects definitively, reworked. Thus his Cleopatra represents not only the sexual temptress but a freshly individual brand of sexuality.

Part III takes account of the fact that such redefinitions of sexuality were achieved by means other than these figures of antiquity. As important as fresh readings of the ancients in shaping people's ways of regarding sex were the multitude of moral and devotional books, not least the newly accessible Bible, which address the issue. Dramatizations of woman's social role provide the focus of this third part. Plays are discussed as they observe not only marital traumas but the economic problems of the brothel; not only patterns of heterosexual relationship but that web of emotional and practical support which women provide for one another. Behind these plays is no canon of classical texts but the great socio–sexual debate, running for centuries but formalized and energized by print on a scale impossible in an oral culture. Indeed, the scale is such that it goes beyond a quantitative to become a qualitative change; and Shakespeare's sexual language and preoccupations are as sensitive a gauge of such change as we have.

PART I
Shakespearean Images and the Paradox of Print

1

The Shakespearean Reputation

In the *Sunday Times* (17 June 1993), John Peter gratefully reviewed David Thacker's Stratford production of *The Merchant of Venice* for laying 'to rest the venerable nonsense that this is an anti-semitic play'. He poses another touchy issue when adding that 'it has no more to do with Jewishness than Othello has with blackness'. Yet in an adjoining article, the director confesses that he has had to perform a few gyrations in order to bring the play into line with current sensibilities, coming 'to the conclusion that in the light of 20th-century experience, Shakespeare would be likely to withdraw permission for the play to be performed in its present form'. He is sufficiently confident about this that he can reconcile his approach with the claim that he is 'against rewriting Shakespeare'. This is not 'manipulating or distorting his plays to suit current tastes or particular ideologies', but getting into the dramatist's mind to see what shifts a reincarnated Shakespeare would wish to introduce for the modern audience. He is not to be taken as a playwright who opens up a complexity of Elizabethan attitudes, antisemitism and all, but is stuck with the responsibility first thrust on him by Jonson in a commendatory poem prefacing the 1623 folio of the plays: 'He was not of an age, but for all time!' Given such a responsibility, it would be no escape route to suggest that the racism in *Merchant* is not endorsed by the dramatist. Once accept that Shylock's Jewishness is an issue and Shakespeare must be culpable for supplying the antisemite with such powerful ammunition; once concede culpability on the racist front and the cherished idea of Shakespeare as source of revelation for our own troubled times begins to sicken.

In that same commendatory poem, Jonson compares Shakespeare to some of the ancient dramatists, thereby affirming the immortality which playwriting might confer. Elizabethan dramatists enjoyed little prestige for their work; even the printed plays were regarded as ephemeral, as the linking of 'pampheletes, playes and balletes' indicates in a 1559 parliamentary bill on press censorship.[1] This was the situation which Jonson, determined to advance the dignity of playwriting, finally overturned by including his plays in the 1616 collection of his *Workes*. It was in the next decade that the label 'classic' became attached to the literature of the ancients; and while the term 'modern classics' belongs to the eighteenth century, Jonson is already setting Shakespeare amongst the standard authors. Shakespeare himself utilizes the cliché of the immortalizing power of poetry in his *Sonnets*, which are held to confer their benefit on both author and subject.[2] That he failed to extend the proposition to his theatrical writing was perhaps no more due to historical conditioning than to his consciousness of the collaborative process through which plays found their way to the stage.

But the notion of the classic Shakespeare has its problems for those considering the theatrical conditions in which he worked. They must welcome, amongst the various liberating ideas to enter Shakespeare criticism in recent years, the questioning of authorial primacy – a convention as subject to change as any other. Clearly Shakespeare raises in acute form the question of what it is that we understand by the author; for, more than poet or dramatist he is cultural icon, a construction of critical and uncritical discourses. He serves as a brand name, so Harold Hobson, reviewing the Hall and Barton *Henry VI* of the Stratford quatercentenary season, began with the claim that plays by Shakespeare's contemporaries put on as part of the bardic celebrations had served to demonstrate the poverty – Shakespeare apart – of the Elizabethan theatre. The only 'unfamiliar work of high talent' proves to be *Henry VI*, which 'is worth, for anything the stage today has been able to show to the contrary, all the rest of the Elizabethan output added together'. That *Henry VI* proved unfamiliar is hardly surprising since in this production 'Barton and Shakespeare are co-authors': thus writes Bamber Gascoigne, who in his *Observer* review credited Shakespeare only with 'the raw details', which Barton turned 'into our contemporary idea of drama'. He adds:

One can see just how much of 'Henry VI' is Barton's at the British Theatre Museum, where his various drafts are on view with the new words typed in red. There are stretches, particularly in the council scenes, where the red lines march solidly down page after page, interrupted only by occasional brief black objections, such as 'away with him!'.[3]

Since Shakespeare the man has faded into convenient obscurity, the name is shorthand for the work; and the work is apt to serve as a kind of tarot pack. So John Peter insists that '*The Merchant of Venice* is a tough play because you have to make up your own mind' – always provided, of course, that you don't opt for a racist reading. But nineteenth and earlier twentieth-century critics showed no embarrassment over the racist issues, or indeed the feminist ones, preoccupying recent commentators. What worried them was the possibility that the classic Shakespeare might enjoy sexual banter. Coleridge's way out of the dilemma is to maintain that 'the disgusting passage of the Porter' in *Macbeth* is 'an interpolation of the actors', an idea not entirely without merit.[4] If such passages could not be unloaded, then the debased taste of the groundlings was held responsible. Quiller-Couch and Dover Wilson dislike the part of Paroles, supposing that Shakespeare '"wrote in" this stuff for some popular low-comedian'.[5] But they do 'note how compactly the whole Paroles business can be put into square brackets, . . . and cut out of the story, like a wen, without the smallest detriment to the remaining tissue'. Perhaps those square brackets betray nostalgia for the Coleridgean solution of some lesser hand at work; they certainly intimate that such material is extraneous to the Shakespearean artwork.

But in the seventeenth century, this class of material is recognized as very much part of Shakespeare's authorial identity. John Johnson, in *The Academy of Love* (1641, p.99), puns on the vaginal two-leaved book and that phallic fescue from *Two Noble Kinsmen* (II.iii.35), describing how 'the young sparkish Girles would read in *Shakespeare* day and night, so that they would open the Booke or Tome, and the men with a Fescue in their hands should point to the Verse'. More directly, Cartwright's commendatory poem prefacing the folio edition of Beaumont and Fletcher's plays (1647) glances disparagingly at Shakespeare,

Whose wit our nice times would obsceannesse call,
And which made Bawdry passe for Comicall.

But Freeman, in 'To Master W. Shakespeare', allows the poet mastery in both virtuous and vicious subjects, *The Rape of Lucrece* balancing '*Venus and Adonis,* / True modell of a most lasciuious leatcher'.[6] The latter work established Shakespeare's reputation as erotic poet. Middleton, in *A Mad World, My Masters* (1604–7) I.ii.48 links it with Marlowe's *Hero and Leander*, 'two luscious marrow-bone pies for a young married wife', the marrowbone being a popular aphrodisiac. Brathwaite, *The English Gentlewoman* (1631, p.139), cautioning that '*Books* treating of light subiects, are Nurseries of wantonnesse', specifies that '*Venus and Adonis* are vnfitting Consorts for a Ladies bosome'. This receives confirmation of a kind from Cranley's *Amanda; or the Converted Courtezan* (1635), where, topping the list of Amanda's favourite 'amorous Pamphlets' is *Venus and Adonis*, followed by the epyllia of Beaumont and Marston.[7] What constitutes a poetry of arousal evidently varies from age to age, though literature can usually furnish something to this end. So in 1583 Philip Barrough, *The Methode of Phisicke* (p.142), can advise on sexual impotence: 'Let the patient sleepe in a soft bedde, and let him reade things that do stirre vp lust, or let him heare them read'. Giordano Bruno found that 'the Song of Songs gave him an erection'[8]; but by the 1590s Shakespeare's poem would have been an obvious text to prescribe.

In addition, the poem was evidently taken as a manual of rhetoric. A lawyer's clerk in Markham's *Dumb Knight* (1607–8) III.i claims this '"Maids Philosophy, or Venus and Adonis"' to be 'A book that' all of his profession 'is beholden unto'.[9] He chooses to quote that especially popular stanza of human topography, one line of which turns up in Baron's *Fortunes Tennis-Ball* (1650. p.2) as: 'VENUS would be's Parke, if he her Deere'; Brathwaite, *Strappado for the Diuell* (1615, p.82), recalls it when Venus bids Adonis 'leaue to ioy / In Forrest pleasures, . . . / Hauing more store of game within thy parke'. In *The New Married Couple* (*c*.1675), the bride imitates Venus, inviting her husband to 'Graze on my soft Lypis; if those Hills be dry stray [further] down where Fountains lye'.[10] Shakespeare's poem continues with reference to 'Sweet bottom-grass' (l.236), which itself finds an echo in 'Young Strephon and Phillis' (pre-1720)[11] where the lovers 'sat on a Hill' and, in their cavortings, 'fell soft on the Grass at the Bottom'. That this too contains a buried allusion to pubic hair is confirmed when the refrain varies to 'Thou'rt all kind, and all soft at the Bottom'.

But his dramatic bawdry prompted imitation too. As Dover Wilson pointed out (Cambridge New Shakespeare, 1936), Hamlet's 'rank sweat of an enseamèd bed' (III.iv.82) relates to his disgusted perception of the marriage couch as 'nasty sty' via the wooldyer's use of hog's lard as 'seam'. That Fletcher recalls the passage in his *Triumph of Death* (1612) vi.121 is made probable by that inverted reference to Claudius at 'prayer': 'take him dead drunk now without repentance, / His leacherie inseam'd upon him'.[12] *A Canto on . . . the D[uke] of M[onmouth]* (1681) associates Monmouth with the Falstaff of *2 Henry IV* both for his cowardice, and because one day he may cry '*A Pox of my Gout, a Gout on my Pox*'.[13] One of Shakespeare's more tortuous references to syphilis found an echo too. Doggerel in *Love's Labour's Lost* (IV.ii.56) beginning:

> The preyful Princess pierced and pricked a pretty pleasing pricket.
> Some say a sore, but not a sore till now made sore with shooting

plays on 'sore' and 'pricket' as terms respectively for four-year-old and two-year-old bucks. That the soreness which comes with 'shooting' (covertly sexual emission) is due not to friction but pox becomes clear in the last two lines, proliferating sores finally doubled by a pun on the Roman numeral 'l'. But 'sore' and 'ell' (the phallic yard) also contain genital puns:

> If sore be sore, then 'l' to 'sore' makes fifty sores – O sore 'l'!
> Of one sore I an hundred make by adding but one more 'l'.

This is Holofernes's 'extemporal epitaph on the death of the deer' following his refusal 'to abrogate scurrility'. Nabbes recalls it in *Totenham-Covrt* (1633–4) I.v, where the deer becomes 'lac'd mutton'. He plainly accepts the pox sense after a servant describes sending a 'Fawne to a wanting poet . . . who . . . will . . . dresse it in some lamentable *Epitaph*'. Through his further generosity, 'A longing Lady in the strand had a *pricket*. Then I sent a *soare* to Barber-Surgeons Hall'.[14]

If audiences could grasp this allusion, they would have had no trouble in recognizing Dekker's burlesque of *Romeo and Juliet* in *Satiromastix* (1601), with its death-simulating drug: 'sh's deathes Bride, he hath her maidenhead' (V.i.168). He borrows Shakespeare's vaginal joke about falling 'into so deep an O'

(III.iii.90) when a gentlewoman's 'tis – ô a most sweet thing
to lye with a man' is answered: 'tis a O more more more sweet
to lye with a woman' (I.i.17).[15] But it is *Othello* – acknowledged
by Rymer to be the most highly rated tragedy 'acted on our
English stage'[16] – which prompted most imitation, especially of
its bestial imagery. Given the symbolic identity of the creatures,
it is hard to be certain whether expressions like that in Cleland's
Memoirs of a Woman of Pleasure (1748), where a whoremonger
'look'd goats and monkies at' Fanny Hill,[17] are indebted to
Othello, III.iii.408. But when Sampson, in *The Vow-Breaker* (c.1625)
II.ii.162, envisages a woman who has broken her troth-plight as
'More prime then Goates, or Monkeys in their prides', 'prime' is a
telltale Shakespearean idiosyncrasy.[18] Thomas Blount's *Academie of
Eloquence* (1654, p.226) glances at 'the Beast with two backs, which
the knavish *Shakespear* speaks of', a recurring association. Brown,
in *Letters from the Dead* (1702), wonders: 'what other business can
a man and woman have in the dark, but, as the fellow says in the
Moor of Venice, to make the beast with two backs?',[19] and Samuel
Cock, *A Voyage to Lethe* (1756, p.35), writes of what 'Shakespeare
beautifully calls *The Beast with two Backs*'. But the expression was
common in French from the fourteenth century, and may have
entered English colloquial use before Shakespeare borrowed it.[20]
Ford is notably influenced by *Othello*, still recalling the plot in his
tragicomedy *The Lady's Trial* (1638):

> His friend hath set before him a bad woman,
> And he, good man, believes it.   (IV.i)

Earlier, he had turned it into Caroline tragedy (*Love's Sacrifice*
?1632) and farce (*The Fancies, Chaste and Noble*, 1635–6). Iago's
suspicion that 'the lusty Moor / Hath leapt into my seat' (II.i.294)
is just one specific recollection in the former (II.iii): 'Doubtless the
youth aims to be duke, for he is gotten into the duke's seat'. And
in the latter, Iago's brute image of 'an old black ram . . . tupping
your white ewe' (I.i.88), is effectively transferred to the husband:
'this ramkin hath tupped my old rotten carrion-mutton' (IV.i). But
it is Iago-Spadone who derides the victim as a monster (III.iii).[21]
Although this cuckoldry gibe is commonplace, the association with
Othello (IV.i.60) is clearly shown by Ned Ward, *The Rambling Rakes*
(1700, p.8), where a wife is 'as Notified for an Intreaguer at *Cupids*,
as her Husband for one of *Othello*'s Monsters'.

Ford's *Fancies* has a remarkable borrowing from *Henry V*, the husbandly injunction to 'Keep your bow close, vixen' (III.iii),[22] seeming to combine elements from the Shakespeare quarto and folio and perhaps indebted to a third, performed version. Thus Pistol's parting words to his wife in the 1600 text are: 'Keepe fast thy buggle boe', a marked improvement on folio's 'Keep close, I thee command' (II.iii.57). But Ford's metaphor, corresponding to the phallic arrow, is more commonplace than Shakespeare's buggle boe, primarily a goblin or bugbear, but also 'an ugly wide-mouthed picture carried about with May games'.[23] The latter provides sufficient basis for its vaginal appropriation, also found in Shirley's *Gentleman of Venice* (1639) I.i, where Malipiero offers to bribe a relative with his list of courtesans, 'which shall tumble, and keep their bugle-bows for thee'.[24] It served as title of a 1670s fornication ballad with the punning refrain, '*to shoot in the Bugle-bow*'.[25] Here, too, is probably the key to *Antony and Cleopatra*, III.xiii.111, where Antony describes Cleopatra as 'a boggler', one prone to use her bogle boe.

Clearly Shakespeare enjoyed a considerable reputation for erotic and bawdy writing during the seventeenth century, a reputation once again well appreciated. It is Eric Partridge who best represents that return swing of the pendulum after the discomfort experienced by Victorian critics. He supposes that the world's greatest writer and wit must necessarily excel in the matter of bawdry. Amongst contemporaries, only Jonson and Beaumont and Fletcher 'are as smutty', though less witty.[26] 'Smutty' is too loaded; and besides, if density and intricacy are to be the criteria, dramatists like Barry, Mason or Sharpham crammed a good deal more into their one or two plays than Shakespeare can match at his bawdiest; while, as a serious exponent of sexual imagery in both comedy and tragedy, Middleton is at least Shakespeare's equal. But these lesser mortals have no chance against the Shakespearean hype.

Whatever the contribution of this sexual material, it is evident even from what has been said here that Jonson, with his own vested interest, played a conspicuous part in ensuring Shakespeare's posthumous reputation as a dramatist. Jonson's efforts were part of a growing cultural emphasis on the writer rather than the product. It is the way that this new set of assumptions battles with the old in Shakespeare's theatre which is the subject of the next chapter.

2
Performance versus Text

AD LIBBING AND THE 'BAD' QUARTOS

While Chapter 1 examines the Shakespearean reputation and dimensions of his canonical status, this chapter is partly concerned with the growing significance attached to author over work in the Jacobean theatre, where it became a major force for change. Alan Sinfield[1] discusses how this author principle has acquired a political function, serving to smooth out the knotty, contradictory elements in the text – or rather, in the performance: it is the theatre director (or reader as director) who supplies, or declines to supply, unity. Thus its role today is the reverse of what it was in Shakespeare's time. What was at the outset a radical force is now a traditionalist barrier against a resurgent selfconsciousness on the modern stage. It remains a formidable power, though contradictions which earlier critics strove to resolve have become appreciated for their very rawness by those following the insights of Brecht. Congruity and coherence have lost their axiomatic acceptance, and the extent of the change may be measured by recalling Bradley's refusal to accept as Shakespeare's this couplet spoken by Lear's fool:

> She that's a maid now, and laughs at my departure,
> Shall not be a maid long, unless things be cut shorter.
>
> (I.v.49)

The lines are 'incongruous' as well as 'grossly indecent'. Worse still, they are '*irrelevantly* indecent and evidently addressed to the audience, two faults which are not in Shakespeare's way'.[2] The process is double-edged: interpolation serves as alibi for anything found distasteful by the critic; but there is nothing more distasteful than interpolation. Lesser critics than Bradley, to escape the prospect of Shakespeare's victimization by ad-libbing clowns, declare 'that he wrote them such inimitable parts in order to save them from yielding to that temptation in his plays'. Doris Fenton recalls this view, in all its circularity, while assembling evidence for widespread improvization on the Elizabethan stage. She also emphasizes that her main concern, direct audience address, went into steep decline from about 1616, whereas 'almost two-thirds of the existing plays written before 1616' possess this feature.[3] It is one which lends itself to improvisation, and the decline she registers keys with the growing text-consciousness which has been noted from around that date.

That text-consciousness, chiming with the improved status of the dramatist, brings ad-libbing into disrepute. This is very plain in William Prynne's attack: 'Yea sometimes such who act the Clowne or amorous person, adde many obscene lascivious jests and passages of their owne, by way of appendix, to delight the auditors, which were not in their parts before'.[4] He is in no doubt that a play performance will be more inflammatory than a play-book, with its 'lively representations of Venery, . . . lascivious tunes and dances'. But it is his bias about the relative authenticity of what is played and what is printed which makes interesting comment on how print had changed people's assumptions.

Prynne was writing in the 1630s, but an earlier generation of theatre-goers would have expected more from their afternoon's entertainment than a play performance, scripted or unscripted. David Wiles, arguing 'for the importance of studying the actor as much as the writer', stresses the significance of those 'Jigges Rymes and Daunces' which regularly featured as anti-masque to the main item on the programme until 1612, when they were suppressed by an order issued at the Middlesex General Session.[5] This represented a tightening of control over a theatre where, although designed as an instrument of authority, entertainment was too apt to dissolve into potentially subversive routines. For the modern play-reader, to recognize that the last words or action would not have concluded the entertainment in early seventeenth-century theatres must affect response to the play. This remains the case, though the ephemeral nature of much that went on means that usually we can only guess at the forms it took. Thomas Platter of Basle, who saw a performance of *Julius Caesar* at the Globe in 1599, was able to enjoy both the play and the dancing which concluded the entertainment.[6] Indeed, plays were not only equipped with a tailpiece, but had the dramatic frame breached, both between and within acts, by what a more conservative genre consciousness than the Elizabethans possessed would consider alien intrusions. Although Platter records that the intervals in performances he attended were given over to the selling of refreshments, he makes suggestive reference to comedies (a category in which he includes *Julius Caesar*) 'wherewith folk make merry together'. His picture suggests some likeness with court masque, where barriers between audience and performers regularly collapsed. Puttenham (1589), ostensibly examining the ancient theatre, is probably extrapolating from 1580s practice when describing how 'betweene the acts' a vice would appear and give 'a crosse construction' to what had gone before.[7] But that such neat counterpoint was not always to the fore is clear from Lyly's apology, in the prologue to *Midas* (1589–90), for a '*Hodge-podge*' theatre:[8] the very one which Shakespeare inherited and exploited.

But as we have noticed, Shakespeare's later working years were marked by rapid cultural changes. Probably Dekker panders to recent legislation when, in *A Strange Horse Race* (1613), he deplores the way that 'the finishing of some worthy Tragedy' leads to 'a nasty bawdy Iigge'.[9] But that suppression-order chimes with larger historical movements from fluidity to fixation, beginning with the professionalizing of the theatre itself. Now that what constitutes legitimate theatre has been defined, the tidying-up process becomes a more subtly effective means of control than attempts at outright suppression. The author principle makes its contribution in providing a sharply focused area of responsibility; and it is consolidated by insistence on adherence to scripts. Shakespeare's position is pivotal in this. Towards the end of his career, the prologue to *Henry VIII* warns austerely that there will be disappointment for those expecting

> to hear a merry bawdy play,
> . . . or to see a fellow
> In a long motley coat guarded with yellow

(i.e., he has omitted the king's jester, Will Summers, who had been so conspicuous in Rowley's *When You See Me, You Know Me*). But Jonson, in the Induction to *Bartholomew Fair* (1614, p.130), hints that even in his late plays Shakespeare had no aversion from 'the concupiscence of Iigges', begetting '*Tales, Tempests*, and such like *Drolleries*'.[10]

How much ad-libbing this might have accommodated is a

moot point. While an element of extemporizing continued on
the London stage through the seventeenth century and beyond,
it could never occupy the important place that it did in Italy.
There the *commedia dell' arte* continued to flourish because Italy
stubbornly resisted the spread of print culture. In Britain, the fixing
capacity of print fostered a new sense of 'correctness': hence the
move towards standardized spelling. Another consequence was the
elevation of creative over executant artist. This is very noticeable
with the printing of musical scores, but the previous chapter
acknowledges a similar swing in the Stuart theatre. The idea of
the definitive text and the increased prestige of the writer are
two sides of the same coin. But this latter development need
not stand in complete contrast to the older, freer model. A
compromise position was reached in musical development which
may well illuminate what took place on the London stage. In fact,
it may supply an analogy both for the extemporal tradition and the
author–player relationship. By the mid-sixteenth century, musical
improvisation was becoming systematized, the patterns established
being still operative in early nineteenth-century Italian opera. An
anecdote of the bass Louis Lablache describes his singing in an
Italian opera with Malibran, who thought to discountenance him

> by introducing ornaments and caprices of extreme difficulty,
> which it was the business of Lablache to imitate. But the trap
> laid for this vocal Hercules availed only to cause a display
> of his agility; note after note, trait after trait, shade after
> shade, did Lablache reproduce in falsetto, the fioriture which
> Malibran had taken such pains to mature. On meeting behind
> the scenes, Malibran could not help expressing to Lablache her
> astonishment at the ease with which he had surmounted such
> difficult passages, and the latter, with his usual *bonhommie*, replied
> that he had not been aware of the difficulty.[11]

But in his 1829 *Méthode de Chant*, he insists that improvisation
should follow lines set out by the composer, so he is at one with
the critic of the *Musical Times* who in September 1850 took Jenny
Lind to task for introducing into *Messiah* 'cadenzas more fitted to
Bellini than the sublimity of Handel'.[12]

It was recognized that the vocal line was often somewhat sketchy
to give the singer ample scope for embellishment. Singers performing with the kind of tact advocated by Lablache might achieve a

form of creative collaboration with the composer ruled out by later nineteenth-century conditions. In the presence of a third element, the expectantly responsive audience, it made possible that special kind of spontaneity which needs a convention of disciplined freedom. It also requires a delicate balance of forces which would be easily upset by the egoism of either writer or executant.

One can only speculate whether some such balance was achieved in the changing conditions of Shakespeare's theatre. But one of its members, the clown Kemp, shows the suggestive influence of *commedia dell'arte*;[13] and the still relatively free and open style of the public theatre would seem to provide fertile ground for just such fruitful collaboration. Until fairly recently, however, textual editors have tried to ignore the element of instability engendered by Shakespeare's working conditions. Editorial mediation obliterated traces of fluidity through commitment to the idea of a Shakespeare who never blotted line and a bibliographical preoccupation with the textual singularity which that was supposed to imply. If the textual archaeologist was not always confident of finding what he sought, he was in no doubt about his objective. But it was one based on preconceptions which had no precise counterpart amongst Shakespeare's generation of playwrights. Historical and professional conditions in which he operated make the quest for Shakespearean authority behind every line or even every scene seem not only vain but actually misconceived. As Stephen Orgel says, 'when we make our editions, of Shakespeare or any other dramatist, we are *not* "getting back to the author's original text." We know nothing about Shakespeare's original text'. He summarizes conditions under which an Elizabethan playscript was produced:

> The company commissioned the play, usually stipulated the subject, often provided the plot, often parcelled it out, scene by scene, to several playwrights. The text thus produced was a working model, which the company then revised as seemed appropriate. The author had little or no say in these revisions: the text belonged to the company.[14]

This is a persuasive fleshing-out of known facts, and perhaps consciously reminiscent of Hollywood, another set-up which refuses to regard its scripts as sacrosanct .

The transitory nature of theatrical performance means that a printed text is often taken for the play; and ironically such traces as early performance has left behind are themselves to be found principally in texts (often the less good ones according to the usual criteria). The so-called 'bad quartos' are described by Hart as 'not the corrupt abridgment of Shakespeare's complete text, but . . . a report of what had been spoken on the stage; its immediate source was the official acting version'. He offers evidence of theatrical cuts in the accepted quartos as well as the more problematical ones, though the counter-possibility of an assistant scriptwriter's additions is not considered.[15] Harry R. Hoppe[16] suggests of bad quartos that absence of speeches during scenes of lively comic action probably indicates that 'dialogue had degenerated in the course of time to mere ad libbing and horse-play'. But again the evidence may be turned around: there is no guarantee that what good quartos provide for such scenes are the author's original suggestions rather than a record of stage improvisation.

The 1597 ('bad') quarto of *Romeo and Juliet* gives some glimpses of performance behind the text, including a few bawdy examples. When Peter protests that had he seen a man use the nurse 'at his pleasure . . . my weapon should quickly have been out; I warrant you, I dare draw as soon as another man' (II.iii.147), 1597 reads: 'I would soone haue drawen: you know my toole is as soone out as anothers' (l.74).[17] This might represent Kemp's smoother lead-in to bawdy clowning; but another part of the curtain lifts when Juliet's words about neither 'hand, nor foot, . . . / nor any other part / Belonging to a man' (II.i.82) are unconsciously parodied by the nurse: 'his leg excels all men's, and for a hand and a foot and a body, though they be not to be talked on, yet they are past compare' (II.iv.40). Here the 1597 quarto hints at the way this was played for verbal humour: 'he is not a proper man: and for a hand, and a foote, and a baudie, wel go thy way wench' (l.78). The forced pronunciation turns 'body' into a suggestive adjective, which discreetly loses its noun in an evasion.[18]

Nor do 'bad' and 'authentic' adequately sum up the complex relationship between quarto and folio texts of *Merry Wives*. There is no evidence for supposing that the quarto has made a poor attempt to produce the folio text, an undertaking which would require strangely static theatrical conditions. Certainly quarto's Mistress Quickly sounds 'authentic' as she blunders into bawdry, claiming that she has her employer's confidence since he 'puts all his priuities in me' (B3; *OED* from *c*.1375). Again, the differences in Ford's quarto speech after the line, 'There's a hole made in your best coat',[19] when he reflects on his wife's supposed adultery (III.v.130), give a distinct impression of considered change. In the 1602 quarto, Ford piles up the images of infidelity:

> cuckold, wittold, godeso
> The diuel himselfe hath not such a name:
> And they may hang hats here, and napkins here
> Vpon my hornes.   (E4)

This is not blank verse, but it is compressed, racy, theatrically effective. That 'godeso' was replaced by a repetition of 'cuckold' in the folio presumably reflects the 1605 'Act against Swearing'. This form of the Italian *cazzo* (penis) assimilates to oaths beginning with 'God's' so as to snag with Ford's 'devil' references (that included here is one of several in the speech). They recall how Beatrice in *Much Ado* II.i.39 imagines herself at hell's gate, meeting with the devil 'like an old cuckold with horns on his head'. But devilish deformity shades into domesticity: Sharpham's jealous knight using the same trope: 'I branch, do I not? am not I a goodly screene for men to hang their hats vpon?'.[20] Ford's 'napkin' figure compresses ideas of cuckolding and bastardy, a commonplace of cheap seventeenth-century print which may have a lost sixteenth-century ancestry. *The New Brawle* (1654, p.4) furnishes an example, with its complaint about a 'husband good for nothing but to be set in a Chimney-corner, to dry pist clouts on his Horns'. Although 'napkin' would normally denote either table linen or handkerchief for Elizabethans, there is a strong likelihood that it means an infant's 'clout' in Ford's speech. This speech is no botch. The swift diversity of images is as 'Shakespearean' as anything else that Ford utters, and better reflects his state of mind than the folio version.

It will be remembered that Prynne's strictures, quoted earlier, attribute the practice of ad-libbing to more than clowns. Peter Davison observes how the bad quarto of *Hamlet* shows Burbage, as Hamlet, to be the most extensive ad-libber.[21] Prynne, of course, addresses bawdy interpolation, and it needs noting that bawdy passages have their own special problems for those concerned with authentication. Oldham in his 'Apology' (1680), scornful of ribaldry as social leveller, is accurate enough in his main contention

that even 'Prentices and Carmen . . . can be smart and witty there
/ For all Men on that Subject Poets are'.[22] Actors no doubt had
as much facility in this way as prentices, carmen or dramatists.
But George Wither puts the matter firmly into the Elizabethan
theatrical context when, in *Abuses Stript and Whipt* (1613, p.224),
he complains that hacks will 'patch vp a bald witless Comedy . . .
with *Ribaldry* / Learn'd at a baudy house'. There may be reluctance
to find a description of Shakespearean comedy in this; but Wither
does offer a glimpse of the kind of refurbishing to which plays of
the period were subject.

BAWDY ROUTINES

Amongst other things, Shakespeare's plays are 'a variety entertainment' (Bradley's withering phrase),[23] products of a theatre where
the genres were not yet separated out. Their variety of form would
readily accommodate input from various sources; it would be a
simple matter, when there is little keying-in of a comic routine to
other elements in the play, for a comedian to introduce his own (or
his gag-writer's) material. Some of the routines to be discussed may
include material of that kind, but they are not chosen on account
of that possibility. Rather, they show one aspect of a mixed form
of theatre, an aspect notably productive of bawdy humour, and
one serving as reminder that dramatic unity was only one option
amongst several. So the routines discussed provide examples of
minimal and substantial integration, together with one where the
incongruity is a cunningly calculated part of the dramatic effect.

But first the simplest form, which is well illustrated by *Two
Gentlemen of Verona*. The play includes traditional double acts,
one of which allows Speed to pun furiously on sheep: 'I, a lost
mutton, gave your letter to her, a laced mutton,' adding of this
alleged whore, 'If the ground be overcharged, you were best
stick her' (I.i.94), blurring slaughter with sexual intercourse.[24] In
another exchange he switches from comic to straight man, feeding
Launce the line: 'how stands the matter with them?'; and Launce
predictably responds: 'when it stands well with him it stands well
with her' (II.v.19). But Launce also provides a solo turn, regaling
the audience with a vaginal joke: 'this left shoe is my father. No,
no, this left shoe is my mother . . . . it hath the worser sole. This
shoe with the hole in it is my mother' (II.iii.14). In sexual lore, both
left foot and left shoe have a feminine association,[25] presumably

an offshoot of Galenic theory that the right testis, the masculine source, is more direct and consequently purer than the left which seeds girl-children.

The style of *Romeo and Juliet*'s opening scene would have been instantly recognized by music-hall audiences, familiar with cross-talk acts. The humour is crude enough, but as it takes on bawdy colouring, the violence of family feud is emphasized as a prelude to the street skirmish which follows:

> GREGORY. . . . the weakest goes to the wall.
> SAMPSON. 'Tis true, and therefore women, being the weaker vessels, are ever thrust to the wall; therefore I will push Montague's men from the wall, and thrust his maids to the wall . . . when I have fought with the men I will be civil with the maids – I will cut off their heads.
> GREGORY. The heads of the maids?
> SAMPSON. Ay, the heads of the maids, or their maidenheads, take it in what sense thou wilt.
> GREGORY. They must take it in sense that feel it.
> SAMPSON. Me they shall feel while I am able to stand, and 'tis known I am a pretty piece of flesh.
>
> (I.i.12)

This is the first of a series of comic turns punctuating the earlier acts of the play. Its genital boast is familiar, and the ugly joke about virgin rape as decapitation certainly became so in early seventeenth-century drama. *Pericles* xix.153 provides a variant when rape is proposed to fit Marina for brothel service: 'I must have your maidenhead taken off, or the common executioner shall do it'. But Sampson's use initiates those reminders running through the play that love and death, or more comprehensively sex and violence, too easily conjoin.

A decade or so after the appearance of the two plays we have been discussing, that tired old tumescence joke reappears when Macbeth's porter begins a double act with Macduff. He explains how drink affects sexual activity: 'it provokes the desire but it takes away the performance. Therefore much drink may be said to be an equivocator with lechery: it makes him and it mars him; it sets him on, and it takes him off; it persuades him, and disheartens him, makes him stand to and not stand to' (II.iii.28). He unravels the paradox, also giving that *equivocator* side-glance at

Jesuit involvement in the topical Gunpowder Treason. But this is a tenuous enough integrating detail in a theatre which could accommodate abrupt mood changes and incongruity as readily as a televiewer might in the course of an evening. But what is remarkable here is that tonal dissonance – between Macbeth's obscene action and the porter's musings on boozy, disappointing sex – seems to be a calculated effect. Earlier another dimension opens up when the latter places himself in the miracle-play tradition as 'porter of hell-gate'. The exchange with Macduff is necessarily brief, since the latter is only too aware that he has 'almost slipped the hour' when he was to awaken the king. But until his entry, dramatic action is suspended. Murder and its consequences can be (almost) forgotten while hell's porter becomes stand-up comic with an open-ended routine. What offers is a notably tense genre opposition: comic turn counterpointed with that knocking at the gate, clamorous appeal for admission by the players in the 'real' drama. Each knock prompts a formulaic response from the porter, 'Knock, knock. Who's there', followed by a gag. At the third knock he jokes about a tailor, stereotyped at the time as both thief and womanizer. Theft confuses with French disease, while the goose is both syphilitic swelling and tailor's smoothing iron, one form of dishonesty threatening hell-fire and the other the burning of pox: 'here's an English tailor come hither for stealing out of a French hose. Come in, tailor. Here you may roast your goose' (II.iii.12). The routine preserved in the folio text presumably represents details of how the scene was worked out for a particular production by dramatist (perhaps) and players. It is clearly designed for topical modification, since it is the form of the comic interlude rather than its details which creates the effect. But there is seldom any departing from the sacred script in modern productions, though Declan Donnellan (irreverent enough to cast the porter as a woman) provides an exception: 'Among those whom she drunkenly observes knocking at the gates of hell is "a stockbroker who applied for a million BP shares and couldna stop the cheque"'.[26] This would surely have been the approach of the seventeenth-century comedian. His problem was very different from that of the modern comic actor, playing to that special Shakespeare audience. His audience needed warming up, by ad-libbing or direct appeal. Shakespeare would have understood the issue here. Whatever his relations with his comics, it is Hamlet, prince of Denmark rather than experienced man of the theatre, who would have 'those that play your clowns speak no more than is set down for them'. Indeed, a seeming dig at irrepressible clowns is perhaps a coded complaint about the interfering great upon whose patronage the very existence of the theatres depended. But that is to anticipate the concerns of the next chapter.

3

Censorship and Evasion

STRUCTURES OF CENSORSHIP

It is the paradox of print that it both divided Christendom and provided powerful impetus towards unity. The religious issues were never distinct from other forces, and Luther's programme of reform went far beyond the Church. His translation of the Bible made its contribution to a unified written language, and so to a raised national consciousness.[1] Symbolizing the English Reformation is the way the old missal variations, from the York use to that of Sarum, became unified in a *common* prayerbook: not just a matter of Church bureaucracy but of state control. Yet the extent of such control betrays the scale of official paranoia over print and the new freedom of access to ideas which went with it. Henry VIII's 'Acte for thadvauncement of true Religion' (1543) ordered that the Bible in English should be read by 'no woomen nor artificers prentices . . . husbandmen nor labourers',[2] this same perceived danger of stimulating thought amongst the unprivileged showing up in later theatre legislation. Spenser's *Faerie Queene* I.i.20, where the monster Error's 'vomit full of bookes and papers was', bears vivid testimony to the way that Elizabethan authority viewed the awful disseminating power of print, and the conflicts of interest which it both articulated and intensified.

Such a climate affected the Elizabethan theatre profoundly. It was shaped not only by direct state intervention but by larger conditions of paradox and opposition resulting from this social revolution. For the shift in emphasis from religious drama to secular was only a preliminary stage. The theatre's professionalizing was the important step, with the establishment of companies and fixed places of operation. Such a development was intimately bound up with print, which had created an appetite for the new. Mass entertainment is voracious: its hacks needed the stimulus of a book culture to meet the continual demand for new plots. Theatrical fare interacted with cheap print as information source and in popularizing ideas. But if print made a professional theatre possible, it was the Tudor authorities who ushered it into existence. If the theatre was to be an ideas channel, then one organized on a professional basis would be easiest to control. So in addition to satisfying his public, the dramatist had to be sure to satisfy the censor.

Before attempting to assess how Shakespeare's dramatic bawdry might have been affected by this circumstance, it is as well to recall something of the manner in which control was exercised over plays both on stage and in book form. The power of print had been quickly recognized: the University of Cologne, where the legalistic framework was developed, being granted censorship rights by Pope Sixtus IV in 1479.[3] Britain and France were two countries where the monarchy adopted analogous procedures of their own. Publishing was kept under tight control during Elizabeth's reign, government restricting the number of both printers and presses at work. Indeed, the Stationers' Company had been granted its charter, just a few months before her accession, primarily as a weapon of control. The several strands of anxiety are caught up in an injunction of 1559 against publications 'heretical, seditious, or vnseemely for Christian eares'.[4] But Kirschbaum, in his useful account of the Stationers' Company (pp.25–86), indicates that the official procedures for licensing set up in that year were too cumbersome. So in practice much of the work devolved upon the Company's wardens, who exercised powers of search, seizure and imprisonment. This situation obtained until 1586, when the Star Chamber decreed that the archbishop of Canterbury and bishop of London take control. Thereafter, the Company confined its licensing activities largely to ephemerae, including playbooks, until responsibility for the latter was arrogated by Sir George Buc who, as master of the revels from 1608, had control of the public theatres.

The theatre's double-edged capacity for political intervention is recognized in the commonplace that 'Tragedy . . . maketh kings fear to be tyrants'.[5] Of course, containment in the guise of conflict is a favourite establishment ploy. But, as Prynne was keenly aware (p. 15 above), there may be a wide gap between the ostensible message and the way that the message is conveyed; or indeed between what purports to be said and what an audience actually receives. Some attempt to deal with this was made by restricting not only what might be played but who played it and where. Like political and economic power, culture would gradually become centred on London, with only a few acting companies permitted. The Queen, on 16 May 1559, just six months after her accession, issued a proclamation directed specifically against 'common Interludes in the English tongue' (learned productions at the universities caused no concern), but bringing the performing arts comprehensively under her control. Performances could take place only by official licence. Utterly forbidden were topics of religion and government, the strict preserve of 'menne of aucthoritie, learning and wisedome' (regarded as a single group).[6] Under 'An Acte for the punishement of Vacabondes' (29 June 1572),[7] players could function only when formed into companies under the protection of one of those men of authority, learning and wisdom, who would be answerable for their good behaviour. The weight of this responsibility is apparent from a letter sent by one of them, the Lord Chamberlain, to the Lord Mayor of London in 1594, permission being sought for his players to perform within the city on the undertaking that 'where heretofore they began not their Plaies till towardes fower a clock, they will now begin at two, & haue don betwene fower and fiue, and will nott vse anie Drumes or trumpettes att all for the callinge of peopall together'.[8] Theatre crowds, like those attending football matches in the earlier part of this century, were viewed as a potential source of riot, or even rebellion.

Up to 1581 much of the regulating of London theatres was undertaken by the city, which is why the companies withdrew to the suburbs. But in that year Edmund Tilney had been granted, as master of the revels, sweeping powers over 'plays, players, and playmakers, together with their playing places', defiance of his rulings being punishable by imprisonment without trial at his pleasure.[9] Profanity, politics and sex were prime targets for censorship. That the latter two are still a source of anxiety to the controllers of popular entertainment is revealed by cuts in televised films between one showing and the next: the Goldie Hawn vehicle *Private Benjamin* recently lost two orgasm jokes which it could ill spare, while *Murder by Decree*, a Sherlock Holmes movie, shed a scene in which the future King Edward VII is booed by a theatre audience during the playing of the national anthem.

Charles I commented on a passage in one of Massinger's plays, 'This is too insolent, and to be changed';[10] it would be interesting to know who mouthed the sentiment in this more recent case. Such mind-changing also occurred in the office of the revels. In 1633, some dozen years after the original licensing, a revival of Fletcher's *Woman's Prize* was blocked 'upon complaints of foule and offensive matters conteyned therein'.[11] However Herbert, then master of the revels, purged the play of 'oaths, prophaness, and publique ribaldry' to such purpose that it was 'Very well likt' in a court performance the next month, as a sequel to *The Taming of the Shrew*.

Fletcher's play will warrant further consideration as evidence of the kind of sexual deletions likely to be made by the censor; but that Herbert's ideal could accommodate sexual scenes and banter is demonstrated by Shirley's *Young Admiral*, held up in this same year as a model of the 'beneficial and cleanly way of poetry' in its freedom 'from oaths, prophaness, or obsceanes'. There is no evidence to suggest that the fourth act, as printed in the 1637 quarto, differs materially from the version so warmly commended by Herbert. But in addition to the scene (iii) where a Sicilian nobleman attempts to rape a fair captive,

> I could have
> The virgins of whole families entail'd
> Upon me, and be brought as duly to
> My bed, as they grow ripe, and fit for coupling,[12]

in IV.i there is bawdy recollection of Jonson's *Alchemist*, where Dapper encounters his Fairy Queen. Pazzorello, desiring to be made 'stick and shot free', fears that payment will be in terms of sexual favours: 'thou wouldst not have me lie with the old witch? what a generation of hobgoblins should we have together!'. Asked what he has about him, his mind still runs on sex, fearing castration rather than a cash demand: 'About me! where? in my breeches? what do you mean? I shall be cut for the stone'. That Germanic myth of the hardman some-times connotes talismanic preservation from venereal disease, and punning reference occurs at the end of the scene: 'If the ladies knew I were stick free, they would tear me in pieces, for my company'.[13]

THE CENSORING HAND

Variation between one text and another of a particular play may yield many explanations. But some of the textual discrepancies between 1594 quarto and folio of *2 Henry VI* strongly suggest censorship. Although that quarto has a 'bad' reputation, parts of it integrate suspiciously closely with the folio text in terms of dramatic action and issues. One of these issues, on which I propose to focus, might be called the print crisis. At IV.vii.31, Lord Say is accused by the rebel Cade of corrupting 'the youth of the realm in erecting a grammar school'; and still worse he has 'caused printing to be used'. That he has hanged men 'because they could not read' (l.41) is sour comment on the 'neck-verse' which, demonstrating a knowledge of Latin, saved felons from the noose. In view of this denunciation of privilege, Say is foolish (or desperate) in trying to gain favour with Cade and his 'men of Kent' by telling them what Caesar, in his *Commentaries*, said of their county. Cade orders the beheading of Say and his son-in-law, declaring that peers must pay tribute for their lives, while every maid getting married must 'pay to me her maidenhead' (l.119), and property owners' 'wives be as free as heart can wish or tongue can tell'. This link between political murder and sexual exploitation is continued in a 1594 scene missing from the folio, where a sergeant asks for justice against Dick, a follower of Cade, who 'has ravished my wife' (l.129). This all too closely echoes I.iii.18, where a man had petitioned the lord protector against 'my lord Cardinal's man, for keeping my house and lands and wife and all from me'. The first petitioner received no more justice than the sergeant does from Cade who, disliking police as instruments of repression, orders him brained 'with his own mace'. The choice of victim is neat: there would have been those in the audience who found that 'the justice of it pleases'. But the repetition of the lord protector's scene is dangerously subversive, ironically placing Cade's moral authority at the level of the aristocracy's. It is unsurprising that this episode did not survive into the folio's copy.

Dick has excused his rape by saying that the sergeant would have arrested him, so 'I went and entered my action in his wife's paper house', and Cade gives him quibbling authority to repeat the act: 'follow thy suit in her common place' (l.131).[14] Although 'house', like 'place', is a familiar enough vaginal term, 'paper house' – Wells and Taylor emend to 'proper house' – has special point here since another charge levelled at Lord Say is that he 'built a paper-mill' (1.35). No paper was manufactured in Britain for more than forty years after Cade's death, but Shakespeare perhaps recalls an episode from 1562, at the start of the French Wars of Religion, when the Huguenots led by Condé threw the paper mills at Essonnes, near Paris, into the river.[15] Both factual and fictional occurrences assert a link between print and oppression. Cade identifies reading, writing and, above all, print as the means by which the proletariat is held in subjection. This is another of print's paradoxes, at once democratizing and divisive. Increasingly by the late sixteenth century, class distinction was measured not by wealth, since the superior merchant class could often outbid the aristocracy, but by education. Culture itself had become divided, the new élitism (rooted in a classical education) proclaiming itself as the only mark of cultivation. 'Burn but his books', urges Caliban, who shares with Cade this perception of the unprivileged about power sources (*The Tempest*, III.ii.96).

With the sergeant disposed of, Cade's followers are impatient to get 'to Cheapside and take up commodities upon our bills' (1.141), Cheapside being not only a major shopping centre but the place of execution where Say has been beheaded. So 'commodities' combines ideas of goods for sale (including women as sexual commodities), and severed heads, Cade's full answer (absent from the folio) making this clear: 'He that will lustily stand to it shall go with me and take up these commodities following – item, a gown, a kirtle, a petticoat, and a smock' (1.143). That his followers must 'lustily stand to it' shows that women are implied in his list of garments. But there is no need to invoke the censor's hand here. This is a theatrical cut to speed up the action, since sex and butchery are sufficiently conjoined in the folio text. Thus the heads are brought in on pikes, and Cade jokes brutally on the authority of Hall's *Chronicle*: 'Let them kiss one another, for they loved well when they were alive . . . . at every corner have them kiss' (1.148). But the 'corner' detail is Shakespeare's own, the public display gratingly at odds with that idea of covert sex usually associated with kissing in a corner.[16]

The obvious possibilities of comparing printed and manuscript texts are impeded by the lack of Shakespeare manuscripts. However, the handful of London theatre plays from his lifetime surviving in both early print and manuscript may add clues to the kind of vagaries that the Shakespeare texts have been subject to. The only two examples from the sixteenth century exist in very imperfect manuscript form. Just one leaf of Marlowe's *Massacre at Paris* has survived, preserving a flurry of puns lost in the printed source: 'a counterfeyt key' for a 'privie chamber', an adulterer filling up his victim's 'rome y^t he should occupie. . . . you forestalle the markett, and sett upe yor standinge where you shold not'. For Greene's *Orlando Furioso*, there exists a manuscript text of the leading role, seemingly 'prepared from the original prompt-copy'.[17] Although the printed text is flawed, it offers an interesting example of what Greg calls 'adaptive shortening', evidently designed to dispose of Orlando's lines on Minerva (l.156): 'I knowe who buggerd Iupiters brayne, when you wer begotten'.

However, there is more substantial evidence from the next century, including complete manuscripts for plays by Middleton and Fletcher, both of whose writing demonstrably touched that of Shakespeare. The Folger manuscript of Middleton's *Hengist*,[18] apparently deriving from a prompt copy, adds little to the sexual content of the quarto. It supplies an incest reference:

Mans scattered Lust brings forth most strange events,
Ant twere but strictly thought on; how many brothers
Wantonly gott, through ignorance of there Births
May match with their owne sisters.

(III.i.90)

And a rapist likens the consequences of his act to the sacking of a town:

For as at a small Breach in towne or Castle
When one has entrance, a whole Army followes,
In Woman, so abusiuely once knowne,
Thousandes of sins has passadge made with one.

(IV.ii.274)

But comic crosstalk between the mayor and a Puritan weaver (III.iii.168) is largely printed. The social climbing mayor, a 'mushrump, that shott vp in one night wth Lyeing wth thy M^{rs}', has his tumescence gibe, 'all the Mistrisses in ye Towne

would never gett the vpp', met with another on pregnancy: 'I
scorne to rise by a Woeman as thou didst: My wife shall rise by
me'. Only the mayor's last word, shifting ground yet again to the
idea of a night-straying wife, is omitted: 'The better for som of thy
neighbors when yo^u are asleepe'; and it is hard to imagine a censor
deleting just this concluding quip.

But as promised earlier, the revival of Fletcher's *Woman's Prize*
provides clearer evidence of the blue pencil at work.[19] Both 'pisse'
(I.i.46) and 'pispots' (IV.ii.2) are missing from the printed text, the
latter replaced by the jocular euphemism 'looking-glasses', first
noted by the *OED* from Fletcher's *Beggar's Bush* (*c*.1615–22).
At III.iii.154, the offending word in 'had I not wife enough /
To turn my tooles to?' becomes 'love' in the folio, while
a dozen lines earlier 'rots take me' is replaced with a dash
(though the folio's *Double Marriage* II.v.44 admits it). Suggestive
reference to

> St. *George* at Kingston,
> Running a foot-back from the furious Dragon,
> That with her angry tayle belabours him
> For being lazie
>
> (I.iii.18)

lacks, in the printed text, its gloss of detumescence: 'His warlike
launce / Bent like a crosse bow lath'. And in the previous scene
(l.52), Livia's 'You shall hear what I do' loses the joking response
'I had rather feel it'. Most of the description of a tanner's wife is
removed:

> her plackett
> Lookes like the straights of Gibralter, still wider
> Downe to the gulphe, all sun-burnt Barbary
> Lyes in her breech.
>
> (II.iv.45)

But a substantial deletion at III.i.51 would have offended on
religious as well as sexual grounds (Henrietta Maria was by now
on the throne), claiming that Catholics

> keepe
> A kind of household Gods, call'd chamber-maides,
> Which being pray'd to, and their offerings brought,

(W.ch are in gold, yet some observe the old law
And giue in flesh) probatum est, you shall have
As good love for your monie, and as tydie
As ere you turn'd your legge ore.

Still more censorship must have gone on. An obvious hiatus at
II.iii.33, calling for some sexual badinage, is acknowledged in
the manuscript with a space left for about six lines.[20] This
might represent Buc's deletions or, if the manuscript's source
had suffered Herbert's attentions, one of the latter's more energetic
obliterations.

The relationship between manuscript, a replacement prompt
book of 1625, and folio text of Fletcher's *Honest Mans Fortune* is
quite different. Although the rejection of a supposed adulteress,
'out howling bitch wolfe' (IV.ii.82), loses the last two words in the
folio, this printed text is generally superior to the manuscript. A
heavily deleted passage in the latter (II.i.17), where an unemployed
servant toys with setting 'vp a male stewes, we shold get more then
all yor female sinners', is reinstated in the folio, which also preserves
another innuendo of homosexuality lost to the manuscript. In fact,
the entire ending where Captain La Poop invites a page-boy 'to
Sea with me, ile teach thee to climb, and come down by the
rope' (V.iv.250), is replaced in the manuscript version. Although
the folio text offers nothing more flagrant than: 'a blind man
by the hand / Could have discoverd the ring from the stone'
(V.iv.*248),[21] this is an instance such as Prynne had in mind,
where there is all the difference between text and stage enactment.
In performance a page-boy evidently had his breeches taken down
to remove doubts about his sex. If the folio text is taken to be based
on a source superseded by the manuscript, it would seem that such
business could pass in 1613, but not in a 1625 revival.[22]

This play is presumably one of those texts on which Moseley
based his claim that his 1647 edition of Beaumont and Fletcher
restored '*Scenes* and *Passages*' omitted from acting versions; but *The
Woman's Prize* sufficiently undermines the idea that it offers 'the
perfect full Originalls without the least mutilation'. He probably
knew the claim was false, and may well have understood that
those 'perfect full Originalls' were an illusion. Besides, *Honest Mans
Fortune* notwithstanding, the censorship of print was as stringent as
that controlling the theatre.

OBSCENITY AND EVASION

That sexual material was apt to fall foul of the main religio-political thrust of censorship was nothing new: our oldest myths entangle sex with shame. For early modernism, the rogue element of sex lies in the fact that fornication is as apt to afford bliss as connections which have the blessings of the Church. It tends to replace spirit with flesh, God with man, hence its potent attraction for writers and expungers who are two sides of the same coin. It threatens to be an alternative religion, and anything so potentially destabilizing must be rigorously contained. But more than politics, sex offends not only through ideas but vocabulary. Political words, often proper names, are proscribed at times. But the proscription ends with the regime, whose life is apt to be measured in decades rather than centuries. Sexual change is slower, and some of its terms have retained a subversive force throughout most of the modern era. Response is ambivalent: Sheffield exemplifies the way that people who use these terms often feel constrained to condemn them. In his 'Essay upon Poetry' (1682), he platitudinously claims that 'obscene words, too gross to move desire, / Like heaps of Fuel do but choak the Fire'.[23] But the idea that the user will have 'pall'd the appetite he meant to raise' prompts two immediate objections: on the one hand prostitutes are well aware of 'dirty talk' as erotic stimulant, while on the other obscenity may have aims quite apart from sexual arousal. And that leaves aside the matter of definition, one which is the limit of my present concern. Some consensus about what constituted obscenity, about what words were unfit to appear in print or on stage, clearly existed in Shakespeare's day. And one obvious way of gauging the gap between stage diction and street vernacular is to see which words have to be smuggled in rather than being used openly.

In 1580, a converted playwright who had come to see theatres as 'meere brothel houses of Bauderie', condemned both plays and 'riming extempore' as insufferable 'in a Christian-weale'.[24] The clown Tarlton, whose career ended about the time that Shakespeare's began, was noted for that extemporizing, and some traces of his stage practice are found in *Tarlton's Iests* (the earliest surviving edition being that of 1613). His impromptu obscenity when a lady threatens to 'cuffe' him is perhaps a regular disguisement like the back-slang noted in Cotgrave's *Dictionarie*: 'Noc. Con, *Turned backward (as our Tnuc) to be the lesse offensive to chast eares*'. Tarlton suggests that by cuffing him she would 'spel my sorrow forward, but spell my sorrow backward, then cuffe me and spare not' (sig. A3). This suggests ways of introducing obscenity in an unscripted but formulaic way, though 'fuck' makes no significant mark on sixteenth-century print. William Dunbar is the first recorded user, and appearances are largely in the Scots poets, amongst whom it was evidently vulgar but not taboo. Its only direct appearance in playbooks is also confined to Lowland Scots examples, Lindsay's *Thrie Estaits* (1602, p.45) and the anonymous play *Philotus* (1603, p.4). Although Florio uses both 'fuck' and 'fucker' for definitions in his *Worlde of Wordes* (1598), London print virtually excludes it up to the mid-seventeenth century. There are carefully veiled appearances in Jonson's *Alchemist* II.vi.34, where reference to cosmetics, 'I doe now and then giue her a *fucus*', is wilfully misunderstood: 'What! dost thou deale, NAB?'; and again in Dekker's *Northward Ho* II.i.98, which also exploits the device of misunderstanding.[25] So when Hans boasts that his father is 'de groetest fooker in all *Ausbourgh*', a whore exclaims 'The greatest what?'. The bawdry is edged with social satire since Augsburg was the home of the great merchant family of Fugger, the name – generic for financier or man of wealth – acquiring pejorative force. A boy in Middleton's *Your Five Gallants* II.iii.186 is addressed as 'my little fooker',[26] ancestor of the Crazy Gang's joke, preserved in the film *Okay for Sound* (1937): 'how's Mrs Farquhar? How's all the little Farquhars?'.

These near-homonyms work differently from Shakespeare's single punning use, which occurs in *Merry Wives*. Here the indelicate syllable is unwittingly introduced in one of the teacher's grammar terms:

> What is the focative case, William?
> WILLIAM. O – *vocativo* – O –
> EVANS. Remember, William, focative is *caret*.
> MISTRESS QUICKLY. And that's a good root.

(IV.i.45)

The joke is emphasized by the teacher's Welsh accent, just as Mistress Quickly's confusion over the Latin makes *caret* the (phallic) carrot, and subsequently travesties the genitive into 'Jenny's [vaginal] case'. Such routines, based on the grammar books – in this case Lily's – were very popular. Very similar are passages in *Two Maids of More-clacke*, the original version of which may date from 1597, the year currently favoured for *Merry Wives*. The play was written by the comedian Armin, who had certainly joined Shakespeare's company by autumn 1599 and may well have been a member for a couple of years by then.[27] The link between the grammatical puns in the two plays is unmistakable, Armin both utilizing the school lesson (sig. B4) and exploiting the Welsh accent (Tutch posing as a Welsh knight). He may have joined the Chamberlain's Men in time to appear in the first production of *Merry Wives*. But that is unimportant if we see this not as authorial indebtedness one way or the other, but as a comic turn being adapted from one play to another. And in that case, we should perhaps consider the lesson scene not as an omission from the 1602 quarto but as an addition to the script which furnished the folio text.[28] It is the second episode in Armin's play which is of present moment:

> TUTCH. With vocatiue ô, your father heares it.
> TABITH. And ablatiue caret, takes his daughter.

(G4ᵛ)

Tutch's 'ô' suggests orgasmic groans overheard by the parent, while Tabitha plays on the idea that 'rough Welch hath got a constering English', i.e. in both languages 'ablatiue caret' (ablative is lacking). But *ablative* also reinforces the lurking phallicism, deriving from a verb meaning to snatch away, or even take by force. The scene is fairly bald, probably needing verbal, and certainly clowning, amplification.

'Cunt' also generates Latin puns, where again the influence of the printed page is often apparent. A knight in Heywood's *Wise-woman of Hogsdon* IV.i[29] is called 'a beastly man' for quoting 'Nobis ut carmine dicunt'; while the joke about spelling *sunt* with a 'c' is popular throughout the seventeenth century and beyond. Shakespeare moves in other directions, Olivia's supposed letter in *Twelfth Night* II.v.88 prompting comment on 'Her c's, her u's, and her t's'. Reassurance to the bawd in *Measure for Measure* I.ii.98, that 'Good counsellors lack no clients', introduces a pun on cunt-sellers which is further refined in Cloten's 'lawyer' (*Cymbeline* II.iii.71) who will help him 'understand' the legal-vaginal 'case'. Less notorious than Hamlet's 'country matters' is the old lady's quibbling on 'count' in *Henry VIII*. This was not originally a stage gag, Valenger finding a place for 'Earles wyfe' in his 'Cockolds Kallender' (*c*.1572): 'Well may thie wyfe a Countes be yf thou wilt be an Earle; . . . / All

Countesses in honour her surmount, / They haue, she had, an honourable Count'.[30] But the pivotal relationship between the two words becomes especially apparent on stage, where the unwary (or over-wary) player might well slip unintentionally into obscenity.[31] Shakespeare had used it before, in *All's Well* II.iii.193, when Paroles, asked if he is 'companion to the Count Roussillon', answers: 'To any count; to all counts'. This catches up the clown's claim (II.ii.29) that he has an answer 'From beyond your duke to beneath your constable, it will fit any question', with play on both the implied 'count' and 'constable'. In *Henry VIII* the pun occurs in a scene which casts an ironic shadow beyond the imminent fate of Katherine of Aragon to that of Anne Bullen. The latter, full of sympathy for the unfortunate queen, is too conscious of the precariousness of power to have any wish to replace her: 'By my troth and maidenhead, / I would not be a queen' (II.iii.23). But her companion, firmly in the medieval *vieille* tradition, declares cheerfully that a bent threepence 'would hire me, / Old as I am, to queen it' (l.36). She would become a quean to become a queen, and eventually she cannot accept that Anne might behave differently: 'for little England / You'd venture an emballing' (l.46, punning on the royal orb and testicles, though 'balls' in the latter sense was seldom recorded outside Scotland before the Restoration). Meanwhile, Anne's admission that she does not even aspire to being a duchess draws a scornful retort which plays off the rank below a duke against the anatomical location, while 'way' shifts correspondingly between path and manner:

> I would not be a young count in your way
> For more than blushing comes to. If your back
> Cannot vouchsafe this burden, 'tis too weak
> Ever to get a boy.

> (II.iii.41)

Poor Anne miscarried of a son, precipitating her downfall; but the irony here is that she will indeed produce 'a gem / To lighten all this isle' (l.78) as the Lord Chamberlain hopes, and it is on that triumphal birth-note that the play ends.

THE FIGURATIVE PHALLUS

Concealed use of the taboo word is just one response to censorship; another is to produce replacement terms which – at the outset at least – are less objectionable. Shakespeare uses a number of such replacements for both of the taboo words discussed. But the practice also occurs amongst penis terms where the situation is less clear cut. The difference lies in the fact that, while varying in acceptability, they are never subject to the kind of evasions employed with 'cunt'. The discrepancy shows up in the first edition of *OED* which, omitting the two foremost obscenities, included most of these penis terms (the second edition still finds no citation for 'club', and 'horn' appears only from 1785). So they stand in marked contrast to the rejected 'cunt', which owes some of its taboo to what is denoted – an evil eye according to one folkloric construction. But probably the latter's distinctiveness, its obscene status, lies in its uncompromising aloofness from metaphor.

Not that metaphorical covering is much in evidence if we return to that last act of *Henry VIII*, where crowds mill about trying to catch a glimpse of the christening ceremony, while the porter restrains them. He jocularly wonders whether there is 'some strange Indian with the great tool come to court, the women so besiege us' (V.iii.33), recalling the coeval *Two Noble Kinsmen* (III.v.134), where the Morris dance includes a 'Babion with long tail and eke long tool'. Probably lurking behind the folklore of the well-endowed coloured man may be discerned a facile equivalence between baboons and Indians; the problem of deciding whether denizens of remote parts are men or beasts being clearly posed in *The Tempest* (II.ii.33), where a 'dead Indian' is conceived as peep-show for the 'holiday-fool'. Such considerations do nothing to diminish the irony of likening the infant Elizabeth's attractions to those of a phallic stalwart.

It may be surmised that 'tool' has a longer history than dictionary evidence (from 1553) will support. Certainly 'yard' originates in the fourteenth-century, sexual adaptation following quickly on the replacement of the ell in 1353 with this official 36-inch measurement. In *Love's Labour's Lost* (V.ii.660), Armado's affected 'I do adore thy sweet grace's slipper' is given a coital intonation by Boyet: 'Loves her by the foot', which Dumaine takes to indicate phallic inadequacy: 'He may not by the yard'. Older still is 'cock', the male domestic fowl, which figures the penis from ancient times. There is a clear record of use in late medieval English verse.[32] That Ophelia, in *Hamlet* (IV.v.59), puns on the euphemism for God in her bawdy song, 'Young men will do't, if they come to't, / By Cock, they are to blame', is confirmed by similar play in Whetstone's *Promos and Cassandra Part 2* (1578) I.iii, when Rosko congratulates himself on the profit he makes as go-between: 'cocke for my gayne doth stand', altogether more calculated blasphemy than Ophelia's.[33] More widespread in Shakespeare's day is the metaphor found in *Henry V* II.i.50, where the aptly named Pistol quibbles on the raising of a firearm's cock in readiness for discharging: 'Pistol's cock is up, / And flashing fire will follow'.

'Cock' in the firearm sense is one of that spate of technical coinages which was part of a general linguistic expansion during the sixteenth century. Amongst notable additions to the sexual vocabulary was the substantive 'prick', formed on the Chaucerian 'pricking', a verb of male activity in coitus. In *Love's Labour's Lost*, an archery scene provides the metaphor for a wit contest in which both men and women are acknowledged to have hit the mark. But Boyet presses on: 'Let the mark have a prick in't' (IV.i.131); and although the prick should provide a specific point of aim within the mark or target, it takes its real meaning from the vaginal identification of 'mark'. The friend in Sonnet 20 is 'pricked . . . out for women's pleasure'; and in *Pericles* xix.42, a brothel attendant declares that the reluctant heroine 'were a rose indeed, if she had but —', being too 'modest' to finish the sentence. But Mercutio is less squeamish, answering Romeo's complaint (I.iv.26) that love 'pricks like thorn' with a recommendation to get rid of a troublesome erection (concealed behind the image of Cupid and his darts): 'Prick love for pricking, and you beat love down'. Substantive use occurs at II.iii.104, where he tells the nurse the time: 'the bawdy hand of the dial is now upon the prick of noon'. Since clocks had only a single hand, the phallic innuendo comes readily even without the reinforcement of 'prick', actually the mark on the dial. Print achieved a new fluidity between noun and verb, in both directions; and the penis noun established itself so firmly in the course of the seventeenth century that it became impossible to use the verb in the way favoured by the old romancers.[34] Indeed, the new literacy furnished its own handwriting quibble (prick as full stop), found in Middleton's *Blurt, Master Constable* (1601–2) I.ii.129, where the constable embellishes with a pun on the vaginal oyster his humorous comment on a pass written by the duke, 'for the duke's hand had a prick in't, when I was with him, with opening oysters'.[35]

The codpiece originated in the fifteenth century; but the obvious transference to phallic use (cf. the French *braguette*) is not recorded before the end of the sixteenth century, by which time the garment had ceased to be worn. The anonymous author of *Wily Beguiled* (1596–1606) alludes to 'a carousing codpiece',[36] and in *Measure for Measure* III.i.378 the image of phallic insurrection makes apt comment on a ruthlessly repressive regime: 'for the rebellion of a codpiece to take away the life of a man!'. But in *Much Ado* III.iii.131, Hercules is confused with Samson, a 'shaven Hercules in the smirched worm-eaten tapestry, where his codpiece seems as massy as his club'. This woven hero is dressed in Tudor style, like the frescoed Adonis found at a St Albans pub in 1986. Tension arises because 'club', and indeed specifically that of Hercules, also had a place in the erotic vocabulary.[37] That this hero had achieved chapbook notoriety is suggested by the fact that 'Hercules's club' was soldiers' slang for a trench weapon in the early seventeenth century. Still, much of Shakespeare's joke lies in Hercules wearing an outmoded style which gave parodic emphasis rather than concealment to the genitals.

Finally, the use of 'horn' for erect penis was as popular with the Elizabethans as it is today; and for them it had the bonus of punning on the cuckold's mythic adornment. So Buckley, 'Oxford Libell' (*c*.1564) describes how a woman learns 'as well to giue as take the horne'.[38] The meanings converge when servants bicker in *Taming of the Shrew* IV.i.23, Curtis's 'Away, you three-inch fool. I am no beast', being answered with a gibe and a boast: 'Am I but three inches? Why, thy horn is a foot, and so long am I, at the least'.[39]

WIT'S BEDLAM

With that 'horn' pun, sexual meanings reinforce one another. But Shakespeare's fools offer other patterns. While puns may be unwitting as well as witty, they are often the province of the witless – the foolish or crazy – who may paradoxically exhibit more wit than the sane. Along with the pun, verse and song are natural vehicles for the fool, since they too have a masking capability denied to more prosaic statements. Veiled utterance could masquerade as nonsense; and even if the fool was detected stumbling into sense he could not be held responsible. This was the grand evasion, for the cunning dramatist could hide from official disapproval behind the fool's privilege. But the mood was right for this ploy in the last decades of the sixteenth century. As mental illness became an increasing problem, so the presses fed people's interest in the subject. Along with progressive thinking, they also fixed older ideas in print; and both provided stimulus to the dramatist who recognized the substantial ironic and satiric possibilities of the fool.

Some of these threads will be drawn together by discussion of *King Lear,* where the divided kingdom reflects a painful rift between James and his Parliament. So much of the action is played out in that borderland where madness and sanity merge; and it is here that sex and power appear as correlatives. The edge with which Shakespeare cuts through the veneer of civilization in this play has probably been sharpened by Montaigne, who understands the power of the word independent of the act it denotes. His aphorism, as rendered by Florio, seems to have established itself as an English proverb: 'Wee have taught Ladies to blush, onely by hearing that named, which they nothing feare to doe'.[40] It recalls how the French princess in *Henry V* III.iv.52, encountering '*De foot et de cown*' as she practises English, is intrigued as well as embarrassed by their resemblance to *foutre* and *con*. Shakespeare had been interested from the outset in how standards of linguistic propriety are socially enforced without prejudice to private behaviour. The bride Lavinia in *Titus Andronicus* II.ii.17, asked if she has been aroused too early, provides unwitting testimony of her husband's renewed vigour: 'I have been broad awake two hours and more'. The pleasure may be taken, but not spoken of – except as the subconscious betrays.

The fool is the voice of the subconscious, closing the gap between instinct and appearance. As both symbol and reflector of disorder, he shows up as illusion the social definition of order. In *As You Like It* Touchstone parodies a love poem, specifically one of those produced by Orlando. The courtship poem, a later medieval favourite, became the staple of Elizabethan anthologies. It is a poem of compliment and persuasion, the objectives of the persuasion being seldom openly declared. Touchstone's game is to draw out, albeit obliquely, what is implicit in the Petrarchan evasion. Indeed the indirection is as important as the bawdry; part of the fun lies in digging it out, just as the sexual kernel must be dug out of his figurative nut:

Wintered garments must be lined,
So must slender Rosalind.
They that reap must sheaf and bind,
Then to cart with Rosalind.
'Sweetest nut hath sourest rind',
Such a nut is Rosalind.
He that sweetest rose will find
Must find love's prick, and Rosalind.

(III.ii.10)

Sharpham's *Fleire* (1606) I.ii.68 makes similar play with the lining of a cloak which is not 'linde through', but 'a good depth in' – and 'Ladies loue to haue it Linde a good depth in'. Touchstone's version convicts Rosalind of whoring so that, like the harvest crop, she must be carted. But thereafter he changes tack. Just as the 'sourest rind' alludes to Rosalind's concealing male attire, so does the final couplet depend on her being thought 'accomplished / With that we lack', as another disguised heroine puts it (*Merchant* III.iv.61). Here, the vaginal rose will only be obtained through the paradoxical discovery that this Rose has no prick beyond that of Cupid's dart.

Clowns' songs are often put to such layered use, though some might be offensively direct. There is a Puritan complaint of 1577 that plays instruct how 'to sing filthie songs of loue'; and Gosson, in 1582, attacks a 'glosing plaie at yᵉ Theater' which has 'enterlarded in it a baudie song of a maide of Kent'.[41] Autolycus may have sung something of the sort, though *The Winter's Tale* offers no textual evidence. Like Shakespeare himself, Autolycus is a mediator between print and oral culture. The broadsides which he offers for sale include

the prettiest love songs for maids, so without bawdry, which is strange, with such delicate burdens of dildos and fadings, 'Jump her, and thump her'; and where some stretch-mouthed rascal would, as it were, mean mischief and break a foul gap into the matter, he makes the maid to answer 'Whoop, do me no harm, good man!' (IV.iv.194).

Innuendo of the vaginal 'gap' perhaps combines with allusion to mouth-pulling, an obscene gesture like the *fico* (both are found in Jan Pollack's *Mocking of Christ*, painted in 1492 and now in the Bavarian State Museum). Those 'delicate burdens' turn up in bawdy ballads like 'The Travelling Tinker' (D'Urfey, VI, p.296), where the tradesman will 'thump, thump thump, and knick knack knock, to do her Business rarely', or Middleton's *Chaste Maid of Cheapside* (1611–13) I.ii.56, where a wittol croons of a substitute phallus in delight that another man takes on his sexual responsibilities: '*La dildo, dildo la dildo, la dildo dildo de dildo*'.

Edgar's 'Heigh no nonny' in *Lear* xi.78 is another such refrain, glossed by Drayton's 'noninos of filthie ribauldry'.[42] In this same speech, Edgar claims to have been a servant and to have done 'the act of darkness' with his mistress, adding that he has 'out-paramoured the Turk'. This is the fool's figurative parading of his genitals, image of that degradation out of which civilized man is thought to have emerged. But Edgar knows better and warns by precept as well as feigned example: 'Keep thy foot out of brothel, thy hand out of placket'. He is one of that 'quartet of near-buffoons – a madman, a fool, a blind man and a feigned demon', as Kenneth Tynan once described them,[43] which exposes that existential absurdity masquerading as civilization in the play. The pretence of civilization is that it has renounced instinct, though it is the blind rage of desire which governs each move in the power game. Lust for political and sexual dominance blurs in Edmund's relationship with Lear's daughters: 'Neither can be enjoyed / If both remain alive' (xxii.62); and this becomes a paradigm for the play's larger corruptions which repeatedly receive sexual coding. So Edgar (xi.69) catches up reference to Lear's 'pelican daughters' with a fragment of coital song: 'Pillicock sat on pillicock's hill'. In this he is entirely at one with the fool, who sings an unsavoury verse on crablice as comment on Lear's folly:

> The codpiece that will house
> Before the head has any,
> The head and he shall louse,
> So beggars marry many.
>
> (ix.27)

Copulation will facilitate the cross-movement of lice – the 'many' that beggars marry – in head hair and pubic hair. That the fool manages to describe the process in suitably veiled terms is indicated by the absence of proper annotation.

But the most significant sex–power link comes with Edgar's song beginning 'Come o'er the bourn, Bessy, to me' – not a lost love-song, but a political broadside – upon which the fool improvises:

> Her boat hath a leak,
> And she must not speak
> Why she dares not come over to thee.

(xiii.21)

The utterances of the mad and foolish in Shakespeare, as Horatio says of Ophelia's, prompt the listener to 'botch the words up fit to their own thoughts' (*Hamlet* IV.v.10). Hence the fool's lyrics have sometimes been botched up with a bawdy interpretation. But the material pattern of sex and politics is already established by Edgar's line which belongs to Birche's 'Songe betwene the Quenes majestie and Englande', written on the accession of Elizabeth in 1558.[44] The fool's words about the boat journey and the woman who 'must not speak', evoke Cordelia, known for her reticence and now domiciled in France. Freud identifies Cordelia's dumbness as a 'death' symbol.[45] But this gains peculiar emphasis here, as she merges with Queen Elizabeth, who will never speak again, having some years since reached that 'country from whose bourn / No traveller returns' (Wells-Taylor's retention of quarto's 'burn' in the *Lear* passage is confusing). Birche's ballad had been written as a love duet between Elizabeth and England, but that love match is over and the present marriage is less happy; hence perhaps the reason for the absence of this passage from the copy on which the folio text was based. The play has been seen as a comment on some of the constitutional problems impeding the Union of the Crowns. This was just one of the difficulties facing James during his first Parliament. The way that Shakespeare uses Elizabeth's birth as a high note on which to end *Henry VIII*, discussed above, finds broken parallel here in this recollection of the optimism attending her accession.

Lear provides a highly charged version of that remark by Montaigne quoted earlier:

> Behold yond simp'ring dame,..
> That minces virtue, and does shake the head
> To hear of pleasure's name:

The fitchew nor the soilèd horse goes to't
With a more riotous appetite.

(xx.1114)

Montaigne's cool rationalism is lost in this daughter-distorted
vision, but the sex–power equation receives its starkest expression
in Lear's recoil from the sulphurous vaginal pit. The pattern of
ironies is intricate, the more so as Lear is unconscious of them
as his companions in derangement are not. His equation is naïve
since, while sexual abandonment and the irrational lust for power
are analogues, they are still more importantly adversaries. The
secrecy which the latter craves is threatened by the former,
which therefore becomes a logical scapegoat. Already *Romeo
and Juliet* darkly hints at this, and Mercutio's bawdy banter
is an exercise in containment. So he slily likens love to 'a
great natural that runs lolling up and down to hide his bauble
in a hole' (II.iii.84), establishing a sex–folly relationship where
genital development balances mental deficiency. He effectively
rejects the sexual enterprise whose comical resilience is affirmed
by the clown in *Twelfth Night* I.v.4: 'Let her hang me. He that is
well hanged in this world needs to fear no colours' (no enemies).
Being 'well hanged', Feste scorns further hanging, though in *Lear*,
of course, the 'fool' is hanged in earnest. But Lear himself, for all
his confusions, is not propelled towards Mercutio's limited (and
limiting) objectives. His role as fool-commentator is as central,
though not so immediate, as that in Lucas van Leyden's influential
woodcut of the Prodigal Son's debaucheries (1519), where the
fool leans through a window to address us. (That he addresses
us as well as the Prodigal is due to the alienation produced by his
fool's garb, meaning that we identify with the Prodigal – the real
fool – rather than the observer-commentator.) Those subjective
distortions which have Lear in thrall, with female sexuality as
presiding demon, are readily decoded by an audience which has
been carefully prepared for the task. Although a more problematic
mediator than Lucas's fool, Lear resembles him in his powerlessness
to intervene in events. But his role is crucial in the revelation of
Jacobean political debaucheries, which are an extreme form of that
socially cultivated distance between the word and the deed.

4

The First Print Era: Reader-Spectator as Voyeur

Protestant thinking on sexual issues gains importance not from its novelty but its wide dissemination. Much of it had been anticipated in the late Middle Ages, part of that northern European restiveness which gave rise to the printing press. But this mechanical innovation made all the difference: Pope John XXI could compile his *Treasury of Health*,[1] including abortion recipes, in a world where books were handwritten, and information consequently restricted. Print demystified, weakening élite privilege of access and therefore the élite themselves, particularly as it encouraged translation. It was a bawd presiding over the rape of knowledge, a disrupter of stable cultural assumptions. Hence the outcry against the printing of theological works, and especially the Bible, in vernacular languages, which dispensed with mediation: that way Protestantism lies. The shift is demonstrated in contrasting altarpiece styles. Medieval altarpieces, with their folding wings, were often kept shut, their secrets disclosed only under controlled conditions. The laity found food for contemplation in the less rarefied pictures on the outside, and the sense of mystery within. Donne perceives a sexual dimension to this when, in 'Going to Bed', he likens clothed women to 'pictures, or . . . books gay coverings'. His mood is essentially Catholic, with women as 'mystick books, which only' the privileged 'Must see reveal'd'.[2] On the other hand, the Lutheran altarpiece of Heinrich Fullmaurer (*c*.1540; Gotha Schlossmuseum) invites perusal. It has double outer wings and inner wings arranged like the leaves of a book – no fortuitous resemblance, as the heavy doses of German text accompanying many of the 157 biblical scenes indicate.

Wyclif's translation of the Bible in the 1380s was a lesser catastrophe in a manuscript world; indeed a French translation of a century earlier seems to have quickly thrown off ecclesiastical suspicion.[3] But the printing of a High German version in 1466, followed by an Italian in 1471, laid the foundations for revolution. There were to be no more Italian editions in early print, Cellini having to rely on this Venetian incunable while imprisoned in the Vatican in 1539. But translations appeared in various other vernaculars during the next half-century. British resistance was finally circumvented when Tyndale had his English New Testament published at Cologne in 1525. His Englishing of *Genesis* issued from Antwerp five years later, a momentous irony as the story of Forbidden Knowledge became available in forbidden form. When Milton handled this story in *Paradise Lost*, he was amongst those who rejected the idea of sex as a sordid consequence of the Fall, condemning those 'hypocrites' who 'talk / Of purity, . . . / Defaming as impure what God declares / Pure' (IV.744). When Adam and Eve seek their 'blissful bower', 'on their naked limbs the flowery roof Shower'd roses' (l.772), delicately suggesting their motions of pleasure. For those of Milton's persuasion, it is in the postlapsarian world that this carnal innocence became tainted by lust. None the less, the forbidden knowledge which Adam and Eve acquire continues to be understood as sex. The newly vernacularized story, treating disobedience, is too obviously powered by sexuality for it to be otherwise. With sexual awareness comes shame and a covering of the genitals; so that the very act of genital display seems to re-enact the Fall. Looking equates with doing, the clearest paradigm occurring in that newly developed mode of pornography. For print gave a new vitality to the myth, and conning the forbidden became an issue in much early modern art, both verbal and visual. Veronese uses the witty ploy of the animated statue not only in his Susanna paintings but in *Venus, Satyr and Cupid*.[4] Here the intimacy of Venus's embrace is coded by her leg slung over that of the satyr. The baby Cupid sleeps, but a marble figure of Pan leers towards the erotic activity with conspicuous excitement. The spectator's role is sharply defined by the statue's response, since he or she too exists in another dimension yet lingers over the libidinous scene with questionable relish.

Just as the narrative aspect of voyeurism is shared by painter and poet, so is the picture–spectator relationship matched by that of text and reader. The bathing scene is a popular vehicle in both media, having Ovidian as well as biblical provenance (Susanna and Bathsheba). The latter was one of two images which came to prominence in the last phase of the manuscript books of hours, the other being Job covered in sores, appropriated soon after to represent the syphilitic. Sidney, in *Arcadia* II.11, pursues the implications of a 'Diana and Actaeon' painting through an elaborate bathing scene.[5] Two princesses go to sport themselves in the river, accompanied by a supposed amazon (actual prince) who affects a cold to excuse 'herself' from participating. The latter carries the voyeuristic burden as they remove 'the eclipsing of their apparel', while another princely lover is subsequently discovered covertly watching from the bushes. But the third and most important voyeur-role is that assumed by the reader, moved by Sidney's heightened account of the proceedings. In *Astrophil and Stella* Sidney plays the game of disclosure differently. The fiction of a courtship takes on added intimacy when he trails the idea of a *roman à clef*, the poet's adulterous attentions to Penelope Rich.[6] But Sidney and the various recipients of the sequence in manuscript copies would have moved in the same court circles. Once the poems were committed to print, these supposed upper class goings-on became public knowledge, revealed to anyone with a few shillings to buy the book. Ostensibly it opens up a courtly lover's private emotions not only to strangers but to those lower in the social scale. Sidney had avoided both the vulgarity of print and the subversive effect of publicizing the social behaviour of a class whose power depends substantially on the maintaining of barriers. But for his literary executors the conflict between keeping distance and making money ended in the opening of palace doors.

Of course the political dimension gets played down as the lure of prestige and profit comes into play. Wendy Wall[7] notes how the issue of gentlemanly propriety could be evaded by a pretence that the text appeared in print without authorial consent; not only protecting the writer but arousing the reader's prurient curiosity. She indicates how often forewords resort to sexual imagery, which offers the text as forbidden flesh and invites the reader to thwart prohibition by partaking – or at least by looking. The practice is persistent, the supposed autobiography of a whore, *The Rise and Fall of Madam Coming-Sir* (1703), being introduced by its author thus:

> I shall not use the Accustomary Policy of my own Sex, and endeavour to strengthen the Readers Appetite, to a short

Entertainment (which as yet lies hid behind the Curtain) by keeping him in suspence with a tedious Preamble; but like a true good Humour'd *Prostitute*, who, at the Expence of a Bottle Resigns her Ultimate, I will open the Secret, and give you leave to enter the Premises without any further Hesitation or Delay.[8]

The Water Poet, publishing a prostitute's character in 1622, justifies giving his 'Booke the Title of a *Whore*' since a book, 'like a *Whore* by day-light, or by Candle, . . . is euer free for euery knaue to handle'.[9] He has in mind a figure which became common currency following its use in Marlowe's *Ovid* (1580s), where the lover declares that even if he sees his lady 'ope the two-leav'd book' to a rival, he will trust her words of innocence 'more than mine eyes'.[10] *The Practical Part of Love* (1660, p.39) describes the chief item in the pornographic library of 'Loves Accademy' as 'a Book that had no Title, and therefore I cannot tell its name; I was almost as much pleased with looking on its outside, as on its inside . . . I could not find that it had above two leaves in it'. Shirley rides the image hard in *The Cardinal* (1641) V.ii, where a lady is described as

A pretty book of flesh and blood, and well
Bound up, in a fair letter too. Would I
Had her with all the errata!

His Catholicism emerges in what follows:

I would print her with an *index*
Expurgatorius; a table drawn
Of her court heresies; and when she's read,
Cum privilegio, who dares call her whore?[11]

The book–woman equation is clearly very fluid. But the patterns of prohibition and authorization with which Shirley plays enforce the parallel between sex and reading. Incautious indulgence in either spells danger: the figure gets its charge from the fact that books in the early modern period were taken seriously, something which only happens today in a totalitarian state. The risks attaching to reader-voyeurism are well expressed by Sandys, who says of the Diana–Actaeon story: '*this fable was invented to shew vs how dangerous a curiosity it is to search into the secrets of Princes, or by chance to discover their nakedness'.*[12]

Shakespeare's (and Fletcher's) one fling at a sexually laden foreword comes in the Prologue to *The Two Noble Kinsmen*:

> New plays and maidenheads are near akin:
> Much followed both, for both much money giv'n
> If they stand sound and well.

This suggests a brothel transaction, the audience eager to take the new arrival's virginity. But the impression is modified by reference to marriage and the bride who, after 'first night's stir / Yet still is modesty'. Her 'noble breeder' is Chaucer, from whose *Canterbury Tales* the plot was taken, and the mood carries over into the play's opening scene with its wedding procession.

But Shakespeare also toys with some of the voyeuristic possibilities of the sonnet sequence. *A Lover's Complaint*, included in the first edition of the Sonnets, has a narrator *en cachette*. But the device is given none of the complexity contrived by Dunbar in 'Tua Mariit Wemen and the Wedo' (*c*.1508). In that poem the voyeur is not there by chance as in Shakespeare, but has deliberately sought to eavesdrop on the three women of the title who celebrate midsummer's night in a garden. He wishes to learn what women talk about when they are amongst themselves, tongues loosened by drink. His eager squirming through the undergrowth shows in that verb, 'so hard I inthrang', which Chaucer invests with such trenchant coital meaning in *The Merchant's Tale*.[13] There is a hint that Dunbar's narrator, comically confused with the poet himself, may be limited to this vicarious penetration of women's secrets.

But Shakespeare can be as sophisticated as Dunbar in exploiting autobiographical confusions. Like Sidney, he builds his sonnet sequence upon them. Teasing begins with the dedication 'TO.THE.ONLY.BEGETTER . . . M^r. W.H.'; and its success is demonstrated by the many attempts to solve this riddle and to identify friend and dark lady. He is still teasing as late as Sonnet 151 when, his 'flesh . . . rising at thy name doth point out thee / As his triumphant prize'. But no distinguishing name appears; he simply calls 'Her "love" for whose dear love I rise and fall' (a love sufficiently defined by cyclic erection and detumescence). The most celebrated sonnet opening in the collection,

Th'expense of spirit in a waste of shame
Is lust in action

(Sonnet 129)

makes that unstoppable drive into the second line a figure of sexual urgency. Meaning pivots on 'spirit',[14] both soul and semen; wasting semen (in waists of shame) reducing the chance of saving one's soul. It is just this damning prodigality which is demonstrated in Sonnets 135–6 by that spate of 'will' puns leading to final 'admission' that poet and protagonist are one. But Will employs will relentlessly. Meanings of desire and determination entangle with the genital sense of will (it is likely that Shakespeare is idiosyncratic with his vaginal meaning, despite the annotation which has accreted about this use):

Wilt thou, whose will is large and spacious,
Not once vouchsafe to hide my will in thine?

(Sonnet 135)

The compliment in the first line is almost obliterated by sexual insult: largeness may be welcome in a penis but never in a vagina. But while connecting the woman's capaciousness with her extreme promiscuity, the Shakespearean lover is still ambitious to 'fulfil the treasure of thy love' (Sonnet 136). In *Hamlet* I.iii.31, Ophelia must not her 'chaste treasure open'; but the dark lady's is all too open, so there is a touch of phallic boasting in the idea that he could fulfil it (fill it full). This appears to be undercut by humility, his penis ready to take turns with those of her many other partners: 'fill it full with wills, and my will one'. But play on the proverbial 'Among a number one is reckoned none' shows the banal truth:

Then in the number let me pass untold,
Though in thy store's account I one must be.

This has something of the flatness of Eliot's lines, 'She turns and looks a moment in the glass, / Hardly aware of her departed lover', the empty coital round caught in the movement of the gramophone record.[15] Shakespeare's lover will settle for a receptacle rather than a relationship. There is a glimpse of quick pleasure, then a tantalizing conclusion anticipating that reference to the dark lady's name mentioned above:

> e but my name thy love, and love that still,
>   then thou lov'st me for my name is Will.

But here the man's name is slipped in. Love my penis and you love me, insists the poet-protagonist, for we have nominal identity. And the unravelling of puns is apt to blur with an attempt to unravel further identities. That 'store's account', the inventory of lovers with its play on cunt,[16] suggests that Will may pass unnoticed emotionally, but not financially. For he is involved with a mercenary lady, and the attentive contemporary reader was evidently invited to wonder which of Elizabethan London's professionals might be indicated. In Sonnet 144, Shakespeare not only ties the two sections of his sequence together, with suspicions that the friend is one of the dark lady's bedfellows, but he recalls the theological imagery of Sonnet 129. These two are the protagonist's better and worser angels, and he imagines 'one angel in another's hell'. Nashe had already borrowed Boccaccio's vaginal figure in *The Choise of Valentines* (*c.*1593), describing a glass dildo moving glibly 'to hell be lowe'; and Marston was just one of many early seventeenth-century users, anticipating Lear's antifeminist ravings in *The Fawne* (1604–6, Act IV: 'above them naught but *will*, beneath them naught but *hel*'.[17] Shakespeare's sonnet use derives its force from the intersection of hell-fire and the burning of pox. Poor Will must

> live in doubt
> Till my bad angel fire my good one out.

But once again the clue proves a dead end for identity-hunters, since a diseased whore would have been no rarity in Shakespeare's London.

Shakespeare's feint at autobiography, implicating the reader in the pursuit of secrets, is matched on stage by other models of voyeuristic invasion of privacy. His best example occurs in *Cymbeline*, following an unwise wager by Posthumus on his wife Imogen's chastity. Iachimo, finding her virtue impregnable, tricks his way into her bedroom concealed in a trunk. The wager resembles that resulting in Lucretia's rape, and this story is in Iachimo's mind as he emerges from concealment:

Our Tarquin thus
Did softly press the rushes ere he wakened
The chastity he wounded.   .

(II.ii.12)

Cymbeline dates from 1609 or earlier, and *Macbeth* is usually assigned
to 1606. In that play, Macbeth will go on his murderous errand
'With Tarquin's ravishing strides' (II.i.55). This is more than some
trite idea of the rape of kingship. The professional killer, who has
created 'Strange images of death' (I.iii.95), is abruptly confronted
with the morality of his trade. He feverishly probes the nature of
murder, and pushes with this image beyond the obvious brutality.
For such crimes as his strike too easily as the commonplaces of
history, less disturbing than the activities of sex-killer or rapist. The
violence of ambition or murder for gain have a facile reasonableness
about them; and this is what the Tarquin figure subverts, suggesting
that actions such as Macbeth's are just as disturbingly perverse as the
sex crime. So too, although Iachimo uses no violence, his violation
of Imogen's privacy and rape of her good name (a social death
almost resulting in actual death) have a sexual edge as darkly
overtoned as that in the Tarquin story. Death the ravisher has
invaded her chamber and remarked her whiteness, 'whiter than the
sheets' (II.ii.16); but it is annexed to that of a marble tomb effigy:

O sleep, thou ape of death, lie dull upon her,
And be her sense but as a monument
Thus in a chapel lying.

(II.ii.31)

Iachimo steals the sleeper's bracelet, love token and vaginal
emblem, and eagerly notes 'On her left breast / A mole' (l.37),
knowledge of which will make her husband 'think I have picked
the lock and ta'en / The treasure of her honour'. The scene ends
with heavy irony. First the mood of rape is powerfully intensified
by the discovery that Imogen has been reading   .

The tále of Tereus. Here the leaf's turned down
Where Philomel gave up.

(II.ii.45)

Then the pseudo-rapist returns to concealment with a reversal of
the lover's plea (Ovid, *Amores*, I.13) for night's horses to slow
down: 'Swift, swift, you dragons of the night'.

When Iachimo returns to Posthumus, his trump cards are Imogen's bracelet and mole. But, holding them in reserve, he first describes the artifacts in

> her bedchamber –
> Where I confess I slept not, but profess
> Had that was well worth watching –
>
> (II.iv.66)

his insinuating parenthesis keeping the real issue in play, honing his accounts of a tapestry of 'Proud Cleopatra when she met her Roman' (l.70), and the wonderfully lifelike carving of 'Chaste Dian bathing' over the fireplace (l.82). The latter subject is obviously apt to the circumstances, but an Italian marble relief now in the Chateau d'Ecouen near Paris, and once the chimney ornament in a house at Châlons-sur-Marne, suggests that it was not uncommonly given this focal placing in home décor. Such décor, like public art, was apt to be chosen for its moral or political message, the principal pictures in Thomas Sackford's 'fyne howse' supplying a good example:

> Yn the haul over the chimney is the story of Sampson and Dalilah gallantly paynted and over the table 2 stories of Joseph and his brethern and at the end the story of Scipio which gave unto Lucius the mayds husband the money that hir parents payd to rawnsom hir.[18]

But bedroom decoration had a further importance, given the influence thought to be exerted by sensory impressions. So in Cartwright's *Ordinary* (1634–5)[19]

> 'Tis thought the hairy child, that's shown about,
> Came by the mother's thinking on the picture
> Of Saint John Baptist in his camel's coat.
>
> (II.iii)

The power of the imagination is similarly attested in Gough's *Strange Discovery* (1640), where it is said that

> *Persina* in the act of generation
> Contemplatively eying the faire picture
> Of beautifull *Andromeda*, and firing
> A strong imagination thereupon,

Conceived in her wombe the very figure
Of *Perseus* Mistris.

(V.vi)

The folklore goes back to the Old Testament. Sir Thomas Browne,
in his *Pseudodoxia Epidemica* (1646: VI.10), alludes to the way
that 'Jacob's cattle became speckled . . . by the Power and
Efficacy of Imagination, which produceth effects in the conception
correspondent unto the phancy of the Agents in generation; and
sometimes assimilates the Idea of the Generator into a reality in the
thing ingendred' (Genesis 30:39), reinforcing with examples from
Hippocrates and Heliodorus.[20]

But there is more involved than occult eugenics. Gayton, in *Don
Quixot* (1654, p.17), would ban women's reading of romances since
they, 'going to bed full of Imagination transgresse in Fancy with
Gondibert, and forget who they are under, or who is over them'.
At any rate, the pattern put before us in those *Cymbeline* scenes
reveals some of the complexity of response generated by the art
of the early modern period. Art as revelation, of the private or
even the forbidden, jostles with the expectation that it exert both
exemplary and sympathetic influences.

PART II
Shakespeare and the Classics

5

Roman Rapes

LUCRECE AS HEROINE AND MAKER

In an age of growing national consciousness, even such mythic British history as *Cymbeline* helps towards the shaping of identity. Given the high estimation in which classical civilization had come to be held, the play is particularly effective in relating the history of these islands to the Roman world. It serves as bridge between those chronicle plays covering later periods of British history and the theatre's ambitious project of popularizing Roman history and thought.

As we have seen, in *Cymbeline*, Shakespeare uses images of rape to open up serious questions about the role of art in an age of print. But rape has a significant place in his work apart from this. There are would-be rapists like Proteus in *Two Gentlemen of Verona* V.iv.57, who would 'woo . . . like a soldier, at arm's end' (i.e. at phallic sword's point); or the boorish Cloten in *Cymbeline* again, who – told by Imogen that her husband's 'meanest garment' is worth more to her than a multitude of Clotens (II.iii.130) – dresses in some of her husband's clothes to add piquancy to his enjoyment of her (III.v.137). Caliban too, his human status confirmed when Prospero teaches him to speak, emphatically proclaims his humanity by attempting to rape the daughter of this man who raped his island. But when Shakespeare gets serious about rape, he turns for his pattern not to the primitive, the denizen of newly colonized territory, but to the classical authors. Questions of immediacy, or of lived as against vicarious experience, hardly existed when it was considered that to read Ovid was to study nature. Sir John Cheke's view that reading the Greek classics (along with the Bible) must needs make 'an excellent man' is approved by Ascham,[1] who allows similar efficacy to the standard Roman authors. Such was the status of those authors that their accounts of Philomel and Lucretia were taken to provide all that needed saying on the subject of rape: Tereus and Tarquin are the archetypal rapists.

Ovid's key place in Shakespeare, as in Elizabethan culture at large, is patent. Ovid for most people meant above all the *Metamorphoses* – and that in Golding's translation. The first part of this translation appeared in 1565, followed by the complete version in 1567. This decade of Shakespeare's birth was a bumper period for Ovidian translations: it saw not only parts of the *Metamorphoses* from other hands, but also Turbervile's complete Englishing of the *Heroides*. However, Golding's book was the most influential, reprinting five times until finally ousted by Sandys's version in 1626: 'wee knowe nott Sandes, nor Ouid from each other', praised Hemminge.[2] But Golding, without professing to match the original's 'pleasant style', does in his 'Preface too the Reader' claim to have made Ovid an English poet. Notably, too, in his dedicatory epistle Golding not only offers a moralized reading of the poem but claims that its contents are in complete harmony with those of the Old Testament: 'he dooth with Genesis agree'.[3] Golding's insistence makes better sense if we recall that considerations in reading both ancient and modern authors were practical rather than aesthetic. The utility value of reading was a key matter for the Elizabethan burgher who scorned idle pleasure. Play and poetry books, or purpose-made anthologies, served as aids to articulacy for those cultivating wit and refinement. So Slender, anxious to court his lady in *Merry Wives* I.i.181, 'had rather than forty shillings I had my book of songs and sonnets here'. A maiden in Taylor's *Divers Crab-tree Lectures* (1639) mocks her tradesman-lover for claiming as his own compliments which she recalls having 'read . . . in Print'; and in Browne's 'Fido, an Epistle to Fidelia', a lady is impressed by the flowers in an admirer's letter. However,

> Her chambermaid's great reading quickly strikes
> That good opinion dead, and swears that this
> Was stol'n from Palmerin or Amadis.[4]

That Shakespeare's own work served such a purpose is indicated by Lewis Sharpe, *The Noble Stranger* (1640: IV [G4]): 'oh for the book of *Venus* and *Adonis*, to court my Mistris by'. But Bowdler, in Heywood's *Faire Maid of the Exchange* (1594–1607), who has 'never read any thing but *Venus* and *Adonis*', finds it ineffectual.

He ruefully reflects that '*Venus* her selfe with all her skill could not winne *Adonis*, with the same words'.[5] However, it was possible to draw more from the poets than a few seductive phrases, or a spurious reputation for wit. The sonneteers, penning anatomies of love, were effectively supplying handbooks of sexual psychology, often the most subtle and penetrating accounts then available. To read them could result in a deepening of perceptions or expanding of the consciousness; hence the quality of personal relationships might actually be improved through acquaintance with love poetry. In a prosaic age, such notions of poetry are shelved as quaintly old-fashioned; but they were of prime importance to those in need of moral or spiritual justification for their reading.

According to Aretino, the fledgling whore must pretend an interest in the Petrarchans, flattering clients by asking them to read a sonnet to her.[6] This is at a fairly humble level of harlotry. But Veronica Franco, one of the great Venetian courtesans, composed her own sonnets to admirers; while perhaps the most celebrated of them all, Tullia d'Aragona, not only published sonnets but held regular literary salons in Rome.[7] What this suggests is that there was a closer relationship between reading or writing about love and actually making it than we would expect today. The nearest twentieth-century equivalent would be the way that, in the 1930s and 40s, people's emotional responses were shaped by cinema, and more recently by television; though these media lack the element of danger attaching to sixteenth-century print, where harsh punishments awaited those who published the wrong thing.

This charting of experience by means of literature (or painting) shows up strongly in *The Rape of Lucrece*. Books have their place in the poem's imagery, the train of events being set in motion by unwise boasting about Lucrece's beauty and virtue: 'why is Collatine the publisher / Of that rich jewel' (l.33). Lucrece's direct experience of duplicity is evidently limited, so that when Tarquin covertly bestows lustful glances on her, she is unable to 'read the subtle shining secrecies / Writ in the glassy margins of such books' (l.101). Later on, this becomes the basis for some crass stereotyping. Very modest experience would disprove that,

> Though men can cover crimes with bold stern looks,
> Poor women's faces are their own faults' books.
>
> (1252)

Such lines would pass from the distressed Lucrece, tormented by fears that her ordeal is written in her blushes. But they are altogether more troublesome from a narrator who is not of that unreliable kind which Gascoigne had developed as a major fictional ploy. Nor will the tone allow the tongue-in-cheek sententiousness adopted as Marlowe's authorial voice in *Hero and Leander* (1593). Lucrece is no Hero who, hilariously 'seeing a naked man, . . . screech'd for fear'.[8] None the less, and it is perhaps worth digressing briefly on the subject of the naked lover, this is what greets the rudely awakened Lucrece: Tarquin, leaving his own bed, had done no more than throw 'his mantle rudely o'er his arm' (l.170). There is no such detail in Shakespeare's sources, and a naked Tarquin is rare in art. One appears in an engraving by Veneziano after a design by Raphael.[9] He is shown poised over his victim, pulling the bedsheets from her naked body. Early states of the engraving anticipate what must follow by including a pair of coupled dogs. But the two engravings of the subject by Aldegrever,[10] dating from 1539 (copying Pencz) and 1553, combine a naked Tarquin with a detail which tantalizingly raises the question of whether Shakespeare came across one of them. For Tarquin uses his knee to force Lucrece's thighs apart, a detail obliquely present in Shakespeare, as the rapist reaches Lucrece's bedroom 'And with his knee the door he opens wide' (l.359). But whereas Aldegrever's Lucretias are naked, Shakespeare's wears a nightgown, which serves powerfully to evoke Tarquin's brutality:

> The wolf hath seized his prey, the poor lamb cries,
>   Till with her own white fleece her voice controlled
>   Entombs her outcry in her lips' sweet fold.

> (677)

OED has a 1546 reference to a nightgown 'furrid withe lambe'; but these lines give the impression of flaying.

However, Shakespeare's acquaintance with Continental prints remains a matter for teasing speculation, whereas the experience of reading clearly provides a significant metaphor in the poem. Shakespeare is as discreet in his handling of the naked Tarquin as he is with that forceful knee. Like the engravers, who portray Tarquin half-turned from the viewer, he uses the rapist's dagger to represent the phallic threat: 'he shakes aloft his Roman blade,

. . . his insulting falchion' (l.505). It is punningly likened to 'a falcon tow'ring in the skies', the commonplace figure of the bird-penis aptly becoming a bird of prey in this rape scene. Lucrece receives a harsh lesson in the reading of character, confronting the protean aspects of lust as she picks at the edges of Tarquin's dissimulation:

> In Tarquin's likeness I did entertain thee.
> Hast thou put on his shape to do him shame?
>
> (596)

Now, too, she is quick to register political implications, moving from a lesser to a larger tyranny:

> If in thy hope thou dar'st do such outrage,
> What dar'st thou not when once thou art a king?
>
> (605)

And she understands how the ruler sets the tone for the ruled,

> For princes are the glass, the school, the book
> Where subjects' eyes do learn, do read, do look.
>
> (615)

It is precisely this exemplary consideration which directs her own suicidal course, for there is continual suggestion that, one way or another, her story will continue to be told. Tarquin's coercion of her had rested on this, for unless she 'took all patiently' he threatened to kill her and place the body of a menial beside her in her bed:

> So should my shame still rest upon record,
>   And never be forgot in mighty Rome
>   Th'adulterate death of Lucrece and her groom.
>
> (1643)

This is a fair paraphrase of Tarquin's threat to have her supposed 'trespass cited up in rhymes / And sung by children in succeeding times' (l.524). And she resorts to similar terms in wishing for perpetual night to hide her shame; for else

the illiterate that know not how
To cipher what is writ in learnèd·books
Will quote my loathsome trespass in my looks.
The nurse to still her child will tell my story,
And fright her crying babe with Tarquin's name.
The orator to deck his oratory
Will couple my reproach to Tarquin's shame.

(810)

Despite some banal contrasting of the sexes, Shakespeare's poem is full of complexity. Whereas it is a common experience in reading fiction to combine a sense of the characters' reality with an awareness that they are a fictional entity, here it is Lucrece who has a sense of herself as fictional character. She possesses that selfconsciousness which occurs in many guises during the first era of cheap print.. As the medium lost its novelty, so the self-consciousness waned. But during the sixteenth century it extended well beyond literary culture: sculptors like Michelangelo and painters like late Titian insistently draw attention to the artistic process. Dramatic art shows an inbuilt consciousness of itself: confused dimensions of reality are a conspicuous feature of that earliest secular drama in English, Medwall's *Fulgens and Lucrece*. The induction, where actors discuss the parts they are about to play, is used by Shakespeare's contemporaries; but it is the multi-talented Baroque artist Bernini who goes the whole way with metatheatre. Filippo Baldinucci (1682)[11] records how in 1637 Bernini made a comedy of two theatres opposite each other, the real audience becoming aware of a second performance in progress behind the curtain. When it was lifted for the two performers to settle which one was real, the fashionable audience saw itself mirrored opposite. The performers compromised by each returning to his own audience, and the unsettling entertainment concluded with the supposed audience taking its leave by coach, on foot, or on horseback.

In somewhat similar fashion, the 'real' Lucrece is intent on shaping the fictional Lucrece. Her preoccupation with story gives a reflexive dimension to the poem: the author is not simply constructing a narrative but, along with Lucrece, examining the process of construction. Having suffered temporary loss of control to Tarquin, Lucrece addresses herself to regaining what is essentially control of her story. For the moment, she *is* the story: 'How Tarquin must be used, read it in me' (l.1195); but she looks for more permanent record. Recognizing the importance of externalities, that what matters is not what she is nor indeed what she does, but what she is understood to have done, she is able to write her own history. She becomes the poet's *alter ego*, a conscious fictionist shaping events into story, thereby conferring meaning on the narrative which is (or purports to be) her life. Shakespeare's way here is quite at odds with that of Chaucer and Malory, who invoke tradition with reminders of what the old book saith. While they aim at fresh insight and refinement, they never seek to break away from a linear history of redactions. On this reckoning, Shakespeare would take his place in a line of descent from Livy's *Roman History*, which contains the earliest account of Tarquin's offence. Instead, he uses a strangely self-aware Lucrece to get behind tradition and into questions about its formation. The all-powerful threat which Tarquin brought to bear was that history would put a false construction on her story, taking her not only for an adulteress, but one who further demeaned herself by sleeping with a social inferior. That threat was avoided by quiet submission. The further temptation is that she will justify her continued existence by the fact that she was forced. Her menfolk encourage this response: 'Her body's stain her mind untainted clears' (l.1710). Even the pragmatic Brutus, with his own historic destiny to fulfil, misses the point. After Lucrece's suicide, he seeks to jolt the grieving Collatine into an appreciation of what must be done:

> Thy wretched wife mistook the matter so
> To slay herself, that should have slain her foe.

> (1826)

Lucrece alone sees there is no option but suicide. That she seizes the violent initiative from Tarquin is a favourite painters' compression, with vicious phallic thrust answered by resolute dagger-thrust. But Shakespeare's Lucrece provides an additional angle: alert to the history- (or myth-) making process, she understands the need to become the image. It is not just that her fate is determined by the sources but that her 'reality', like all the other strands in Roman history, is a narrative construction. The imperatives to which she yields are those of narrative, which call for a good ending. Suicide is the best possible ending, more important than life since it offers literary immortality. Of course, she looks beyond the personal in following the high Roman fashion: it transforms her into a cultural ideal, something which gives sense or identity to that culture.

The disclosure of reality as illusion is something that delighted the elder Philostratus, and Shakespeare may have exerted his limited Greek to cope with him. At least, he seems to have recalled what Philostratus said about perspective in a painting of the siege of Thebes when composing his 'Siege of Troy' set-piece: 'Encompassing the walls with armed men, he depicts them so that some are seen in full figure, others with the legs hidden, others from the waist up, then only the busts of some, heads only, helmets only, and finally just spear-points'.[12] But one bit of painterly 'Conceit deceitful' noted by Shakespeare is more striking than anything in the Philostratus passage:

> for Achilles' image stood his spear
> Gripped in an armèd hand: himself behind
> Was left unseen

> (1424)

and may trace back to the highly influential treatment of *Salome* by Andrea Solario, who arrestingly limits the executioner's appearance to a muscular arm holding out the Baptist's head.[13]

Such details might engage Lucrece the myth-maker, but not the distraught rape victim who looks to the painting for help in making sense of her predicament. Whereas Tarquin would not 'by a painted cloth be kept in awe' (l.245), Lucrece is very conscious of how the story of Troy's fall intersects with her own tragedy. The sexual motive, and the meshing of destruction, treachery and politics, are here shaped into graspable formal structure: 'Thy heat of lust, fond Paris, did incur / This load of wrath' (l.1473). In the immediately preceding lines she seems to discover a common cause of tragedy in female beauty:

> Show me the strumpet that began this stir,
> That with my nails her beauty I may tear.

Afraid to see herself in the pictured Helen, she would do violence to the image as later she is to do to herself. But it is 'perjured Sinon', working like Tarquin 'To make the breach and enter this sweet city' (l.469), who for the moment best focuses her sense of outrage:

She tears the senseless Sinon with her nails,
Comparing him to that unhappy guest
Whose deed hath made herself herself detest.

(1564)

As Shakespeare must have known, this was the treatment accorded
to demons in devotional pictures; there are, for instance, conspicuous signs of worshippers relieving their feelings in this way on a
predella by Uccello now in the ducal palace at Urbino.

But it is with Queen Hecuba that Lucrece chiefly identifies,
drawn by her misery though the woman is old and decrepit, 'Her
blue blood changed to black in every vein' (l.1454). This anticipates
the fancy that some of the dead Lucrece's

blood still pure and red remained,
And some looked black, and that false Tarquin-stained.

(1742)

Gazing at the painted queen, Lucrece

shapes her sorrow to the beldame's woes,
Who nothing wants to answer her but cries
And bitter words to ban her cruel foes.
The painter was no god to lend her those,
And therefore Lucrece swears he did her wrong
To give her so much grief, and not a tongue.

(1458)

As a painted image, she is tongueless – just like 'lamenting Philomel', who appears (l.1079) to mark the coming of unwelcome day.
Rather than the dawn chorus of 'mocking birds', Lucrece would
hear the nightingale, 'Philomel, that sing'st of ravishment' (l.1128).
She will join in close harmony with the sorrowing bird; and instead
of the thorn against its breast 'To keep thy sharp woes waking', she
will 'fix a sharp knife' (l.1136).

Earlier, it is thoughts of vengeance not suicide which seem to be
coloured by the Philomel myth:

let mild women to him lose their mildness,
Wilder to him than tigers in their wildness.

(979)

Lucrece's lines recall that Bacchic frenzy simulated by Philomel
and Procne, when the latter fed her son to her rapist husband.

But it is in *Titus Andronicus* that Philomel's story is more fully utilized.

TITUS AND THE TWO CULTURES

In *Titus Andronicus*, Tamora is both actor and sufferer of revenge. She is the quasi-rapist whom Titus finally surprises with the cannibal feast:

> worse than Philomel you used my daughter,
> And worse than Progne I will be revenged.
>
> (V.ii.193)

There are premonitions of his daughter Lavinia's rape at the outset. About to wed the emperor, she is snatched away by his brother Bassianus, who (betrothed to her) denies that it is '"Rape" . . . to seize my own' (I.i.402). His resolve 'To do myself this reason and this right' (l.279) contains the coital innuendo into which Slender stumbles, in *Merry Wives* I.i.216, when asked if he can love Anne Page: 'I hope, sir, I will do as it shall become one that would do reason'.[14] This idiomatic sense of giving satisfaction, borrowed from the French *faire raison*, comes into sexual and drinkers' use during the 1590s.

But both this and Titus's style are at odds with the way in which Tamora's sons discuss their desire for an adulterous fling with Lavinia. In contrast to the literary culture from which the Andronici draw much of their imagery, these Goths turn to proverb (Tilley, W99, T34):

> more water glideth by the mill
> Than wots the miller of, and easy it is
> Of a cut loaf to steal a shive, . . .
>
> (II.i.85)

It is a popular rather than élite language of sex which follows in the exchange between Aaron, Tamora's lover, and her sons:

AARON. Why then, it seems some certain snatch or so
    Would serve your turns.
CHIRON.   Ay, so the turn were served.
DEMETRIUS. Aaron, thou hast hit it.
AARON.   Would you had hit it too, . . .

> (II.i.95)

Ravenscroft, in his reworking of the play (1687, Act II), finds the metaphor of a hasty meal in Aaron's first expression:

You intend her then but for a running-Banquet
A snatch or so, to feed like men that go a-hunting.[15]

Aaron's other terms are sexual clichés, the 'hit it' being enshrined in a popular song (*Love's Labour's Lost* IV.i.124).

What Aaron forces on our attention is that a coarse mode of speaking about sex may signal a similarly coarse mode of behaviour. Hence he sidesteps the problem of persuading Lavinia to infidelity by proposing rape. He does this by borrowing Demetrius's adultery image of striking 'a doe' and bearing 'her cleanly by the keeper's nose' (II.i.93), suggesting that in the forest they may 'strike her home by force, if not by words' (l.119). Ironically, the hunt reflected in this figure has been proposed by Titus, but Tamora sees it as her opportunity to destroy the Andronici. She would have Lavinia murdered after her rape:

First thresh the corn, then after burn the straw.
. . . when ye have the honey ye desire
Let not this wasp outlive, us both to sting.

(II.iii.123)

Again the familiar images come, Shakespeare using honey for sexual sweets in *Troilus* II.ii.143, when Priam reminds Paris that his brothers fight while 'You have the honey still' (i.e. Helen in his bed).

With Bassianus butchered, Chiron excitedly proposes to drag his body

to some secret hole,
And make his dead trunk pillow to our lust.

(II.iii.129)

This reference to the hole is echoed by Lavinia who, rather than suffer defilement, would prefer to be killed and tumbled 'into some loathsome pit' (II.iii.176). In the event, it is her brothers who take a sympathetic tumble into 'the swallowing womb' (l.239). Armin may have been sending this up in *The Valiant Welshman* (1610–15, sig. D4ᵛ), when Morion falls into a ditch while trailing his beloved Fairy Queen. His servant, answering his call for help, asks 'where are you? I thought you had been in the hole by this time'. But the tone is far from farcical when one of Lavinia's brothers wonders:

> What subtle hole is this,
> Whose mouth is covered with rude-growing briers
> Upon whose leaves are drops of new-shed blood . . . ?
>
> (II.iii.198)

These bloodstained briers bespeak both murder and symbolic deflowering, the double function of this hole confirmed by their suggestion of a woman's pubic hair. They offer a sinister variant of the folktale: the sleeping beauty in Grimm's *Little Brier Rose* is protected by a hedge of briers before being awakened to love, the briers being not simply a protection for virginity but a symbol of that untrodden way.

Yet even while this hole echoes Lavinia's fate, it is an emblem of Tamora, the devouring mother in whom sex and death coalesce. Woman-as-landscape is double-sided: it figures Lavinia as passive and vulnerable, but Tamora as dangerous, entrapping. Titus catches something of her danger through the imperial lion figure, as well as the interlock of power and sexuality:

> She's with the lion deeply still in league,
> And lulls him whilst she playeth on her back, . . .
>
> (IV.i.97)

But much of the plotting is undertaken by her lover, Aaron, first of those evil buffoons who exercised a lasting fascination over Shakespeare. Aaron keeps up his black banter in the face of torture and death, sardonically relating how Tamora's sons

> cut thy sister's tongue, and ravished her,
> And cut her hands, and trimmed her as thou sawest.
> LUCIUS. O detestable villain! Call'st thou that trimming?
> AARON. Why, she was washed and cut and trimmed, and 'twas
> Trim sport for them which had the doing of it.
>
> (V.i.92)

Trimming applies to both the rape and mutilation, association of ideas adding another pun when Lucius describes their behaviour as 'barbarous'. As with the business of the hole, part of the effect depends on the near proximity to farce, the popular joke being exemplified in Ford's *Love's Sacrifice* (?1632) III.i, when a womanizer dares one of his quondam bedfellows to 'roar about the court that I have been your woman's-barber and trimmed ye'.[16]

Whether they are using folk expression or street language, the Gothic faction's mode of sexual utterance is demotic as against the Andronici's reliance on book culture. Part of the contrast comes from the radically different perspectives of the two groups, respectively perpetrators and victims of sexual violence. But this is only a surface manifestation of the deep cultural divide, one that reflects the changed face of Shakespeare's own society. Aaron prevents it from becoming too schematic, his own linguistic habits straddling the two cultures. He concedes that 'Lucrece was not more chaste / Than this Lavinia' (II.i.109), a tale recalled (III.i.296) when Lucius determines to 'make proud Saturnine and his empress / Beg at the gates like Tarquin and his queen' (after the younger Tarquin's rape of Lucretia). And Aaron it is who, inspired by Ovid's ugly tale, instructs how they must deal with Lavinia. This

> Philomel must lose her tongue today,
> Thy sons make pillage of her chastity . . .
>
> (II.iii.43)

If Aaron is a poor advertisement for the benefits of a classical education, Titus (with his well-stocked library) effectively routs the proposition that reading good books is an improving activity. He approximates to the Renaissance idea of the *homo universale*, man of war and of cultural refinement. But reading the best authors seems neither to have expanded his humanity nor sharpened his intelligence. Having brought Tamora a captive to Rome and made a funerary offering of her eldest son, he still contrives to believe that she will be grateful to him for her advancement to the imperial throne (I.i.393). On the other hand, Tamora's sons seem not to have given education a chance. When Titus sends a coded warning, Chiron recognizes it as

> a verse in Horace, I know it well.
> I read it in the grammar long ago.
>
> (IV.ii.22)

Even at school it was a second-hand encounter, merely a grammarian's example that he had had drummed in to him. It means nothing now when he and his brother sound more of the street than of élitist education. By contrast, Lavinia is compared with Cornelia, type of the Roman educationist, for her literary nurturing of her nephew (IV.i.12). Likewise, when Titus's brother finds her raped and mutilated, he immediately resorts to the bookish parallel:

> sure some Tereus hath deflowered thee,
> And, lest thou should detect him, cut thy tongue.
>
> (II.iv.26)

But her brutalizing goes beyond that in the story:

> Fair Philomel, why she but lost her tongue
> And in a tedious sampler sewed her mind.
> But, lovely niece, that mean is cut from thee.
> A craftier Tereus, cousin, hast thou met,
> And he hath cut those pretty fingers off
> That could have better sewed than Philomel.
>
> (II.iv.38)

After this, there is little point in Lavinia's fumbling through the pages of Ovid to reveal her plight, especially as she communicates more precisely by tracing in the sand '*Stuprum* – Chiron – Demetrius' (IV.i.77). But it is a mode of apprehension in a different sense, linking the book culture of Shakespeare's day with that of the Andronici, as Lavinia rummages through the library for a copy of the *Metamorphoses*. Moreover, as *Cymbeline* confirms, Shakespeare is intrigued with this text's use as stage property. Nor is he the only one. Hemminge, son of one of Shakespeare's actor-friends, recalls both plays in *The Fatal Contract* (edn 1653) II.ii. It may be supposed that his own taste for the theatre of his father's day is articulated by the lascivious queen, eager for her lover: 'Come shall we Act *Landrey*?'. When Landrey asks what they are to act, she wantonly replies: 'Nothing that's new, old Playes you know are best'.[17]

In this same scene, the queen's son is bent on rape:

> Methinks I stand like *Tarquin* in the night,
> When he defil'd the chastity of *Rome*, . . .

Like Shakespeare's Tarquin, the rapist reflects that

> Her vertues more than beauty ravish'd me,
> And I commit even with her piety
> A kind of incest with Relligion.

And while he watches, his victim reads in Ovid of 'Poor ravisht *Philomel*'. *Titus* is recalled in the character of a (supposed) Moor as arch-plotter, Dekker's *Lust's Dominion* (1600?) showing similar indebtedness with 'Eleazar, the son of Aaron' (Numbers 25:7). But it is the Ovidian link which is most striking. Ovid himself, at the conclusion of his account of Lucretia's rape in the *Fasti* II.856, alludes to Tereus. And in the Elizabethan poets, rape brings mention of Lucretia or Philomel like a conditioned reflex. But if the victim Lavinia offers a prime example, her tormentress Tamora provides a no less striking model of another kind.

6

Sexual Temptresses

Titus Andronicus was a highly influential play, and even Jonson's gibe in the *Bartholomew Fair* induction acknowledges it as a dramatic landmark. Unlike *Antony and Cleopatra*, the source of which is the ever reliable Plutarch, *Titus* offers an invented picture of the late Roman Empire deriving, if from a printed source, from cheap fiction. Cleopatra's story was well known to the Elizabethans. She was presented as sexual temptress in plays before and after Shakespeare's; in *Caesar's Revenge* (*c.*1592–6), both Julius Caesar and Antony succumb to her, the latter being one of Garzoni's 'Amorous Fooles'.[1] But Shakespeare's version was crucial. Fletcher and Massinger, in *The False One*, avoid competition by turning back to 'Caesar's amorous heats'. They claim in the Prologue that their presentation of Cleopatra's first affair is something which 'the Stage yet never knew', and perhaps they believe it. But in any case they are conscious of only one rival. Decoded, their statement means that Shakespeare has left no scope for reworking 'her fatall love to Antony'. That relationship, in Shakespeare's hands, goes beyond revaluation. Instead, what his Cleopatra provided for contemporaries, like Theda Bara's vamp-image in the silent cinema, was nothing less than a reconstituted idea of the sexual temptress.

Even so, *Antony and Cleopatra* depends to a degree on audience preconceptions about the story. Plutarch's *Lives* was one of those ancient texts habitually used to unravel some of the complexities of the early modern period, achieving print in a Latin translation by 1470. The account of Antony and Cleopatra was particularly influential, and is significantly recalled by the Inca Garcilaso de la Vega (*c.*1590) when he describes the meeting of the conquistador Hernán de Soto and the mistress of Cofachiqui in Florida. She crossed the river in a canoe 'covered with a great canopy and adorned with ornaments . . . . Although less spectacular in grandeur and majesty, this scene indeed resembles that one in which Cleopatra went forth to receive Marc Anthony on the river Cydnus in Cilisia'.[2] Likewise, although *Titus* has no classical provenance, those attending that play would have found acquaintance with 'Ouids Booke' to be at least as helpful as it was supposed to be for those reading the Water Poet's character of *A Whore* (1622).[3] Further, the latter's mock-declensions and other playfulness with Latin suggests that it was not only the learned who would have taken pleasure in the play's scattering of Latin tags. For there was more to this than delight in linguistic exoticism. With the shifting of the old power base, which brought money into the hands of the vulgar, the new social demarcation was through education – classical education.

This social shift is represented in *Antony and Cleopatra* by Octavius Caesar, who demonstrates how the bourgeois's singleminded concern with advancement has appropriated an aristocratic paradigm of power. It may be that Shakespeare's Caesar would have elicited more sympathy in Jacobean times than is usual today. Brathwaite's *English Gentleman* (1630, p.316) includes him as an 'heroicke instance' of virtuous conduct: '*Cleopatra* in the last tragicke Scene of her disasters, kneeling at the feet of *Caesar*, laid baits for his eyes; but in vaine; her beauties were beneath that Princes chastitie'. In Shakespeare he exhibits the virtue of success, which has no time for grand passion; his operations reflect the way that Elizabethan *Realpolitik* has superseded chivalry. Chivalry itself may have been largely political convenience; yet there are those like Antony, or Hotspur in *2 Henry IV*, who invest it with moral meaning. But just as in the latter play Prince John has no compunction about betraying the rebels to their death, so Antony wastes his breath in expecting Octavius to meet him in single combat.

It is a truism that Shakespeare uses the classical world to distance socio-political comment. *Titus* was almost certainly written and produced in the three years following the assassination of Henry III of France, when British interest in French affairs may be gauged by some forty surviving tracts on the subject. Anxiety would have focused on Elizabeth's foreign policy, about which no public comment was permitted. It is hard to imagine such a major preoccupation of the time failing to colour Shakespeare's writing in some way. But if he was consciously aiming at topicality in *Titus*, a possibility to be considered below, he would need to have been more than ordinarily circumspect.

These were early days in his career, whereas *Antony and Cleopatra* belongs to his peak period. But the plays have more in common than a setting in the Roman world. Both Tamora and Cleopatra become spoils of war, the one paraded in Rome and the other desperately avoiding that fate. They both enjoy political power, Cleopatra as Queen of Egypt and Tamora, if no longer queen in her own right, as imperial consort. But quite as important as their status in the socio-political scheme is their possession of an older, mythic power as archetypes of female sexuality. That this is probably their closest tie will be seen in what follows: Tamora belongs to the secret, impenetrable forest, while Cleopatra is a Venus presiding over the waters – or even a 'serpent of old Nile'.

TITUS ANDRONICUS: PATTERNS OF SEX AND WAR

The French Wars of Religion, supplying material for the London stage as well as for wall-hangings,[4] continued through most of Elizabeth's long reign. She had supplied short-lived military aid when the first of them broke out in 1562. But she had no further opportunity for direct intervention until, with the assassination of the last Valois king in 1589, the Huguenot Henry of Navarre succeeded to the French throne. Now, as the Catholic League called for Spanish aid, she countered by assisting Henry. Since she had replied to the Armada with a new policy of aggression both on land and sea, financial and military aid for Henry was dangerously stretching her resources. So, from October 1589, she turned for help to the German Protestant princes, and in May of the next year her financier-agent Palavicino was pressing the Landgrave of Hesse for 'horse and foot this summer'. She would contribute to the cost despite already shouldering 'so great a burden of war'.[5]

In 1593, Henry wrong-footed both the Spaniards and the Catholic League by his politic conversion to Catholicism. Thus ended Elizabeth's chief worry over Spanish influence in France. But the fear of Spanish control over Channel ports was real enough in 1590 for her to make a military alliance with Henry and Protestant Germany a priority. Her intriguing caught the attention of the popular press. A broadside engraved by the monogrammist BHKNGF, *Mitt Fusstretten Handt drucken vnnd Lachen* (With Foot-treading, Hand-pressing and Laughing I can make all Three into Fools),[6] shows Elizabeth flanked by French and German admirers: she holds the Frenchman's hand and treads upon the German's foot. Hovering at a distance, a Spaniard receives her smile and flatters himself, like the other two, that he will soon enjoy her favours. Harms, noting that foot-treading blends flirtation with mastery and subjection, relates it to a German saying about women having men under their slipper, which originates in a marriage custom. But the signal crops up from north (Dunbar) to south (Aretino), though closest to the engraving is Field's mention, in *Amends for Ladies* (c.1611), of

> A Lady that will wring one by the finger,
> Whil'st on anothers toes shee treads, and cries
> By Gad I loue but one, and you are hee:
> Either of them thinking himselfe the man.[7]

(I.i.109)

That the artist's images had European currency is significant since, although the place where this print originated is unknown, most of them were produced in the great German commercial centres where they would cater for an international clientèle. The engraving adopts a pattern found in adultery prints as well as borrowing the device of the fool commenting through a window which originated with Lucas van Leyden. In this case he points at Elizabeth with one hand while making the sign of horns with the other. Unlike the erotic fools being played upon by Elizabeth, this fool understands his condition and its inescapability. He is an outsider, ironic onlooker on human folly, but he has a clarity of vision enabling him to comment on political-sexual deceptions which lead men into folly.

This would not have been the Queen's first appearance in Continental caricature. In November 1583, 'licentious pictures of Elizabeth and Anjou' were available on the streets of Paris; and again in 1587, following the execution of Mary Queen of Scots, pictorial comment was made by the rival Parisian factions. In the former case, Elizabeth appeared on horseback, 'her right hande pullynge vpp her clothes shewinge her hindparte'.[8] In the more decorous German broadside she receives no verbal identification, and indeed Harms rules out any political content. He does this on two grounds, the first being the protagonists' lack of resemblance to contemporary rulers. But this has little weight for an age when the physical appearance of the powerful was relatively unfamiliar. It is notable that, whereas the men are labelled with their nationalities, Elizabeth is not. The artist does seem to have some acquaintance with representations of Elizabeth; authentic portraits of the 1580s show the same pointed chin and high forehead graced with a pearl that are shown here. But she is more decisively identified by her way of choreographing power moves as sexual manoeuvres, notably through decades of diplomatic marriage negotiations.[9] Harms's second objection rests on the presence of the Spaniard as third target for Elizabeth's sexual blandishment. But Elizabeth was widely considered to be hedging her bets through peace talks with Spain at the very time that she was intriguing for a northern European Protestant alliance. Rumours to this effect were rife during July and early August 1590,[10] which is a good clue to the exact date of the broadside. Nor were they so implausible. Her greatest fear was of a Franco–Spanish alliance against her. A Protestant France was one way in which this could be avoided; but equally effective would be the country's fragmentation, which was the Catholic League's ambition.

It was while the doctrinal and political uncertainties of France's future were still a major preoccupation of British foreign policy that *Titus Andronicus* was written: the balance of evidence, as weighed by Eugene Waith, pointing to 'a date preceding 1592'.[11] Given tight censorship, the play could make no direct comment on the diplomatic or military manoeuvres of the time in the way of that German broadside, but those events would have coloured its writing and reception. Thus Elizabeth, for logistical reasons and because her subjects had a proper distaste for foreign service, was inclined to pay other nations to fight on her behalf. But the more aggressive policy adopted in the wake of the Armada meant the levying of county militia for dangerous service overseas. Hot service in France or the Low Countries (the genital 'Netherlands' of *A Comedy of Errors* III.ii.143) became a favourite joke of the 1590s and after. The soldier Bowyer, in *The Trial of Chivalry* (1599 or so) II.i,[12] reflects that he has acquitted himself well in the field, but France holds a worse hazard: 'And I could scape (a pox on it) th'other thing, I might haps return safe and sound to England'. This displacement on to venereal disease is a measure of the apprehension felt by those called up for the war.

It is a weakness of Shakespeare's play that the ordinary soldier's

lot is ignored; though the realities of military action are all too
clear in Titus's loss of more than twenty sons in battle against
the Goths:

> Five times he hath returned
> Bleeding to Rome, bearing his valiant sons
> In coffins from the field.

(I.i.33)

But this last dead son is accompanied by the spoils of victory. The
scene was eloquently presented in Deborah Warner's Stratford
production: 'Suddenly the curtains at the back of the stage are
thrown apart to reveal Titus, the triumphant general, grinning
astride a row of prisoners yoked like oxen, and we realise what
the true face of this harsh, barbaric yet decadent society really
is'.[13] This is a long way from that opposition evoked by Frances
Yates of 'the good Titus' against 'the wicked Saturnine', whose
imperial shortcomings are finally repaired when Lucius, 'the just
man', assumes the purple.[14] It is this just man who cries out for a
blood sacrifice:

> Give us the proudest prisoner of the Goths,
> That we may hew his limbs and on a pile
> *Ad manes fratrum* sacrifice his flesh . . .

(I.i.96)

And he re-enters satisfied that 'Alarbus' limbs are lopped / And
entrails feed the sacrificing fire' (l.143). That Lucius's prominence
in this affair came about through deliberate revision is clear from
a redundant passage where Titus claims to have already 'Done
sacrifice of expiation, / And slain the noblest prisoner of the
Goths' (after I.i.35). It is not so clear whether the reviser is
Shakespeare or a collaborator; but the same vein is followed when,
returned to power, Lucius condemns not only the Moor Aaron but
his baby:

> First hang the child, that he may see it sprawl –
> A sight to vex the father's soul withal.

(V.i.51)

The child's life is spared not as an act of mercy but as a bargain for
a full confession from the father. While Lucius keeps his bargain,
he finds another torture for Aaron, who is buried 'breast-deep'

in the ground and slowly starved to death (V.iii.178). There is nothing casual about the anachronism when Aaron sees Lucius equipped 'With twenty popish tricks and ceremonies' (V.i.76). It at once distinguishes him from the amoral pagan Aaron and alienates him from an Elizabethan Protestant audience. Hence his arrival at the head of an army of Goths – not in the chapbook version – does more than locate the fictitious history in the period of Rome's decline, when the Gothic threat produced at one time military confrontation and at another uneasy alliance. It also offers a disquieting reflection of current events as the Catholic League invited a Spanish army on to French soil.

It is at least tantalizing that, while the name of the Emperor Saturninus is, as Yates observes, 'the evil opposite of the golden age of Saturn', Elizabeth's senior adviser Burghley was nicknamed 'old Saturnus . . . a melancholy and wayward planett, but yett predominant here'.[15] Not that he is seriously represented in the guise of the emperor any more than is Elizabeth in that of the empress. Tamora is not Elizabeth, but she may offer a glance at the latter's possibly over-confident intriguing: 'it shall become / High-witted Tamora to gloze with all' (IV.iv.34). And the ironic allusion to her as Diana gets added bite from the goddess's place in Elizabethan iconography. As we have noticed, Elizabeth's virgin status by no means impedes sexual representation of her political power. Tamora is no virgin, but she is presented as both servant of Venus and (sarcastically) a Diana, while her blackamoor lover (rival of Saturninus) is temporarily a saturnian, diametrically opposed to the venerean:

> Madam, though Venus govern your desires,
> Saturn is dominator over mine.

> (II.iii.30)

He has arrived for no love-tryst, offering only an illusion of phallicism:

> My fleece of woolly hair that now uncurls
> Even as an adder when she doth unroll
> To do some fatal execution . . .

> (34)

For 'these are no venereal signs', his mind being set on revenge and death which supply more of an erotic charge than Tamora's body.

When the emperor's brother Bassianus enters a moment later, he affects to wonder whether he has discovered Tamora 'Or is it Dian, habited like her' (l.57). But Tamora angrily retorts that had she

> the power that some say Dian had,
> Thy temples should be planted presently
> With horns, as was Actaeon's, and the hounds
> Should drive upon thy new-transformèd limbs, . . .
>
> (61)

The grim irony is that she does have some such power, and her sons will be the hounds to despatch Bassianus and force his bride. This Lavinia, daughter of Titus, is both self-righteous in her chastity and mistakenly confident of her own power as she turns the Actaeon reference into a reproach of Tamora's adultery:

> 'Tis thought you have a goodly gift in horning,
> And to be doubted that your Moor and you
> Are singled forth to try experiments.
> Jove shield your husband from his hounds today.
>
> (67)

Saturninus had used the moon-goddess as compliment to his chosen empress,

> That like the stately Phoebe 'mongst her nymphs
> Dost overshine the gallant'st dames of Rome, . . .
>
> (I.i.313)

But now the figure rebounds as comment on his cuckolding. Royal adultery was a political as well as sexual offence; but the Actaeon story was often straightforwardly political in application. Spenser, in *The Faerie Queene* VII.vi.45, borrows the absurd rapist Faunus from Ovid's *Fasti* (II.307) as an Irish Actaeon spying on the bathing Diana. This neo-Actaeon is wrapped in 'Deeres-skin' and hunted; but this time the hounds are unsuccessful. The offended Diana–Elizabeth curses Ireland and leaves it to its wild beasts and wilder men. (If this national withdrawal never quite occurred, the episode strangely prefigures the way that Spenser himself was driven out in 1598.)

It is apt to recall, in connection with Tamora, that Diana could exhibit more than chaste anger. The lascivious quail was her sacred bird, and her arrows were regarded as the cause of sudden death, especially to maidens and wives. Her darker origins are apparent even in Chapman's obscure compliment to Elizabeth, *The Shadow of Night*, published in 1594, the same year as the first quarto of *Titus*. Diana-Elizabeth, while 'shunning faithlesse mens societie', will yet 'Commit most willing rapes on all our harts'.[16] But she can be more than metaphorically harsh towards those who offend her:

> Diseases pine their flockes, tares spoile their corne:
> Old men are blind of issue, and young wiues
> Bring forth abortiue frute, that neuer thriues.

(33)

He borrows here from Callimachus's *Hymn to Artemis*, but he gives a still more lurid picture of her depredations as she shoots some, while others 'hir doggs eate' or 'her monsters carried to their nests' and 'Rent . . . in peeces' (l.37). She is 'Enchantresse-like, . . . / Circkled with charmes, and incantations' (l.28), recalling Horace's Epode V.37, where the witch Canidia makes her appeal to 'Night and Diana' as she prepares to sacrifice a boy so 'that his marrow and his liver, cut out and dried, might form a love-charm'.[17]

It is this unbenign aspect of Diana – and Chapman knows 'she is *Heccate*' (l.45) as well as Elizabeth – which best agrees with the lust and cruelty of Tamora. Once within the forest, the latter finds herself. This is her tangled domain, where she will ensnare those who enter unbidden. As forest creature or enchantress she is an archetype of female sexuality. And that sexuality, like Diana herself, may be benign as well as destructive. This is apparent in the harmony which she has achieved with her surroundings, as she awaits her lover. The birds provide music for this assignation, while the snake as yet 'lies rollèd in the cheerful sun', though its phallicism and implicit menace emerge in those lines already noted on Aaron's 'woolly hair'. For her, it is a spot where Aeneas himself might have forgotten his divinely appointed task to found Rome; though this second Dido's lover seeks to destroy not build. But destruction is far from her present mood, as she muses on that tranquillity which will follow rapture: 'Our pastimes done', the distant sounds of the hunt and the birds' melody will serve as 'a nurse's song / Of lullaby to bring her babe asleep' (II.iii.13–29). This is benign, procreative. But the dreamy Venus becomes an outraged Diana when the enemy intrudes. Indeed, the whole episode serves as a sustained pun on venery: as Dekker and Webster put it, 'hunting, and venery are words of one signification'.[18] Now Tamora chooses to see with her enemies' eyes this 'barren detested vale' (l.93) shaded with 'moss and baleful mistletoe', where 'nothing breeds / Unless the nightly owl or fatal raven' (the latter a betraying gloss on Lavinia's 'raven-coloured love' accusation). Tamora has aligned herself with these sinister birds as breeder in this place, a bestial alliance with darkness already insisted on by Bassianus, who sees her

> Dismounted from your snow-white goodly steed,
> And wandered hither to an obscure plot,
>
> (II.iii.76)

in order to mount (or be mounted by) an evil black one.

But there is more here than a sense of Aaron as embodiment of evil. Unlike the audience, Bassianus has not been given any basis for such a view beyond the man's colour. But that is enough. He expresses repugnance for a liaison between a Moor and a white woman, the miscegenation issue being sharpened later when the product of the liaison, a black baby, turns up in crucial scenes. On the baby's first appearance, Aaron has to protect it from slaughter by its half-brothers, on account of its betraying blackness:

> sanguine, shallow-hearted boys,
> Ye whitelimed walls, ye alehouse painted signs,
> Coal-black is better than another hue
> In that it scorns to bear another hue.
>
> (IV.ii.96)

'Sanguine' and 'shallow-hearted' do not mean red-faced and cow-ardly (Waith) but bloodthirsty and unfeeling. The 'whitelimed walls' recall the Bankside tavern-brothels whose signs, painted on white walls, were visible across the Thames. Painting, with its cosmetic connotations, often suggested whores. So sexual corruption is doubly signalled: contempt for the brothers' white faces, foppishly painted, becomes the black man's reflexive answer to colour prejudice. Later, Lucius adds a dimension of blood-guilt, declaring the baby 'Too like the sire for ever being good' (V.i.50), an idea well understood through the Christian-Jewish polarities. Black is decidedly not beautiful in this play, but nor are the Romans whiter than white. Black and white are no safer moral guide than the oppositions of Roman civilization and Gothic wilderness. That linking of wilderness with danger and depravity which is allowed to overlay Tamora's earlier forest idyll does not entirely invalidate the latter. There are two sides to the forest as there are to Diana-Tamora. If Tamora's objectives are sexual betrayal, as a spoil of war she had little say in the marital transaction. Further, Saturninus's sexual interest in her at the very moment when he was expecting to wed Lavinia (I.i.261) betrays his own insecure commitment to marital fidelity.

Tamora had arrived in Rome defeated and demoralized, only to be faced with Titus's decision to sacrifice 'The eldest son of this distressèd Queen' (I.i.103). She has a dire introduction to the Roman victors' clemency when her pleas for his life are ignored. Violence begets violence: war requires its ritual sacrifice, and this in turn incites vengeance against the entire Andronicus clan. It is understandable that Roman civilization has less appeal for Tamora than the peace of the forest; and there is scope in this scene for the actress to open up a vein of sympathy which will complicate audience response to her subsequent villainy. In this way, her relaxed mood beneath the trees works like Titus's later anguish: it offsets the fact that, under stress, both Roman and Gothic cultures will accommodate atrocity. The moral confusions are taken over from Ovid. When Titus likens Lavinia's fate to Philomel's, 'Forced in the ruthless, vast, and gloomy woods' (IV.i.53), he purports to find description of such a place in the *Metamorphoses*. But, in Golding's workmanlike rendering, evocation of the scene stops short at 'a pelting graunge that peakishly did stand / In woods forgrowen' (VI.663). What Ovid does exploit is the feigning of Bacchic frenzy by Philomel's sister Procne, during which she butchers her son and feeds his flesh to her rapist-husband. This is rooted in the fable of Agave's murder of her son in a drugged Bacchic rage, both stories appearing in Nonnos's *Dionysiaca*, a lush amplification of Euripides's *Bacchae*. But in Shakespeare it is not the forest creature Tamora, encourager of rape and murder, but her Roman enemy who resorts to cannibalism. Just as Procne's horrific response prevents us from aligning with her against her rapist-husband, so here it is clear that neither Roman nor Goth monopolizes depravity. In theory at least, the play offers a cooling reminder to British bellicosity that a war's formal end does not conclude the brutality. That Titus has been often seen as a noble embodiment of the (Roman) military ethic shows up the problems of criticizing that ethic. For it is war which has accustomed him to bloody murder; and if it disguises itself as honour reflex when he cuts down his son early on, it emerges in all its grisly reality at the Thyestean banquet.

SALT CLEOPATRA

Some cheap fiction achieves impact through its use of archetypes. But Shakespeare's source for *Titus*, assuming that he turned to an ancestor of the eighteenth-century chapbook version, offered nothing of the kind. It is Shakespeare's Tamora rather than the chapbook empress who belongs to the forest, symbol of female sexuality. Bartholinus explores the symbolism, saying of the vulva that '*Plautus* calls it *Saltus*, a Wood or Grove'.[19] But Brathwaite, glancing at another archetype, suggests that this '*grove* . . . might be styl'd Loves-watring place'.[20] And water is the province of Cleopatra, another sexual temptress who, like Tamora, is intended to embellish a Roman triumphal procession. But folk images are overlaid with literary culture. Bullough notes how Plutarch lies behind Shakespeare's 'glowing sympathy which perceived grandeur in the most deplorable sins of passion and the inevitable dooms they brought', while North furnished his translation with 'some splendid prose which kindled Shakespeare's imagination'.[21] But it is not Shakespeare's intention to allow the folklore to be obliterated. Water is traditionally associated with woman, being identified as the source of all life in various cultures. Shakespeare makes the association with the dark lady, 'the bay where all men ride' according to Sonnet 137. Her insatiability is stressed in Sonnet 135: 'The sea, all water, yet receives rain still', a sentiment recalled in *The Costlie Whore* (c.1620) III.i, where the duke seems intent on marriage with one 'whose body is as common as the sea / In the receipt of every lustfull spring'.[22]

'Lustful' is the minimal gloss usually provided when Pompey describes Egypt's queen as 'Salt Cleopatra' (II.i.21). But this meaning, from Latin *saltus* (leap), surely links with the sexual sea-figure by way of the chemical compound sense. Burton, in *The Anatomy of Melancholy* (1621) 3.2.2.1, finds salt placed by Gomesius amongst those things accustomed to provoke uncontrollable lust, finding confirmation in Venus's emergence from the salt ocean and the derivation of 'salacity' from 'salt'. Salmon, in his *New Method of*

Curing the French-Pox (1690, p.30), is similarly impressed with these
details: "Tis by reason of the Salts with which the Seed abounds
that Voluptuous Men are called *Salaces*, which is derived from
Sal, and *Venus* is . . . *orta mari*' (sea-born). They have point in
view of Cleopatra's devotion to Venus (the activity if not the
goddess). As soon as Shakespeare's play shifts back to Alexandria,
reminiscence of the prank played on Antony by Cleopatra adds
another dimension:

> 'Twas merry when
> . . . your diver
> Did hang a salt fish on his hook, which he
> With fervency drew up.

(II.v.15)

Although this episode derives from Plutarch, Shakespeare gives
new emphasis through that erotically charged 'fervency', as well
as the preceding speech where Cleopatra determines to

> betray
> Tawny-finned fishes.
> . . . and as I draw them up,
> I'll think them every one an Antony.

Cleopatra was first seen by Antony as a goddess on the water,
Plutarch detailing the care which she devoted to this grand
appearance. It was a power play, since she answered Antony's
summons by deliberately choosing a slow means of transport. But
this touch of rebellion was greatly strengthened by the calculated
eroticism. Her attendants were attired like Nereides and Graces,
'and there went a rumour . . . that the goddesse Venus was come
to play with the god Bacchus' (Antony having been extravagantly
feted as Bacchus during a visit to Ephesus).[23] Shakespeare follows
North's Plutarch closely when Enobarbus describes this floating
masque, with Venus-Cleopatra fanned by 'pretty dimpled boys,
like smiling Cupids':

> The barge she sat in, like a burnished throne
> Burned on the water. The poop was beaten gold;
> Purple the sails, and so perfumèd that
> The winds were love-sick with them. The oars were silver,
> Which to the tune of flutes kept stroke, and made

The water which they beat to follow faster,
As amorous of their strokes.

(II.ii.198)

In those last lines he figures what he takes to be Antony's masochistic obsession, which will override political good sense and draw him back to Egypt. The whole speech is heavy with irony, coming as it does immediately after Antony has agreed to a political match with Caesar's sister, Octavia.

Enobarbus has no doubt of Cleopatra's power as sexual enchantress, and Antony too (IV.ix.12) calls her 'this great fairy'; or in IV.xiii, 'This grave charm', 'gipsy', 'spell', and 'witch'. Her name frequently appears amongst the heroes of alchemy, a reputation linked with her trick of dissolving a pearl.[24] Indeed alchemy is supposed to have originated in Egypt with the god Thoth, identified by the Greeks with Hermes (Trismegistus), first of the magicians and inventor of all the arts and sciences (including soothsaying as well as alchemy). The latter word supposedly derives from Arabic *al-kimia*, Egypt being known as the land of Khem or Khame (black earth). The Alexandrian alchemists located in this black earth, the fertile mulch deposited by the Nile's inundations, that original matter which they sought to transmute.

The alchemist's activities are curiously paralleled in the relationship of Antony and Cleopatra. Just as the alchemist's furnace must be maintained at a constant temperature, for overheating would destroy the work, so we are told that Antony's heart 'is become the bellows and the fan / To cool a gipsy's lust' (I.i.9). Fanning has a double function: it may inflame as well as cool, as Enobarbus recalls in his Cydnus speech. In the barge, those 'pretty dimpled boys, like smiling Cupids', had stood beside the queen plying their

fans whose wind did seem
To glow the delicate cheeks which they did cool,
And what they undid did.

(II.ii.209)

Cydnus was the start of an affair which would culminate, like the alchemist's work, with the king and queen united by the fire of love. (That in books of alchemy the erotic figure often appears as a sea-bound coupling has its own irony here.) Antony is sufficiently moved by the phenomenon of the black earth to discourse on the

Nile floods at the banquet aboard Pompey's galley. And, when leaving for Rome, he has protested 'By the fire / That quickens Nilus' slime' (I.iii.68) that he will remain Cleopatra's servant. The fertility process obtrudes all the more strikingly just when he is attempting to break free of Egyptian entanglement. Plainly, he continues enthralled by one who – at moments, and especially near the end – is close to that mystery which the alchemists saw in the energy released by inundation and by sexual union.

Even more than the alchemist, the soothsayer was involved with this inundation. In Lucan's *Pharsalia* X.238, Julius Caesar calls on the soothsaying priest of Isis to divulge the secrets of the Nile's rising; but here Cleopatra's preoccupations set the tone, and he is reduced to reading sexual fortunes in her ladies' palms. 'You shall be more beloving than belov'd', he tells Charmian; and her retort depends on the idea of the liver as seat of love as well as target for alcohol: 'I had rather heat my liver with drinking' (I.ii.19). Her odd echo of the Nativity story becomes a mockery of the old fertility rhythms: 'Let me have a child at fifty to whom Herod of Jewry may do homage' (l.24). Iras's 'oily palm' is ironically reckoned to presage chastity 'E'en as the o'erflowing Nilus presageth famine' (l.44); and asked 'If you were but an inch of fortune better than I, where would you choose it?', she insists: 'Not in my husband's nose' (l.53).

Cleopatra herself is given to such phallic quibbling, ostensibly registering her smallness compared with the burly Antony: 'I would I had thy inches' (I.iii.40). This involves not only female receptivity; it is of a kind with that recollection of a drunken night when she put her 'tires and mantles on him whilst / I wore his sword Philippan' (II.v.22). Antony, descendant of Hercules, had found his Omphale. The myth's humanist message appears on Cranach's series of pictorial renderings from the 1530s, relating how Hercules, given the distaff, becomes subject to his mistress's authority: 'Thus damned lust seizes on great souls, and soft love weakens strong breasts'.[25] Antony's 'dotage' is remarked in the play's opening line; and soon he himself is resolving that 'These strong Egyptian fetters I must break, / Or lose myself in dotage' (I.ii.110). Philo concludes his opening speech as the protagonists make their first entrance. He is not so much addressing his companion, another friend of Antony's, as the audience. His words have a showman's formality, introducing the tableau of Antony,

The triple pillar of the world transformed
Into a strumpet's fool. Behold and see.

(I.i.12)

The visual imagery catches up the verbal, that fanning function
of Antony's heart being externalized by Cleopatra's *'eunuchs
fanning her'* (as the folio stage direction requires). Just how their
eunuch status would have been established on the Jacobean stage
is indeterminable; but it was clearly important to project this
outward sign of Antony's emasculation. The emblem of whore
and fool had its visual configurations too, familiar from woodcut.
Although the form is Germanic, it found its way across the Channel
very quickly. A translation from the French, *The Beaute of women*
(1525?), includes a cut of a naked woman playing a lute, while
a fool sprawls at her feet pointing at her genitals. The original
is probably a drawing by Urs Graf, dated 1523, which spawned
numerous variations, all with the characteristic of the man reduced
to grovelling inferiority. In one by Hans Brosamer (*c*.1530), the
woman holds a mirror and a cosmetic jar, the latter identifying her
as Luxuria and associating her with the harlot Magdalene. Again the
fool points up at her genitals.[26] Antony is such a genitally orientated
fool, in contrast to Caesar's bourgeois sobriety. The lover's values
are immune to logic and indifferent to social norms, though from
a more troublesome perspective his folly becomes a metaphor
for normality. Caesar, like the politically muscular middle class
of Shakespeare's day, suppresses any such intimations and places
reason above emotion. So the Egypt–Rome polarities represent
that Jacobean opposition between the pursuit of sensation and the
moral ideals of the bourgeoisie – ideals of restraint and self-control,
with sexual demands kept within matrimonial bounds. Caesar can
only deplore the way that Antony

fishes, drinks, and wastes
The lamps of night in revel; is not more manlike
Than Cleopatra, nor the queen of Ptolemy
More womanly than he.

*not toll
roles.*

(I.iv.4)

Caesar has a give-away distaste for Antony's Egyptian life, a need
to denounce the things which go to make up the love of Antony
and Cleopatra as wasteful and repugnant. He is genuinely puzzled

by the seeming contradiction between the Antony he admires for the tough endurance shown on campaigns and the chamber warrior who surrenders to sensuality:

> Let's grant it is not
> Amiss to tumble on the bed of Ptolemy,
> To give a kingdom for a mirth.
>
> (I.iv.16)

It is not just that Antony indulges himself at inopportune times. Caesar recoils from the wild, careless abandon of Egyptian court life, and from the depravity and corruption of the body's love:

> If he filled
> His vacancy with his voluptuousness,
> Full surfeits and the dryness of his bones
> Call on him for't.
>
> (I.iv.25)

The consequences of Antony's debauchery serve as an (unheeded) reproach. 'Surfeits' is a splendid word for the writer who joys in compression, since it embraces both the over-indulgence and the price paid – two kinds of sickness. But Caesar also glances at syphilitic damage in terms used by Davies of Hereford, *Scourge of Folly* (1610, Epig. 13), where a whore's 'bones that full of marrow were, / Are dry and rotten'.[27] Caesar's musings are interrupted by the arrival of a messenger with news of support rallying to Pompey, yesterday's man, against the triumvirs; but his image of the fickle plebs betrays how his mind still runs on Antony:

> This common body,
> Like to a vagabond flag upon the stream,
> Goes to, and back, lackeying the varying tide,
> To rot itself with motion.
>
> (I.iv.44)

Indeed, his very next words, delayed by the arrival of more news, are: 'Antony, / Leave thy lascivious wassails' (l.55). But the water-weed figure, where the 'common body' might be taken as a whore whose looseness brings inevitable disease, easily evokes Antony's life-style, as he yields to the eddies of delight; for rot, like bone damage, often appears in syphilis contexts.[28]

'Idleness' is the word used repeatedly to connote the relationship between Antony and Cleopatra. When Antony chides Cleopatra for being almost 'idleness itself', she answers with a paradox of sexual pleasure:

> 'Tis sweating labour
> To bear such idleness so near the heart
> As Cleopatra this.

(I.iii.93)

Their coupling together is not confined to the bed; nor is the friction, for Cleopatra can recall how she has laughed Antony 'out of patience' (II.v.19). None the less, they have the same idea of fun, often riotous, extravagant fun. Together they are a wild pair, but they live for each other. So when Antony has left for Rome, Cleopatra's days are empty. She talks vaguely of drinking mandragora, 'That I might sleep out this great gap of time / My Antony is away' (I.v.5). Or as a tepid diversion, she would make Mardian the butt of her bawdy humour: 'I take no pleasure / In aught an eunuch has'. Later, however, when Charmian declines to play billiards, Cleopatra concedes that

> As well a woman with an eunuch play'd
> As with a woman . . . .
> And when good will is showed, though't come too short
> The actor may plead pardon.

(II.v.5)

But she has scant interest in short wills, and comes to life only at memory of passionate moments shared with Antony or the little games they played together. Her listlessness is apparent in her prurient enquiry about whether Mardian has 'affections'. 'Indeed?', she exclaims when he answers affirmatively, a perfect feed for his bawdy wit:

> Not in deed, madam, for I can do nothing
> But what indeed is honest to be done.
> Yet have I fierce affections, and think
> What Venus did with Mars.

(I.v.15)

He significantly assigns the active role to Venus, another such evocation of eager lust as Cleopatra provides in demanding news of Antony:

Ram thou thy fruitful tidings in mine ears,
That long time have been barren.

(II.v.24)

This Cleopatra is something of the man-devourer portrayed in
Venus and Adonis, who could oversway her Mars, 'Leading him
prisoner in a red-rose chain' (l.110). But Shakespeare's queen has
another face. There were those, and Boccaccio will serve as an
example, who showed Cleopatra using her beauty in the service
of greed and lust; but Chaucer could place her as the first of his
Good Women, 'For love of Antony that was hire so dere'. Collected
editions of Chaucer had made his *Legend* readily available since
1532; and Boccaccio's *De Claris Mulieribus* had been reprinted
still more freely, though in Italian translations not English.[29]
Shakespeare seems intent on combining both traditions, making
Cleopatra neither wholly admirable nor entirely disreputable.
Enobarbus is her keenest observer. He resorts to sexual derision
when anticipating how she will play the prima donna on hearing
that Antony must leave. She will die: 'I have seen her die twenty
times upon far poorer moment. I do think there is mettle in death,
which commits some loving act upon her, she hath such a celerity
in dying' (I.ii.134). This earns no rebuke from Antony, whose love
for Cleopatra is of a kind which can accommodate such criticism.
Besides, Enobarbus is in no doubt about her allure; Antony 'will to
his Egyptian dish again' (II.vi.126). It is he who provides testimony
that she is very special, stressing

Her infinite variety. Other women cloy
The appetites they feed, but she makes hungry
Where most she satisfies.

(II.ii.242)

But the crucial statement is his Cydnus speech, describing how
she could transform a journey of submission into her own erotic
triumph. Later, she will take the ultimate step to avoid submitting
to Caesar and becoming a showpiece in his triumphal procession.
She knows how she would furnish matter for street-ballads or
stage farce. The travestying of classical subjects which followed
their new familiarity through print here merges with popular libel.
Growing literacy made this a weapon of the humble as well as the
elevated, of women as well as men. The 'scald rhymers' feared by

Cleopatra might include the likes of Joan Gomme of Thetford, Norfolk, brought to court in 1606 'for that she hath made and doth exercise the makeinge of libellous and lascivious ballads by and of her neighbors'.[30] Jacobean stage convention was more restrictive, so Shakespeare has the boy-player of Cleopatra draw attention to himself in a way which skirts self-mockery, quaintly apprehensive of seeing

> Some squeaking Cleopatra boy my greatness
> I'th' posture of a whore.

> (V.ii.212)

If this is a reminder that no mere player can *be* Cleopatra, it is notable that her finest moment, on the Cydnus, must be left to Enobarbus's reporting. On that occasion she had been the cynosure not on Roman terms but her own, as deviser of this river spectacle. In Enobarbus's fancy, the very air would have 'gone to gaze on Cleopatra too', but for creating a vacuum (II.ii.224). Indeed, the air and the seeming handmaidens of Venus who sailed the barge combine in an image of potent eroticism (flatulence being thought a prime factor in the mechanism of erection):[31] 'the silken tackle / Swell with the touches of those flower-soft hands' (l.216). This leisurely pleasure-boat supplies a fitting emblem of what her subsequent life with Antony will entail, as they let pleasure take them on its slow stream.

A watery ambience suits this Venus-Cleopatra. According to Plutarch, she instigated the sea-fight with Caesar. In Shakespeare, Antony has been dared to it by Caesar, which effectively deflects blame for this military blunder from Cleopatra. But she is quick to approve: 'By sea – what else' (III.vii.28); and she points to Egypt's naval strength: 'I have sixty sails, Caesar none better' (l.49). She is angry with Enobarbus for speaking against her 'being in these wars' (III.vii.3). It is as well that she fails to catch his remark that

> If we should serve with horse and mares together,
> The horse were merely lost; the mares would bear
> A soldier and his horse.

> (III.vii.7)

This recalls her own words of frustration at her lover's departure: 'O happy horse, to bear the weight of Antony!' (I.v.21); but it is also broadly accurate, as subsequent events demonstrate. Enobarbus cautions her that already it is being 'said in Rome / That Photinus, an eunuch, and your maids / Manage this war' (III.vii.13). This is yet another instance of how Antony's subjection to Cleopatra is figured as gelding or effeminacy. Nor is Cleopatra's playing with masculine roles any less problematic. In Shakespeare's culture, and here lies Cleopatra's dilemma, rulers customarily led their troops in action, while women were excluded from the battlefield. In such a culture women, when the bullets fly, do as those American servicewomen did in Panama City: they run.[32] This is an eminently sane response for those outside the cult of heroism. But it destroys Cleopatra and Antony in a world which recognizes war as the ultimate sanction of political power. Although love has challenged the ascendancy of that power, it has by no means rendered war unthinkable.

Cleopatra is not embarrassed by the tensions arising from her status as both woman and monarch, for the real conflict lies elsewhere. This play is a particularly complex example of that popular sub-genre which deals with the tug-o'-war between political responsibility and sexual desire. Queen Helen, in Sidney's *Arcadia*, is in just this predicament; but she consoles herself for putting love before duty with the reflection that 'my people . . . are content to bear with my absence and folly'.[33] Cleopatra spares not a thought for her people, but is wholly preoccupied with Antony's absence or presence. She has found Antony's absence in Rome almost unendurable, and it is her determination not to be separated from him again which propels her into the sea-battle. Nonetheless the consequences described by Antony's friend Scarus result from her sex and Antony's sexual bondage. Scarus has witnessed 'Yon ribaudred nag of Egypt' – preferable to the Wells–Taylor emendation – fly like a cow stung by a gadfly. And Antony (sustaining the derogatory figures) followed her 'like a doting mallard' (III.x.10). Antony is rueful rather than contemptuous, though saying much the same thing:

> Egypt, thou knew'st too well
> My heart was to thy rudder tied by th' strings,
> And thou shouldst tow me after.

> (III.xi.56)

But his words catch the intense physicality of their relationship, and he can console himself with a kiss. This receives a telling gloss from Enobarbus when Cleopatra, anxious about her own degree of culpability, is told that Antony alone is to blame 'that would make his will / Lord of his reason' (III.xiii.3). Shakespeare clearly fears that his audience will slide over this point if he fails to hammer it home with almost Hollywood-like persistence. The scene is an interweave of humiliation, anger and recriminations, out of which Antony emerges ready for 'one other gaudy night . . . . Come on, my queen, / There's sap in't yet' (III.xiii.185). This is heroism of a kind; but Enobarbus cannot appreciate it, and defeatedly resolves to abandon his fallen hero.

Enobarbus has been a reliable commentator on events, his own bias not blinding him to the queen's attractions. But now he can only despair at Antony's abandonment of military sense. Goethe finds in the play a supreme demonstration of the way 'that enjoyment and activity exclude one another',[34] and it is clear that Antony, through his love for Cleopatra, has lost his grip on military-political affairs. But the play shows the perspective of world leaders to have no obvious advantage over that of the lover. The context of mortality makes the lust for power appear as trivial as the other kind; arguably more so, since sexual lust furnishes reproduction as a constructive response to mortality, whereas political ambition is an attempt to push it from the mind. Boccaccio, in that hostile picture of Cleopatra deriving from chroniclers like Josephus, hardly distinguishes between the two lusts, whereas the Chaucerian model finds a connection between love and goodness. Shakespeare will not go so far: the wonder of love is not as a virtue-instiller. But neither does he attempt to render the two lusts as one, though they are apt to converge: those watery episodes on the Cydnus and at Actium each represent entanglements of sex and power.

Even the shift of focus in the later stages of the play to the nexus of sex and death is not the fresh departure that it might seem. Cleopatra, as she prepares for suicide, can identify this step with her first sight of Antony: 'Go fetch / My best attires. I am again for Cydnus / To meet Mark Antony' (V.ii.223). Antony will encounter death like an eager bridegroom (IV.xvi.100), and Cleopatra perceives its stroke 'as a lover's pinch' (V.ii.290). Sex and death are enmeshed from the start. News of Fulvia's death requires Antony's departure for Rome to conclude 'The business she hath broachèd in the state'; but Enobarbus quibbles that 'the business you have broached here cannot be without you, especially that of Cleopatra's, which wholly depends on your abode' (I.ii.164). He has already rendered Cleopatra's sexual ploys as 'celerity in dying' (l.137); and when she confronts the finality of death, some of her most moving speeches are touched with the carping tones and pettiness which she has adopted earlier. But they are transfigured so that it is sorrow, shame and fortitude which adopt the outlines of that old, shabby jealousy when Charmian dies ahead of her:

> If she first meet the curlèd Antony,
> He'll make demand of her, and spend that kiss
> Which is my heaven to have.
>
> (V.ii.296)

Her trickery precipitates Antony's death; but all the splendour and passion of their relationship inheres in her valediction:

> O, withered is the garland of the war.
> The soldier's pole is fall'n
>
> (IV.xvi.66)

Fanny Hill's periphrasis, 'I was content . . . with having rais'd a maypole for another to hang a garland on',[35] shows how this might easily slip towards grossness. But recollections of military achievement and May Day romps combine into solemnity. That vaginal (rose) garland, a favourite figure of German folksong but little used in English[36] (though Shakespeare may have recalled it when naming Guildenstern's companion), indicates that Antony is to have no successor in Cleopatra's bed. She seems unable to think of their love except in the most strongly physical terms. This is very clear in that later encomium, where her implicit association with the sea plays its part. She envisages Antony as a Colossus, following that interpretation of the *Greek Anthology* (VI.171) which has the statue straddling the harbour entrance of Rhodes: 'His legs bestrid the ocean; his reared arm / Crested the world'. In this case he bestrides her harbour, a sexual commonplace.[37] That 'reared arm' too carries phallic resonance; Marston's *Malcontent* (1600–04, V.i) makes meaning reference to those who would 'trie the strength of a mans backe, and his arme', while Urquhart (1653) corroborates with his picture of the 'labourer of nature' which 'grew marvellous long, fat, . . . stirring and Crest-risen'.[38] Cleopatra maintains the pattern:

> For his bounty,
> There was no winter in't; an autumn 'twas,
> That grew the more by reaping. His delights
> Were dolphin-like, they showed his back above
> The element they lived in.

> (V.ii.85)

Bounty, sexual largesse, this was the strong-backed Antony's outstanding quality. Coital indulgence served only to increase his ardour; but the animalism is tempered by the rhythmic grace of the dolphin.

So the double aspect, identified here with Boccaccio and Chaucer, is kept in play to the very end. We are not shown any alchemical mystery of sensual stupor transformed or spiritually regenerated. Cleopatra briefly acknowledges the change which death will bring as she becomes 'fire and air' (V.ii.284), leaving behind her 'other elements' – sea and black earth, both emblems of fertility. But such refinement is only an oblique reminder that she is the very embodiment of Egyptian creation myth: the 'serpent of old Nile' bred on the river's mulch 'by the operation of your sun' (I.v.25; II.vii.27). If her death is somehow transcendent it is also undeniably sensual. The use of the clown to bring in 'the pretty worm / Of Nilus' (V.ii.238) demonstrates this duality, a serio-comic restatement of that key fertility motif. The basket of figs as camouflage for the worm derives from Plutarch. But it takes on special aptness here. The fruit's aphrodisiac properties are noted in Benvenuto's *The Passenger* (1612, p.175), where it is explained in King's translation that 'figges . . . aide sperme'. But the vaginal sense also comes into play, an Italian use familiar to Elizabethans through the 'fico' gibe: 'There are but few descendants of *Adam*, that . . . would have refused to taste of that figge' (p.271). Some authorities identify the fig with the Forbidden Fruit of Eden, which anticipates the present sex-death collocation; and there is the further irony that in ancient lore the fig tree quells the fiercest passions.[39] So the phallic worm arrives nestling amongst vaginal figs. Tool of both death and life, it also becomes suckling infant taken to Cleopatra's breast. The richness of overtone which the clown brings to his account of the creature begins with that seeming verbal slip: 'his biting is immortal' (V.ii.241). Behind this lies the popular figure of pregnancy as poisoning,[40] so Cleopatra's own 'Immortal longings' (l.276) have a procreative colour. The clown's routine needs tighter control than that in *Macbeth*. It includes pertinent jesting over 'a very honest woman, but something given to lie, as a woman should not do but in the way of honesty', who though 'she died of the biting of it . . . makes a very good report o'th' worm' (l.246). Sex overrides death here; or rather, this is orgasmic death produced by the phallic worm; and it is unnecessary to distinguish between meanings when the clown wishes Cleopatra 'joy of the worm' (l.255). Her suicide, inability to live without Antony, demonstrates the heights which her love can reach. This point remains despite that rival concern about becoming a degraded captive. Whatever the mixture of motives, she can still make her dying a magnificent expression of her love for Antony: 'Husband, I come' (l.282).

Cleopatra's well-attested artistry in dying reaches an erotic high-point in this scene. Jacobean respectability would have frowned on her total absorption in passion even unto death; but Shakespeare puts her within reach of current orthodoxies through her fidelity to Antony. There is no inclination to take some court flunkey or stable-boy during his lengthy absence; instead she settles for the harmless diversions offered by eunuch or ladies in waiting. Her lovers represent a correlation of sex and power; Antony ill-humouredly recalls that he found her

> as a morsel cold upon
> Dead Caesar's trencher; nay, you were a fragment
> Of Gnaeus Pompey's.
>
> (III.xiii.117)

But while power has an erotic fascination for her, clearly there is more to it. She makes no attempt to ensnare Octavius Caesar. He has the power but not Antony's romantic view of power, and would be no substitute in her bed or heart. Whereas in Plutarch there would have been no chance of Cleopatra's weaving her spells about Octavius, Shakespeare gives the actor scope to show it differently. Even in death, and Octavius betrays himself a little in bearing such witness, she retains her own awesome power:

> she looks like sleep,
> As she would catch another Antony
> In her strong toil of grace.
>
> (V.ii.340)

7

Trojan Whores

The prologue to *Troilus and Cressida* announces a stage epic. This is achieved linguistically as 'princes orgulous' are described coming

> To ransack Troy, within whose strong immures
> The ravished Helen, Menelaus' queen,
> With wanton Paris sleeps.

The pompous-sounding archaism and the neo-latinism 'immures' (walls) anticipate the ironic use of latinate diction in the body of the play. This stands in teasing relationship to 'that fatal classical misconception of all ancient poets which the humanists have fastened upon our education – the spectral solemnity, the gradus epithets, the dictionary language, the decorum which avoids every contact with the senses and the soil'.[1] But that hint of soil and senses in the reference to Helen's abduction will be graphically confirmed by Thersites's summing up of the Trojan War: 'All the argument is a whore and a cuckold. A good quarrel to draw emulous factions and bleed to death upon' (II.iii.71).

Shakespeare uses Thersites to undermine epic values because they are substantially military values, preaching the ethic of heroism. Epic representation of war, like the Romans' ruthlessly efficient practice of it, provided both a model and a justification for the Renaissance. But for the moment Shakespeare keeps up the heroic front, declaring

> that our play
> Leaps o'er the vaunt and firstlings of those broils,
> Beginning in the middle, starting thence away
> To what may be digested in a play.

He will follow the Horatian prescription, *in medias res*; and Horace was still, as he had been for centuries, the most influential literary

theorist in Shakespeare's day.[2] Indeed, Shakespeare's beginning
thus and finishing his play well before the war's end recalls the
plan of the *Iliad* rather than that of medieval Troy-books. None the
less, despite Rossiter's belief that since 'The Troilus and Cressida
story is medieval and chivalric, . . . it is this which is deflated' rather
than the world of classical epic, the distinction had been eroded by
no less a theorist than Cinthio.[3] He argues, in his *Discorso intorno
al comporre dei romanzi* (1554), that the single-plot Homeric epic
and the multi-plot medieval mode are of the same genre. In this
defence of the Ariostan method, he advisedly retains the term
romanzo, since he sees this medieval form as mediator between
ancient and modern heroic poetry.[4]

Elizabethan disputants over the nature and purpose of poetry
borrowed their arguments from the Italians, amongst whom the
debate had taken place in the years before Shakespeare's birth.
Almost without exception, those who valued poetry considered
epic (especially Virgilian) the highest form, fulfilling most com-
pletely the function of teaching virtue through noble example. In a
letter prefacing his second instalment of Homer translation (1598),
Chapman – intent on releasing some of that poet's power to his
unlearned contemporaries – sees his task as a 'meanes to the absolute redresse or much to be wished extenuation of all the unmanly
degeneracies now tyranysing amongst us'.[5] He attacks Scaliger for
that 'diminution of Homer'[6] which was fairly widespread. Cinthio
finds Homer hampered by the vulgarity of his age which he cannot
choose but reflect. Hence Virgil is the safer model, since he 'always
attained to the grand and the magnificent and avoided the baseness
unworthy of the heroic style'.[7] For him, epic takes as its hero the
performer of illustrious deeds, deeds which should be honourable
as well as exceptional.[8] But Shakespeare goes well beyond those
Homeric improprieties which offended Cinthio. Heroic decorum
belongs to the world of classicism whereas *Troilus and Cressida* is
Shakespeare's most complete embracement of *manierismo*, with its
tense recognition that there is no absolute truth or morality, but
that all is relative.

According to High Renaissance thought, the task of the poet
was not simply to imitate nature but to select those parts of nature
deemed permanent. It was because Homer found many permanent
things to imitate that he survived. But while acknowledging this,
his detractors deplored the manners and mythology dispensed in

his poems as transient and temporary. The Mannerists swept this debate aside, denying permanence in nature, as they helped to negotiate change from universalism to pluralism. There was no longer one holy, apostolic Church, reflecting the oneness of God: schism bred sectarianism. The role of the printing press in this momentous shift has already been noticed. While it brought into easy reach the ancient preachers of heroic virtue, it also led to a critical scrutiny of their values. Print gives a measure of permanence, yet at the same time exposes that illusion of stability which is the basis of classicism.

Even the early Reformer Tyndale, intent – according to Foxe[9] – on bringing the Scriptures within reach of 'a boy that driveth the Plough', found the press double-edged. It could be used to spread the word of the Devil as well as that of God. In his *Obedience of a Christen Man* (1528, p.20), he charged that the papists 'permitte & sofre you to reade Robyn hode & bevise of hampton/ hercules/ hector, and troylus with a tousande histories & fables of love & wantones & of rybaudry as fylthy as herte can thinke'. This is of present interest, indicating that chapbook versions of the Troilus story as well as ballads were in sixteenth-century street currency. The first printed book in English was Caxton's *Recuyell of the Historyes of Troye* (1475?), demonstrating keen interest in the subject amongst well-to-do readers; but those of more modest means and reading ability were in a position to measure Shakespeare's treatment against received versions of the story. So there is no need to postulate any special audience for the play on the grounds of accessibility. Equally beside the point are those attempts to explain away Shakespeare's surprises and distortions in his handling of familiar material by unearthing precedents. None of his sources provides anything like his concentration of discords. Upsetting of expectations by violating norms is the very stuff of Mannerist art. Astonishment and disquiet are the aims, and they would have been excited here by the matter as well as the manner. Indeed, the play is likely to have caused problems not through inaccessibility but its opposite, making freely available ideas which were deemed appropriate only for an élite (see p. 27). Antique Scepticism was widely encountered by that élite through Latin translations of Sextus Empiricus, published at Paris, Antwerp and Geneva in the 1560s, while Montaigne supplied an updated version. But Montaigne is resolutely conservative in a way that the message of *Troilus* is not. As Ellis-Fermor claims, many of the play's 'main issues depend . . . upon the question of whether value is absolute or relative', its writer being 'a man to whom values have become suspect'.[10] Hence it is likely to have been the authorities rather than Globe audiences who would be disconcerted by ideas which, conventionally disguised in earlier Shakespearean plays, are here exposed nakedly as ploys for holding the many in subjection to the few.

Epic values tend to concern themselves with manly virtues, expressed in the Renaissance as battlefield or boudoir heroism. But as 'New Philosophy call[ed] all in doubt',[11] a 500-year-old courtly-chivalric tradition was as open to questioning as any other. The confusion of Mars and Venus, which runs through the play, was a still older tradition. Wind traces the classical origins of that 'combination of a martial spirit with amiability [which] was so essential and natural to the Renaissance code of chivalry'. Love chastens Strife to produce Harmony; but these opposing qualities coincide 'In the perfect lover . . . because he – or she – is the perfect warrior'.[12] Mars and Venus converge in the opening lines of the play, when Troilus decides to disarm:

> Why should I war without the walls of Troy
> That find such cruel battle here within?

He finds himself 'Less valiant than the virgin in the night' (I.i.11), meaning that he would yield to his opponent. That yielding on the battlefield is a different proposition from willing sexual surrender is characteristically ignored; it accords with Aeneas's proposal to take the field 'with a bridegroom's fresh alacrity' (IV.iv.145). Eventually, having witnessed Cressida's betrayal, Troilus is ready to proclaim his anguish 'In characters as red as Mars his heart / Inflamed with Venus' (V.ii.167) – a far cry from the neo-Platonists' conception of Venus's chastening power.

But it is no genuflecting to tradition or acknowledgment of sex and violence as heady theatrical combination which keeps the two continually entangled here. Rather, Shakespeare puts it to us that the relationship is culturally determined, sex having had a well defined role as provoker of combat since at least the twelfth century. With the shift from the old heroic mode to the courtly-chivalric, it behoved the warrior both to protect allegedly weak women and to impress undoubtedly nubile ones.[13] Even

Ulysses's notorious 'degree' speech is touched by sexual issues. He describes how that 'universal wolf' appetite, 'seconded with will and power' and feeding on all, will 'last eat up himself' (I.iii.122) – a characteristic of 'lechery' according to Thersites, as he watches a fight between 'the wenching rogues' Troilus and Diomedes (V.iv.31). But the symbolic link between lust and other – notably the economic – appetites is conspicuous throughout the play. Whereas Ulysses's theme is 'The specialty of rule' (I.iii.77) and its neglect in the Greek camp, he evades Agamemnon's appeal for a remedy, responding tangentially with a picture of Achilles and Patroclus passing their days 'Upon a lazy bed' (l.147).[14] The homosexual nature of their relationship is emphasized in Marlowe's *Edward II* (1591–3), when the Gaveston–Edward liaison is mirrored in the way that 'for Patroclus stern Achilles droop'd'.[15] It is made still more emphatic here as Achilles's 'lazy bed' becomes his 'pressed bed' (l.162), the implications of the epithet borne out when Pandarus ushers Troilus and Cressida into 'a chamber with a bed – which bed, because it shall not speak of your pretty encounters, press it to death' (III.ii.203). At II.i.115, Thersites comments more forthrightly on the relationship, referring to Patroclus as 'Achilles' brooch' – or 'brach' in Rowe's generally accepted improvement on Shakespeare. Patroclus is a 'brooch', a jewel, as a mistress might be described who has been won and worn. He may be 'Achilles' male varlet' or 'masculine whore' (V.i.15), but is none the less anxious that Achilles risks being loathed as 'effeminate' (III.iii.211) for his refusal to fight. This is part of the pressure exerted on the hero by Ulysses, who urges that 'better would it fit Achilles much ∕ To throw down Hector than Polyxena' (III.iii.200); the double applicability of the verb intimating Achilles's equivocal sexuality or even that ascribed to the Elizabethan actor, apt to mistake 'the Woman for the Boy in Womans attire' or 'the Boy . . . for the Woman'.[16]

Ulysses's smooth duplicities are evident even while he addresses the Greek high command. Although he includes himself amongst those mimicked by Patroclus for Achilles's delectation, the hamming performances he describes are those burlesquing Agamemnon and Nestor. This is but the first occasion on which he betrays a taste for making others squirm. But when Patroclus plays at being Agamemnon and Nestor we recognize a miniature of the play's entire action. The effect is characteristically Mannerist, with

distinctions set up between art and life only to be broken down
(distinctions are finally routed by Pandarus).

But in the wake of Ulysses's speeches, Aeneas arrives from
Troy with a different kind of identity-questioning. His failure
to recognize Agamemnon's 'most imperial looks' (I.iii.223) makes
ironic comment on that doctrine of degree which has just
been articulated. Agamemnon, already unsettled by accounts of
Patroclus's mockery, is uncertain whether Aeneas is baiting him.
The actor might play it either way, and certainly Aeneas recognizes
Achilles readily enough later on (IV.vi.77). But the idea of the
natural, commanding leader, perhaps even hedged about with
divinity, suffers another blow when Ajax – albeit distracted by
a new sense of importance – mistakes Thersites for Agamemnon
(III.iii.253). On any orthodox scale, Thersites is at the opposite
extreme to majesty. Puttenham describes Homer's original as a
'glorious noddie', and in Heywood's *Iron Age* (1612–13) III.i,
Thersites takes pride in his 'hutch-backe' because 'whom Nature
. . . most deformes, they are best arm'd below'.[17] But Shakespeare's
Thersites describes Agamemnon as a whoremonger, 'one that loves
quails' (V.i.48), which further erodes distinctions.[18]

Ajax uses Thersites for his entertainment as Achilles uses
Patroclus, delighting in his wicked caricatures of the Greek
leaders. Ulysses complains that these unruly elements rate action
above thought. They deride the general staff, calling its activity

> 'bed-work', 'mapp'ry', 'closet war'.
> So that the ram that batters down the wall,
> For the great swinge and rudeness of his poise,
> They place before his hand that made the engine.
>
> (I.iii.205)

The sexual overtones are unmistakable: 'closet war' is evidently
fought by chamber-warriors; whereas the active principle is figured
with ponderous phallic power. Such resentment of staff officers was
prevalent amongst front-line troops in the Great War. But another
parallel with that more recent conflict is the serious peace initiatives
taken by the Greeks. The peace proposal made during the play
is not the first attempt by the Greeks to conclude hostilities.
Hector's mention of having met Ulysses 'on your Greekish
embassy' (IV.vii.99) obliquely recalls earlier peace talk. It is one
of several moments in the play where Shakespeare is not simply

allowing his audiences to draw on their reading experience but is positively requiring it. Whatever the shortcomings of the Greek generals, they are too practical to cherish war for its own sake. Their new proposal is beautifully simple, stipulating only the return of Helen. But it has no more success than the Kaiser's initiative of December 1916, and the ostensible reasons are much the same. Peace with honour can be achieved only through victory. The warrior mystique governing Trojan response is much the same as that encountered by the actress Lena Ashwell when she ventured the opinion, in a 1918 officers' mess, 'that war was no solution of differences' since men could be killed easier than ideas. This was after four years of carnage, yet 'The whole mess fell upon me with the argument that war was the great means of bringing out what was finest and best in man'.[19] It is noteworthy that the first modern revivals of Shakespeare's play took place in Germany during the sabre-rattling build-up to the Great War, the mood of the play agreeing with that of satirical papers like *Simplicissimus*.

Just as the discourse led by Ulysses amongst the Greek leaders is heavily qualified by ironic juxtapositions, so the Trojan council called to discuss the Greek peace terms is placed in the compromising frame of Hector's challenge. Sexuality is inseparable from his warrior image. His challenge to the enemy claims that 'He hath a lady, wiser, fairer, truer, / Than ever Greek did compass in his arms' (I.iii.272). If this challenge meets no response, he will assume that 'Grecian dames are sunburnt and not worth / The splinter of a lance' (I.iii.279). But Agamemnon affirms that there will be no shortage of champions, since any soldier worth his salt is a lover. Hector, having begun with a reasoned plea for returning Helen to her husband since the cost of keeping her had already been so bloody, performs a complete *volte face* and immediately recalls his 'roisting challenge' (II.ii.207). Paris has naturally urged Helen's retention, speaking (as Priam puts it) 'Like one besotted on your sweet delights' (l.142). He has 'the honey still' while his brothers have 'the gall', anticipating those great capitalist wars of the future where the prize goes not to the winning tribe but to a privileged minority. Inevitably, he insists that sexual enjoyment is not his guiding motive: 'I would have the soil of her fair rape / Wiped off in honourable keeping her' (II.ii.147). While acknowledging some disgrace, he introduces the paradox of 'fair rape'. Boccaccio, although presenting Helen as a wanton, supplies opposing accounts of her abduction, one in which she leaves willingly with Paris, and the other in which she is enforced.[20] Paris's reference to 'the ransacked queen' (l.149), recalling the Prologue's linkage of ravished Helen and ransacked Troy, argues enforcement (cf. *Rape of Lucrece*, l.838, where Lucrece is 'robbed and ransacked by injurious theft').

But it is Troilus who most vehemently rejects peace as the price of Helen. To Hector's rational arguments he responds that reason emasculates, making 'livers pale and lustihood deject' (II.ii.49). Hector's 'Brother, she is not worth what she doth cost' (l.50) transforms board and lodging into vistas of heaped corpses. But Troilus turns it into a debate on whether value is innate or arbitrarily imposed. There is an odd criss-cross here, Hector's realist approach taking an idealist turn while Troilus's idealism is subverted by his choice of image:

> We turn not back the silks upon the merchant
> When we have soiled them; nor the remainder viands
> We do not throw in unrespective sewer
> Because we now are full.

(II.ii.68)

In the same speech, when he talks directly of Helen, he elevates his tone:

> she is a pearl
> Whose price hath launched above a thousand ships
> And turned crowned kings to merchants.

(II.ii.80)

But although he finds a more romantic way of acknowledging her destructive power than Hector, his own image of merchandise persists. His entire case boils down to Helen as 'a theme of honour and renown, / A spur to valiant and magnanimous deeds' whose fame will 'in time to come canonize us' (II.ii.198).

By contrast, Diomedes – contemptuous of Menelaus, who 'like a puling cuckold would drink up / The lees and dregs of a flat 'tamèd piece' (IV.i.63) – sees her as a broached cask (''tamèd piece'), its contents grown flat. This is in response to Paris's question,

> Who in your thoughts deserves fair Helen most,
> Myself or Menelaus?

(55)

It offers a parody of Paris's Judgment, one interpretation of which was that awarding the apple to Venus had brought a temporary end to strife.[21] But the more traditional reading was that it had set in motion the processes leading to the ten-year Trojan War. Diomedes's pragmatic view of things might have been a route towards ending the war. But at this very moment he is on a mission to bring Cressida to the Greek camp, which turns into his own small-scale re-enactment of Helen's rape. His resentment that 'For every false drop in her bawdy veins / A Grecian's life hath sunk' (l.71), is easily seen by Paris as a chapman's ruse, dispraising 'the thing that you desire to buy'. Although this implies that the Trojans are no traders, both sides regard her chiefly as a commodity, a sexual trophy for which they contend. Troilus puts it cynically in the first scene: 'Helen must needs be fair / When with your blood you daily paint her thus' (l.90). Already, allusion to face-painting puts her into Diomedes's trollop category. She is evoked through images requiring very little pressure to yield a bawdy sense. Hector's response to Menelaus's welcome, 'By Mars his gauntlet, thanks', contrives a cheap taunt about her continuing vaginal orientation: 'Your quondam wife swears still by Venus' glove' (IV.vii.62). (Menelaus might well have said, with Armin, that Helen is 'the gloue, which still I seeke to weare'.)[22] Earlier, Thersites asserts that Ajax 'Has not so much wit . . . As will stop the eye of Helen's needle, for whom he comes to fight' (II.i.80). This declares him witless; but a subordinate idea catches the prevailing mood of warring for a placket, placing his brains between his legs.[23]

Helen herself appears only briefly in the play. Pandarus goes to visit Paris, and a brothel mood is evoked in readiness for Helen's appearance. Pandarus affects urgency; his 'business seethes', and a servant mutters: 'Sodden business! There's a stewed phrase, indeed' (III.i.40). The brothel sense of 'stew' is often overtoned with that of syphilitic scalding, though Fletcher's *Island Princess* (1619–21) I.i.8 goes directly to the latter sense when Piniero is warned off wenching, which would 'stew my bones'. 'Sodden' acquires a similar sense, Jonson, in *Cynthia's Revels* (1600–1) IV.v.47, using 'sodden *Nymph*' as the insulting equivalent of 'poxed whore'.[24] Helen's conversation is less spiced with bawdry than Cressida's, and by no means proclaims her a 'sodden nymph'. But when Pandarus mentions that 'My niece is horrible in love with a thing you have, sweet Queen' (III.i.94), she clearly registers a genital innuendo in 'thing', responding: 'She shall have it, my lord – if it be not my lord Paris' – lover as phallus. And when he reassures her that 'she'll none of him. They two are twain', she retorts: 'Falling in, after falling out, may make them three', remarking the procreative possibilities of reconciliation.[25] But what creates the atmosphere is not risqué exchanges but the availability of a musical instrument to Pandarus, as if he visits a barber's shop – or a brothel. Then there are the tactile experiences discovered by Helen's 'white enchanting fingers', which will soon be used ambiguously to 'disarm great Hector' (III.i.148). But now, as they caress Pandarus's forehead, we recall the chin-chuck – a favourite amorous signal – which Troilus is said to have received when Helen 'puts me her white hand to his cloven chin' (I.ii.115). Cressida wonders 'How came it cloven', and is told ''tis dimpled'. The dimple is supposedly 'a certain prognostick' of an amorous disposition, even though Shakespeare's Lucrece possesses one (*Rape of Lucrece*, l.420). According to Fletcher, *Maid in the Mill* (1623) II.ii.160, '*Venus* has the . . . sweetest dimple hole'; and in 'Katy's Beauty' (pre-1720) a sympathetic explanation is afforded as far as the female sex is concerned: Katy's 'Chin's adorn'd with a Dimple, / Like the Charms above her Knee'.[26]

When Helen strokes Pandarus's forehead it evidently puts him in mind of dimples, and he sings of Cupid's shaft which wounds no deer 'But tickles still the sore' (III.i.116). This 'sore' is both a buck of the fourth year and the vulva. Thus in Shakespeare's 'Fair was the morn' (*Passionate Pilgrim*, 9), Venus demonstrates to Adonis where another 'sweet youth' was wounded by a boar: 'See in my thigh, quoth she, here was the sore. / She showèd hers; he saw more wounds than one, / And blushing fled'. In Pandarus's song, the tickling produces orgasmic 'dying', rendered by a series of 'groans' and titters. When Pandarus groans in earnest, Helen takes it to mean that he is in love 'to the very tip of the nose' – in this context an unmistakable phallic displacement recalling that in *Antony and Cleopatra* (p. 88 above). The prevailing mood of decadence is rounded off when Paris languidly declares that 'I would fain have armed today, but my Nell would not have it so'. Far from propelling him into danger, this mistress provides him with an excuse to avoid it, sensibly finding a display of manly prowess in bed preferable to that in battle.

Cressida is associated with Helen early on: 'An her hair were not somewhat darker than Helen's – well, go to', declares Pandarus, adding: 'An she were not kin to me, she would be as fair o' Friday as Helen is on Sunday' (I.i.41, 75) – Cressida's week-day looks match Helen's Sunday best. In this same scene, Troilus speaks of her in imagery that he will use of Helen later: 'Her bed is India; there she lies, a pearl' (l.100). To couch with her would be to know the riches of India, the wealth of its sea-bed. She is a prize for this merchant-venturer, and Pandarus will be the vessel to transport him to her. But so far the resemblance between the two is superficial. Helen is what Cressida will become when she is prostituted to the needs of a ruling élite. For the moment, when Pandarus asserts that Helen loves Troilus 'better than Paris', Cressida can retort that 'she's a merry Greek indeed' – a whore (I.ii.105). As for her praising him, 'I had as lief Helen's golden tongue had commended Troilus for a copper nose' (l.100). The suggestion is that Helen's 'golden tongue' would be as spurious as a copper nose, no cause for praise since it is the sign of a drunkard or, more literally, a disguise for nose mutilation – often enough caused by pox. In this scene Cressida shows her own mettle, wittily evading Pandarus's attempts to enthrall her with Troilus. Representations on the latter's behalf are repeatedly undercut with bawdry. Despite his youth, boasts Pandarus, he will 'within three pound lift as much as his brother Hector'; and she responds wryly: 'Is he so young a man and so old a lifter?'.[27]

She mocks attempts to prove Helen's love for him with a quibble on phallic erection: 'Troilus will stand to the proof if you'll prove it so' (l.125). Pandarus's cake-making image in the first scene is recalled here when he suggests that 'birth, beauty, good shape' are the 'spice and salt that season a man' (l.249). Beryl Rowland[28] has unravelled the sexual implications of that first image, and now Cressida proceeds to discover some here: 'Ay, a minced man – and then to be baked with no date in the pie, for then the man's date is out'. The humour is fairly tangled, 'minced' indicating effeminacy or even emasculation in this out-of-date man. But the counterpart to the vaginal 'pie' (the popular figures are of cutting up or having a finger in) is clarified by Tom Brown (1700), whose Aesopian fable of marriage as the buying of dates ends by warning against the relationship though there are 'twenty women in our neighbourhood that long to be fingering your dates'.[29]

Nestor allows Cressida to be 'A woman of quick sense' (IV.vi.55), with mental agility and sensuality jostling in that last word. And she readily nonplusses Pandarus: 'You are such another woman! One knows not at what ward you lie' (I.ii.254). But this prompts another rush of quibbles, based on the 'watch and ward' phrase, with verbal fencing underscoring the old link between sexual and martial combat: 'Upon my back to defend my belly, upon my wit to defend my wiles, upon my secrecy to defend mine honesty, my mask to defend my beauty, and you, to defend all these – and at all these wards I lie at a thousand watches'. Pandarus is reduced to a feed for this dazzling comedienne: 'If I cannot ward what I would not have hit, I can watch you for telling how I took the blow – unless it swell past hiding, and then it's past watching'. Reference here to the betrayals of pregnancy indicates that this is more than fun. It shows her lively apprehension of sexual vulnerability. This becomes still more emphatic when Pandarus offers to bring 'a token from Troilus', and Cressida rounds on him: 'By the same token, you are a bawd'. When he leaves, she muses that she already inclines towards Troilus without any nudging from a go-between. But she understands that harsh cultural difference between those who do and those who are done: 'Yet hold I off. Women are angels, wooing; / Things won are done. Joy's soul lies in the doing' (I.ii.282).

Troilus has tried to talk her out of her fears, but she recognizes fear tempered by reason as a sane combination (III.ii.68). This contrasts with Troilus's position, during the Trojan council meeting, that 'Manhood and honour / Should have hare hearts' if reason were allowed sway (II.ii.46). That the echo is deliberate is clear from the cross-talk over monsters. There are none such 'In all Cupid's pageant', reassures Troilus; and Cressida responds with phallic levity: 'Nor nothing monstrous neither?' (III.ii.71). Troilus, seemingly oblivious to the joke and innocent of double meaning, answers: 'Nothing but our undertakings', which he represents as clichés of weeping seas or taming tigers at a mistress's behest.[30] But then he comes to the real 'monstruosity in love, . . . – that the will is infinite and the execution confined; that the desire is boundless and the act a slave to limit' (l.78). It is at this point that Cressida recalls the hare reference from the earlier scene with devastating irony: 'They that have the voice of lions and the act of hares, are they not monsters' (l.84). The issue is one quizzically raised by Montaigne (III.v: 'Upon Some Verses of Virgil'): that while women are subject to social restraint far beyond that imposed on men, their sexual stamina is embarrassingly superior; and Cressida rubs the fact in.

When these lovers awaken after their one night of passion, it is to find that the lark has roused 'the busy day', and that in turn 'the ribald crows' (IV.ii.10). Right on cue, Pandarus enters crowing. Cressida's insecurity has shown in her search for reassurance: 'Are you aweary of me?' (l.9), and her reproach that

> You men will never tarry.
> O foolish Cressid! I might have still held off,
> And then you would have tarried.

> (IV.ii.18)

The old skill in badinage, which the actress will often render as a defensive posture, has gone, and she is vulnerable to Pandarus's prurient clowning. She weakly protests that 'You bring me to do – and then you flout me too', and he exploits her embarrassment further: 'To do what? To do what? – Let her say what. – What have I brought you to do?' (l.30). Then he turns his attention to Troilus: 'Alas, poor wretch. Ah, poor *capocchia*, has't not slept tonight? Would he not – a naughty man – let it sleep?'. The phallic application of *capocchia* is clear from its basic meaning, the knob of a stick. This is Pandarus affecting to be one of those Italianate blades who pepper their talk with expressions like *cazzo*.[31]

That Troilus and Cressida respond quite differently to Pandarus's teasing has nothing to do with innate characteristics. It reflects the way that fornication is taken to be a guarantee of masculinity, yet a betrayal of femininity. When more ribald crows come knocking at the door, Cressida seeks to protect her modesty while Troilus chooses to misunderstand:

> My lord, come you again into my chamber.
> You smile and mock me, as if I meant naughtily.

> (IV.ii.39)

Troilus, unattuned to Cressida's sensitivity, discerns innuendo of the vaginal chamber.[32] But the contrast is no greater than that drawn from Troilus by the prospect first of Helen and then of Cressida being surrendered to the Greeks. As we have noticed, sustained, impassioned rhetoric is called forth in the first case. But in the second, he asks resignedly: 'Is it so concluded?'

(IV.ii.69). The essential difference between the two is that Helen's return would have ended the war, whereas Cressida's surrender is expected to improve Trojan fighting power. But here, as so often, the play depends for ironic impact on external knowledge of events. It assumes an audience of readers who will recall that in exchanging Cressida for Antenor the Trojans receive a traitor into their midst who will make Cressida's sexual betrayal seem trivial.

Besides, now the Trojans have made Cressida a whore in the war game, the Greeks will make her a whore in the love game. She has scant choice in the matter. Arrived amongst the Greeks, she is greeted by Agamemnon. 'Our General doth salute you with a kiss', observes Nestor, who shows the perception and mannerisms of Justice Shallow.[33] But Ulysses thinks ''Twere better she were kissed in general' (IV.vi.20). What follows is akin to the stylized rape in Edward Dmytryk's *Shalako* (1968), where Apaches circle a captive and bandy her from one to another. Ulysses has set this degrading affair in motion, and he also joins in taunting the cuckold Menelaus. Patroclus has taken Menelaus's turn in the kissing ritual, declaring 'thus popped Paris in his hardiment' (1.29) – with the implication that Mercutio draws from 'pop 'er in' (Poperinghe: *Romeo and Juliet*, II.i.38).[34] And as Menelaus and Cressida dispute, Ulysses intervenes:

> It were no match, your nail against his horn.
> May I, sweet lady, beg a kiss of you?

> (IV.vi.47)

But he grows resentful when Cressida prefers a verbal skirmish. It is at this point that Nestor commends her wit, but Ulysses condemns her in terms which are all the more unfair because it is he who has exposed her to promiscuous handling:

> Her wanton spirits look out
> At every joint and motive of her body.
> O these encounterers so glib of tongue,
> That give accosting welcome ere it comes,
> And wide unclasp the tables of their thoughts
> To every tickling reader, set them down
> For sluttish spoils of opportunity
> And daughters of the game.

> (IV.vi.57)

This keys with the friendly meeting of Hector and Achilles in the next scene (l.123), when they take lascivious pleasure in locating those parts in the other's body where they will thrust their weapons. Hector realizes that he is being sized up for the kill: 'O, like a book of sport thou'lt read me o'er'. He is apt to think of mankilling as sport; that Greek in rich armour, of whom more anon, is a 'beast' to be hunted down and flayed. Like a rapist, Hector relishes in anticipation the sick urgency with which he will strip off his victim's harness: 'I'll frush it and unlock the rivets all' (V.vi.29). But here the heroic rivals are drawn together, like Sidney's princely combatants, in a quasi-erotic way, 'as in two beautiful folks love naturally stirs a desire of joining'.[35] So that book of venery is not so far removed from Ulysses's figure of unclasping tables. This is a vaginal figure belonging to the age of print, that 'two-leav'd book' which Marlowe chose to introduce into his translation of Ovid's *Elegies* III.xiii (see p. 49). Unclasping tables is analogous to Cressida's 'juggling trick: to be secretly open', as Thersites puts it (V.ii.25); and that latter phrase whispers more than paradox. Genital exposure and a book of secrets with its forbidden reading have their point of intersection in the Genesis story.

In *1 Henry VI* V.vi.68, when Joan of Arc claims to be with child, it is suggested that 'She and the Dauphin have been juggling': Wells-Taylor argues unnecessarily for a turned letter which would make it 'ingling'. Cressida is similarly targeted for gossip before she has had time to find a Greek partner. But the foreshortening has dramatic point as Thersites asperses Diomedes: 'They say he keeps a Trojan drab, and uses the traitor Calchas his tent' (V.i.93). It underscores Ulysses's mention of Calchas and Diomedes attending a feast, the latter giving 'all gaze and bent of amorous view / On the fair Cressid' (IV.vii.166). Ulysses has plainly heard the rumour. He has an ear for such things, surprising Achilles with his knowledge that the latter is 'in love / With one of Priam's daughters' (III.iii.187). So, too, it must be knowledge of Troilus's relationship which prompts him to ask the latter whether Cressida had a Trojan lover 'That wails her absence' (IV.vii.173). Already there is a hint of that malice which Troilus mistakes for courtesy when Ulysses takes him to see Cressida's infidelity with Diomedes.

This betrayal scene is deftly arranged as Cressida spars with Diomedes before capitulating, while Troilus and Ulysses watch.

In addition, Thersites provides intermittent commentary so that the audience's attention is continually being redirected. Ulysses shows something of Iago's delight in manipulating, his one concern over Troilus's mounting passion being that the noise 'draws ears hither' (V.ii.184). In conducting Troilus to the scene he makes clear that Cressida's supposed slight still rankles. His betraying words as she enters, 'She will sing any man at first sight', are amplified by Thersites: 'And any man may sing her, if he can take her clef. She's noted' (V.ii.10). Her alleged skill in musical sight-reading has generated a pun on musical sign and vaginal cleft paralleled in Dekker's *Noble Spanish Soldier* (*c*.1625) IV.ii.12, where Baltazar, asking 'What Crotchet' fills the betrayed Onaelia's head, is answered: 'No Crotchets, 'tis onely the Cliffe has made her mad'.[36] And Thersites is quick to comment as 'the devil Luxury with his fat rump and potato finger tickles these together!' (V.ii.55) – presumably alluding to a penis stiffened by the aphrodisiac sweet potato.[37] For Troilus, the world of certainties has collapsed. He rejects the evidence of his senses: he is not deceived by Cressida but deceived into thinking 'Diomed's Cressida' is his. This goes way beyond the Euripidean model of the two Helens in ambiguity. He has made the demoralizing shift from an undivided world to a 'Bifold authority' (V.ii.147), emerging painfully in this congested speech as full-fledged Mannerist hero.

The play is intent on doing more than pitting ideals against the pressure of realist thought: that of hierarchy against the threat of encroaching chaos, or chivalric restraint against the demands of total war. As it happens, both of these examples come under compressed scrutiny in that episode where Hector kills a man who flees for his life merely to acquire his 'goodly armour'. Early on (I.ii.225), Troilus had been hailed by Pandarus as 'the prince of chivalry'; but by now it is Hector who most merits that title. On this same day, that of his death, he has taken the field despite the entreaties of his wife and sister, holding 'honour far more precious-dear than life' (V.iii.28). Even so, when he declares himself 'today i'th' vein of chivalry', his choice of phrasing suggests that his chivalry is a matter of whim – like Richard III's 'giving vein'. Troilus cautions against this 'vice of mercy . . . Which better fits a lion than a man', and in so doing accords with a tag, given spurious Virgilian authority by Caxton in this same context, that 'ther is no mercy in bataill'.[38] When Hector insists that it is 'fair play' to let a defeated opponent live, Troilus rightly scorns it as 'Fool's play'. While war can accommodate claims of kinship or a chivalric freemasonry, it is inimical to this more expanded notion of fair play. The earliest recorded use of the phrase is in Shakespeare's *King John* (V.ii.118). But it occurs here with searing irony, for the action has amply demonstrated that war is not play, and is emphatically not fair.

It is interesting to find O.J. Campbell insisting repeatedly that this play does not represent an attack on war as an institution, but on war marred by 'insubordination to rightfully constituted authority'.[39] He further claims that to detect anything like pacifism here is to be guilty of anachronism, choosing to ignore the impact of Erasmus on sixteenth-century thought. Indeed, war as robbery and murder writ large was a view developed from St Augustine.[40] Of course, Campbell was writing in 1938, when the peace movement of the 1920s and early 30s had collapsed under the weight of Hitlerism. Less transparent, though strangely commonplace, is his determination to have on his side a writer so culturally distanced from himself. But Shakespeare, emphasizing the pettiness of the Trojan quarrel, seems aligned with Erasmus who is 'ashamyd to remember for howe lyght and vayne causes christen princes prouoke the world to war'. Erasmus commends democracy as a way of curbing the tendency to war, which should not 'be moued for the pleasure or lust of one or two', but only 'taken in hand by the consent of all the people'.[41] Ovid suggests that the lover, laying siege to his lady, is better placed than the Greek commander at Troy in not having to share credit for victory with any troops (*Amores*, II.xii). But war in this play, like love, is understood as an élite activity, taking scant account of the commoners' role or opinion.

However, the question of estate is obliquely addressed in the episode of the 'goodly armour', which crystallizes questions not only about the conduct of war but also about 'rightfully constituted authority'. Here Hector forgets his notions of chivalry and fair play out of desire to possess what Lydgate[42] describes as the bejewelled armour of 'a Grekysh kyng' (Caxton[43] calls him a 'moche noble baron of greece'). Either way, Yoder's attempt to rationalize Hector's behaviour by urging that the laws of chivalry do not apply to 'common soldiers like the nameless Greek' is inept.[44] Although Shakespeare specifies neither king nor baron, it is obvious that only one of superior rank would be wearing armour fine enough to arouse Hector's rapacity. Indeed, this is another of those moments which Shakespeare expects audiences to fill out from their reading. Hector's quarry is a king or nobleman, yet flees in terror for his life like any lesser mortal. Advantages of birth or breeding control neither cowardice nor the acquisitive drive at this point. Shakespeare puts an awkward question: if the élite behave *in extremis* like other men, what justifies their privileged position?

Maurice Keen shows how, by the fifteenth century, the code of war had been given a rational and commercial basis, though 'still spoken of in the language of chivalry'. Thus Castiglione avers that 'in wars the true provocation is glory', though Shakespeare – through Hector's behaviour – points to the tensions produced by the shift.[45] The economic appetite, as contemporary satirists tirelessly insist, had lost the old religious sanctions and had become a glorious end in itself. So neither Homeric nor any other gods have a role in this play, though Shakespeare does invoke an older moral disposition . Drawn by the glitter of battlefield spoils, Hector – in a tradition used by Chaucer's Pardoner – finds Death. The 'putrefièd core' (V.ix.1) which is revealed under the glittering armour mirrors his own corrupt mortality.

It has already been suggested that Hector and Achilles meet in lust, their two encounters purposefully framing Hector's 'rape' of that richly accoutred Greek. Having played fair by an out-of-condition Achilles, he is rewarded by having the latter catch him unarmed before sending his Myrmidons to make the kill. But Achilles has no compunction about taking the credit:

> On, Myrmidons, and cry you all amain,
> 'Achilles hath the mighty Hector slain!'

> (V.ix.13)

Thus are heroic reputations made. Indeed, we are tempted to ask whether the fame of these epic warriors is worth more than the notoriety attaching to the names of Pandarus and Cressida. The players in the love-comedy are strangely conscious of destiny. If 'As true as Troilus' never quite achieves the proverbial status envisaged by Troilus, Cressida's idea of the notoriety that would be contingent upon her falseness is fully realized in the abusive 'kite of Cressid's kind', and the way that later ages will call 'all brokers-between panders' (III.ii.199).[46]

The relationship between past and present, between play-world and that of the audience, finds more direct affirmation when Pandarus, left alone after the lovers have gone to bed, addresses the audience directly:

> And Cupid grant all tongue-tied maidens here
> Bed, chamber, pander to provide this gear.[47]

(III.ii.206)

But the tone has changed substantially between this speech and the last lines of the play. For it is Pandarus and not Thersites – despite the latter's view of the disorder and impermanence masked by our illusions having prevailed – who delivers the epilogue in which he inculpates the present with the vices of the past. This time, his play-world shattered, he steps out of the dramatic frame to harangue not 'tongue-tied maidens' nor even 'daughters of the game'. Instead, the *ami* has become bawd and identifies with the 'Brethren and sisters of the hold-door trade' found in the audience.[48] By this stage he has succumbed to 'the Neapolitan bone-ache', wished by Thersites 'on those that war for a placket' (II.iii.18). Both this 'ache in my bones' and 'rheum in mine eyes' (V.iii.107) are pox symptoms supposedly shared by those galled geese of Winchester in the audience.[49] By this final speech, one so clearly integral that it is hard to see why some critics view it as an excrescence, his mortality hangs on the temporary reprieve of the sweating tub. Moving from his play-world to the different reality of Elizabethan London, Pandarus confounds dramatic illusion to make past and present one, emphasizing how the mythic past is a projection designed for present political ends.

In conclusion, it is worth noting the burlesque strain which had entered Renaissance epic, following the huge success of Pulci's fifteenth-century *Il Morgante Maggiore*. Before the eighteenth century, when its other virtues began to feed into English writing, Cervantes's *Don Quixote* was chiefly influential in the same way. Ridicule of the classical epic reached new blatancy with Restoration pieces like Cotton's *Virgil Travestie* (1664–5) and Scudamore's *Homer Alamode* (1681); and it was in the wake of their popularity that a semi-burlesque epic, by Shakespeare's contemporary Tassoni, was translated by Ozell as *The Rape of the Bucket* (1713). But Spenser as well as Shakespeare had already picked up the strain during Elizabeth's reign. One such *Faerie Queene* episode, where the giantess Argante thunders into view with the Squire of Dames draped across her saddle bow (III.7.43), is a grotesque parody of Venus and Adonis. Written soon after Shakespeare's poem on the subject, it has something of the Shakespearean tone – of which more will be said in Part III.

8

Cupid-Adonis:
'Prettie Boyes' and 'Unlawfull Joyes'

Cinthio has reservations about Ovid as epic poet since he 'followed too much his own sweet will, so that his works are . . . overly soft and luxuriant'. He should have been more 'profound', less 'licentious'.[1] But the Ovidian influence on Shakespeare was profound; and Francis Meres, who had a taste for pairing ancients and moderns, was persuaded that 'the sweete wittie soule of Ouid liues in mellifluous & hony-tongued *Shakespeare*, witnes his *Venus and Adonis*, his *Lucrece*, . . . &c.'.[2] However, Shakespeare's easy familiarity with Ovid's *Metamorphoses* allows him to relate to the poem in his borrowings in an intricate and complex way. Thus the opening stanza of *Venus and Adonis* depends for its effect on readers' recognition that 'Rose-cheeked Adonis' – who loved hunting, though 'love he laughed to scorn' – and 'Sick-thoughted Venus' have little direct connection with their Ovidian counterparts.

But these neo-Ovidian poems were designed to give pleasure to those who knew the original; and a refined pleasure in this case might come from recognition of how the context in which Ovid places the story has left its impress on Shakespeare's poem. It is Orpheus who elects to sing (in Golding's translation)

> of prettie boyes
> That were the derlings of the Gods: and of unlawfull joyes
> That burned in the brests of Girles.
>
> (X.157)

Propriety requires that he begin with Jove's rape of Ganymede, but it is the story of Apollo and Hyacinthus upon which he dilates. The mood created by these stories of boy love has its reflex in Shakespeare's poem, assisted by the way that his Venus assumes the masculine initiative. A parallel with Hyacinthus's story is clear enough; for just as the latter's tragic accident is softened by his yearly renewal as a flower, so the blood shed by Adonis becomes an anemone.

However, more striking than these overtones from other sections of the Orphic song is Shakespeare's omission of what had been an essential part of the story. According to Ovid, Venus's passion for Adonis resulted from the accidental grazing of her breast by one of Cupid's arrows. Shakespeare eschews this mythic explanation along with any allusion to Cupid. Indeed, perhaps literalizing the way that Ovid represents the stricken Venus as forsaking her customary haunts, including heaven itself, he shows her – until the final stages of the poem – grounded, subject to human limitation, where the divine Venus would have been sexually irresistible. The inclusion of Cupid is customary in paintings of the subject, as an oblique allusion to the accident. But a year or two after Shakespeare completed his poem, Annibale Carracci painted his version, now in the Kunsthistorisches Museum, Vienna, with Cupid actually grazing his mother just as Adonis comes upon the pair.

This is Ovid plain, central to the composition being the interlock of gazes, proclaiming love at first sight. But another painter will better serve to illuminate the darker recesses of Ovid's narrative, as well as Shakespeare's own recognition of them. In the early 1530s, Bronzino was working for Bartolomeo Bettini, a friend of Michelangelo's. The centrepiece of the room he was decorating was to be a painting of Venus and Cupid by Pontormo, after a design by Michelangelo, now in the Accademia, Florence. Cupid clambers over his mother, kissing her and holding an arrow which Venus casually fingers. Bronzino's first important picture depicts the animation of Pygmaleon's statue (Palazzo Vecchio, Florence), a story used by Orpheus as a transition from those of boy love to that concerning Myrrha's incestuous love for her father which spawned Adonis. The Ovidian passage and Pontormo's painting were the joint inspiration, years later, for Bronzino's remarkable *Venus, Cupid and Jealousy* (Szépmüvészeti Museum, Budapest). According to Ovid, when Adonis was born 'Even Jealousy personified would have praised his beauty, for he looked like one of the naked Cupids painted in pictures' (Innes renders *livor* as 'Jealousy', and *Jealousy* in the picture-title rests on Vasari's description)[3]. Ovid approximates a film-maker's dissolve as he shifts from Adonis to Cupid and back again. The fleeting years take Adonis from blooming infancy, through youth into still more beautiful manhood. Now (Innes again) he has become 'the darling of Venus, and avenged the passion which had assailed his mother'; and Ovid proceeds to explain how this new passion has arisen: for while Cupid was kissing Venus, an arrow sticking out of his quiver had grazed her. The wound proves unexpectedly deep, anticipating the phallic wound which Adonis is to receive in the groin from the boar – though it is Shakespeare rather than Ovid who clarifies the nature of the latter.

Cupid has expressly denied that his dart wounded Myrrha with incestuous desire (*Metamorphoses*, X.311). But his childish kisses strangely recall those given by Cinyras to his daughter Myrrha when he seeks to comfort her, kisses which she relishes as more than paternal (362). In his Budapest painting, Bronzino represents Cupid as a youth rather than a child, and Venus directs his arrow towards her thigh. He holds his bow over them in a way recalling its yoking function in marriage portraits.[4] Bronzino's more elaborate version in the National Gallery, London, shows this stripling Cupid kissing his mother and fondling her breast. His knees straddle on a cushion, buttocks thrust provocatively towards the spectator to evoke Ovid's tales of boy love. Venus holds an arrow in one hand and in the other one of those golden apples from Tamasus of which she told Adonis in between love-making. A naked putto is about to scatter roses over the pair, a symbolism used in Milton's *Paradise Lost* (VIII.515) when Adam and Eve pleasure each other in their bower. But Bronzino deals in incestuous passion. Just as Myrrha received her father's seed, so Venus is about to receive that of her son.

Ovid's deliberate blurring of Cupid and Adonis causes the former's relationship with his mother to be contaminated by the main incest story. Bronzino responds powerfully to this in his picture, striking a balance between the child Cupid and the adult Adonis with his voluptuous adolescent. Shakespeare's Adonis is hardly voluptuous, yet he is of an age with Bronzino's Cupid; and the relationship with Venus becomes the more problematic because of Venus's maternal aspect. If her initial behaviour towards Adonis is far from maternal, she yet projects an image of buxom middle age. And when she runs desperately through the forest in search of the boy, she is likened to

> a milch doe whose swelling dugs do ache,
> Hasting to feed her fawn hid in some brake.
>
> (875)

It is this same maternal note which sounds, with increased pathos, as she cradles a flower, all that remains of Adonis, in her bosom where her 'throbbing heart shall rock thee day and night' (l.1186).

If Shakespeare makes no mention of what his Venus wears, we may be sure she is no Giorgionesque nude. Her dress warrants no mention because she may be assumed to wear the customary wardrobe of a middle-aged woman in late Elizabethan society. For, in reducing his goddess to a human scale, Shakespeare gives the impression of a woman at that stage where she is desperate to renew her youth in the arms of a young lover. It is the syndrome memorably explored in Mike Nichols's 1967 film *The Graduate*, where the predatory older woman changes from assured adulteresss to hurt, vengeful fury as her daughter delivers the ultimate wound in supplanting her sexually with the young graduate. Shakespeare has not handled it in quite this way, but the pattern is clear from the start when Venus drags Adonis out of the saddle and tucks him under one arm. The feat depends not on divine power but a sudden, sexually charged surge of adrenalin, and its effect is both alarming and comic. It is significant that Shakespeare chooses to present the besotted urgencies of lust through this Wife of Bath figure who, like the original, is at once shocking and sympathetic.[5] The increasing assertiveness of women in Shakespeare's society was something of a male obsession. Battles for the breeches were a recurrent image, and contemporaries would have recognized Venus's relationship to the new feminism. Venus's oft-noted usurping of the male role is apparent from the first stanza as she confronts Adonis 'like a bold-fac'd suitor'. It is affirmed with calculated crudity as

> Backward she pushed him, as she would be thrust,
> And governed him in strength, though not in lust.
>
> (41)

And this traditionally male posture is insisted on again as she shields the boy from the sun (l.194). Earlier, Venus has achieved mastery over Mars, 'Leading him prisoner in a red-rose chain' (l.110). The mythographers read this as an allusion to the fall of man, which regularly carried sexual overtones like Venus's offer of 'A thousand honey secrets' – though they are to be imparted 'where never serpent hisses' (1.15). If her triumph over Mars affords a glimpse of that neo-Platonist *discordia concors* figure, the purpose is ironic, emphasizing the grotesquerie of the present situation.[6] Venus had tied Adonis's 'lusty courser' to a tree before pushing him on his back and seeking (metaphorically) to 'tie the rider' (1.40). But the literal tethering of the stallion is the more remarkable, since he is the lusty creature that Adonis is not. It demonstrates the sexual power which Venus is accustomed to exercise. The furious tide of her lust is imaged in the stallion's snapping of his girths and crushing of the bit. His one lack, that of 'a proud rider on so proud a back' (1.300), completes his identification with Venus, adding further comment on that reversal of roles which is so prominent a feature of Venus's wooing. Her quasi-masculine assault recalls Orpheus's starting point, the rape of Ganymede.

But Ovid's Venus is hardly more changed here than is Adonis. He has become a fresh-faced boy of whom Shakespeare declares: 'Hunting he loved, but love he laughed to scorn' (1.4).[7] The collocation of 'love' in this line is a suggestive reminder of the double sense carried by 'venery'; medieval attitudes linger sufficiently to point a symbolic connection, an essential similarity, between the two activities, which is of prime importance in the poem. So the opening stanza not only registers the modification undergone by Shakespeare's protagonists, but through this collocation hints at his purpose in refashioning the Ovidian story. Such a hint would be especially clear to the attentive Elizabethan reader, who could hardly fail to realize that expectations in the treatment of the story were being flouted. Meanwhile Adonis remains 'frosty in desire' (1.36); we hear of his 'bashful shame' and 'the maiden burning of his cheeks' (1.49). His youth and inexperience in the face of Venus's impetuous wooing make him appear ridiculous, like a divedapper (1.86). He is tempted by her assurance that a single kiss will buy her off but, when it comes to the point, 'He winks, and turns his lips another way' (1.90): we see the nice adolescent grimacing with distaste. This accords with that other glimpse of him, through Venus's impatient 'What seest thou in the ground? Hold up thy head' (1.118). He is a puling companion for the seasoned vamp, nervously unsure of himself in a new situation. Approaching adulthood is obliquely announced in Lodge's *Rosalynde* by young

Rosader's 'perceiving his beard to bud'.[8] It is in similar terms that Venus acknowledges Adonis's unreadiness, but only momentarily. For his extreme youth is a main source of attraction:

> The tender spring upon thy tempting lip
> Shows thee unripe; yet mayst thou well be tasted.
>
> (127)

She moves fluently into a *carpe diem* argument. This is Lolita in reverse. Her mocking of him as 'no man' (l.215) lacks force after that earlier effusion which finds him 'more lovely than a man' (l.9). So, that Adonis's first direct words are full of childish petulance would be no grave shortcoming in Venus's eyes. Later, however, he is allowed to offer a precise gloss on that alluring unripeness:

> Measure my strangeness with my unripe years.
> Before I know myself, seek not to know me.
> No fisher but the ungrown fry forbears.
>
> (524)

He uses the riding image to like effect, retaining that inversion which allowed Venus to be equated with the stallion. But even after Venus's quasi-surrender of initiative when a more orthodox posture is assumed, he still shows himself unready and 'will not manage her, although he mount her' (l.598).

However, it has been commonly observed that, in his one extended speech, Adonis moves away from insistence on his green years to a direct attack on Venus. He accuses her of promiscuity, and of rationalizing about breed. He has no real basis for the first accusation, and indeed subsequent events indicate just how special Adonis is in Venus's estimation.[9] He is on stronger ground about her rationalizing. The merit of her argument is beyond question; her motives are not. Shakespeare was later to give the argument to Paroles as seduction-ploy; so there is at least room for doubt about Venus's utterances on breed. But it is less important that his charges should be true than that they should be honestly urged. They are. Shakespeare's portrayal of the boy is thin-textured, but the radical changes wrought in the Ovidian character suggest that he was intent on something important. It is at this point, if anywhere, that we glean some idea of what that might be. Adonis's shift of ground, then, from defence to attack should represent something more than a debating tactic. The move from an appeal to his own tender youth to a probing of the love on offer, a shift of focus from self-preoccupation to exterior forces, suggests a measure of emotional development associated with the disturbances of puberty.

There is a continuing primness about him; the adolescent tends to veer between this and crudity in seeking to cope with sexual experience. Venus's assault on Adonis has forced a recoil into primness, with the only suspicion of crudity found in his taste for venery – the boar hunt. He offers a distinction between love and 'sweating lust', whose tyranny is presented in political images which Shakespeare had already used, and was to use again, in the history plays. Spenser, too, presents Britomart's anxiety to distinguish between love and lust as an aspect of her coming of age sexually. A.C. Hamilton detects the onset of menstruation in Spenser's description, and certainly her change of status is symbolized as she sees the vision of Artegall instead of her own reflection in Venus's looking-glass.[10] The Renaissance poets were much interested in this process. A similar moment occurs in *Paradise Lost* where Eve gazes into the lake and is diverted from her own image by an awareness of Adam (IV.460). Lois Potter offers pertinent commentary:

> The fact that she is so quickly attracted to her own image in the water has been taken to indicate a dangerous narcissism in her from the beginning. I take this episode rather as a condensation of the normal process of growing up: the child at first loves only itself, and is drawn to what is like itself, another member of the same sex, before learning to love difference, otherness, in whatever form it may take.[11]

Most immediately significant, however, is Marlowe's deft handling of the subject in *Hero and Leander*, à poem centrally concerned with sexual awakening. Hero's seeking refuge in her bed from the naked Leander is a striking anticipation of that sexual ambivalence which forms the culmination of Shakespeare's poem. Adonis may be the 'orator too green' against Leander's 'bold sharpe Sophister'; but if Leander has the stallion within him (II.141), so has Adonis the boar. This perhaps needs insisting upon, since any untoward pressure on the text would have Adonis eschewing second-generational incest in favour of homosexuality. It is certainly the poem's central irony that he runs from lust in the shape of Venus only to embrace it in the form of the boar.[12] Indeed, Shakespeare prefigures that climactic move when Adonis 'springs' from Venus towards his horse. Just what Adonis hastens towards is made abundantly clear since at that very moment the stallion bursts after the breeding jennet.

It is a presentiment of what is to come when Adonis declares that he knows not love, 'nor will not know it, / Unless it be a boar, and then I chase it' (l.409). Venus first seriously engages our sympathy at a point designed to give anticipatory prominence to the boar. Out of pity she unpredictably releases Adonis, seeking only to arrange a tryst for the morrow. But he tells her he is already engaged to hunt the boar. She collapses, drawing him into a coital position which is especially apt in view of the boar's signification. To his protests she replies that he would have gone by now had he not expressed his intention of hunting the boar (l.613). Her sexual jealousy is very evident here, and becomes increasingly explicit. She warns how the boar 'Would root these beauties as he roots the mead' (l.636), the sexual implication agreeing with that in Dekker's phrase about 'rooting other men's pastures'.[13] Set against this, Venus's trembling 'like an earthquake' (l.648) at thought of what the boar might do to Adonis is, since the boy lies upon her, a parody of coital movement. Their intimate posture is strangely reflected as she envisages the boy's bloody conjunction with the boar, 'Under whose sharp fangs on his back doth lie' (l.663). The boar hunt is like a tribal initiation, by means of which the youth proves his manhood. So it is vain for Venus to recommend less dangerous quarry such as the hare. Don Cameron Allen has been criticized for singling out the hare for extended comment when other animals are also mentioned.[14] But Venus herself dwells on the hare and invites us to find a sub-text. Allen persuasively associates Venus with the creature: 'The ancients thought that hares could exchange sex, and an aggressive masculinity was attributed to the females that suits Shakespeare's impression of Venus'.[15] The hare is, after all, traditionally associated with Venus for its amorousness. But here, as with the stallion, there is no simple symbolic equation. The hare's bewildered terror as it seeks to throw off pursuit is most reminiscent of Adonis's desperate attempts to parry Venus's advances. If it be objected that such an identification would taint Adonis with leporine lust, that is by no means discordant with the poem's movement. At any event, we are thus given ample warning against taking the boar too simply.

The boar has been identified with death, and with the baser urges of Venus as well as with lust in general. Shakespeare leaves us in no doubt about affinities between the creature and Venus, even causing her to admit that

> Had I been toothed like him, I must confess
> With kissing him I should have killed him first.[16]
>
> (1117)

Venus, not 'prick'd . . . out for women's pleasure', may be at a disadvantage in her assertive boy love. But presentiments of death cling about her love-making: she is intent on *smothering* Adonis with kisses; his very words 'she murders with a kiss' (ll.18, 54). Adonis has heard that love 'is a life in death' (l.413); and soon afterwards some of the ambiguities of the phrase are teased out. We find Venus enacting the metaphor when 'at his look she flatly falleth down, / For looks kill love' (l.463). The drama develops with Venus lying 'as she were slain, / Till his breath breatheth life in her again' (l.473).[17] Adonis's kiss of life is translated into amorous terms by Venus, a kind of reversal of those kisses given to Myrrha by her father. She asks:

> Do I delight to die . . . ?
> But now I lived, and life was death's annoy;
> But now I died, and death was lively joy.
>
> (496)

Venus's death here throws light on the eventual death of Adonis. His kiss produces a killing ecstasy, and Venus would have him 'kill me once again!' (l.499). This is typical of the poem in presenting moments of lesser sexual activity in images of total conjuction.[18] Their kissing is such that 'Incorporate then they seem' (l.540) – i.e., one thing in another so as to form one body. The term was in use as coital verb by the time that Iago spoke of the 'main exercise, th'incorporate conclusion' (*Othello*, II.i.262). Indeed, *kiss* itself was a common Elizabethan euphemism for copulation, and death as an image of sexual climax came into vogue in the early 1590s.

In such a context, there is no great difficulty in understanding the boar's killing of Adonis in terms of sexual ravishment. Serena's treatment at the hands of the cannibals in Spenser's *Faerie Queene* (VI.8.37ff.) works in much the same way. In his engagement with the boar Adonis is recognizing one of life's imperatives. Lust is apt to be overwhelming, even destructive at times. But that is no more than medieval tradition from Gottfried to Malory had taught. As A.T. Hatto points out, Gottfried himself used the boar as a figure of overmastering virility in *Tristan und Isolde* 'fouling bed and royal linen with his foam'.[19] Shakespeare stresses the seminal nature of the foam by likening it to milk on the boar's first appearance, and its mingling with blood points to the deflowering of 'maiden' Adonis which has taken place (l.901). The culmination of Venus's fancy that even the wild creatures loved Adonis is reached in her notion that the boar 'thought to kiss him, and hath killed him so' (l.1110). This picks up the earlier collocation of kissing and killing, but we are now more fully conscious of that cyclical pattern of sex and death. It permits us to retain the notion of Adonis's being killed by the boar while superimposing a view of violent sexual awakening. Venus has already declared that, Adonis

> being dead, with him is beauty slain,
> And beauty dead, black chaos comes again.
>
> (1019)

This is very like Othello's 'when I love thee not / Chaos is come again'. The irony there is that Othello never ceases to love Desdemona, even in killing her. There is a similar irony here, for beauty is not slain. It is only a conceit that beauty has died with its embodiment, Adonis; and Adonis himself flowers in his deflowering. The boar means not only death and lust, but the dialectical relationship of the two.

So Venus loves and loses Adonis, and (according to Ovid) his mother (Myrrha) is avenged. If he has behaved to Venus like those 'boys of ice' derided by Lafeu in *All's Well* (II.iii.94), her attempts have seemed gross as well as grotesque, overtoned by those irregular relationships of which Ovid's Orpheus sings. Adonis rejects her ambiguously maternal embrace for the more exhilarating challenges of sexual maturity. In his sexual death he has fulfilled his destiny, while Venus is left to a tragic solitude poignantly evoked in the poem's final, muted stanza.

9

Pox and Gold: Timon's New World Heritage

Shakespearean Mannerism had still to be developed when he wrote *Venus and Adonis*. So his retelling of Adonis's story lacks the cynicism to which Caravaggio was subjecting the boy Bacchus at about the same time. In a painting now in Florence's Uffizi Gallery, he was catering for the paedophiliac tastes found amongst Roman society figures like Cardinal del Monte. Reformation propaganda had exploited such predilections from the time of Tyndale who, in his *Answer to Sir Thomas More's Dialogue* (1530) IV.ii, identifies the Pope with Antichrist for 'setting up in Rome a stews, not of women only, but of the male kind also against nature'.[1] What Caravaggio does is to render his youthful Bacchus with sultry, hooded eyes, plucked eyebrows, dirty fingernails, and a toga which might be a soiled bedsheet, so as to give him a well-used look. But a still more pervasive element of late sixteenth-century art is pox, which had wrought its own changes in the European consciousness with the discovery of the New World. Bacchus is touched by this through the bowl of fruit which he has to hand, much of it rotten. The effect is consolidated by the cup of wine which he holds out to his unseen companion (a role supplied by the spectator) – presumably a pox-poisoned chalice.

The stings of disease accompanying the sweets of sexual passion are still more dramatically presented in Caravaggio's *Boy Bitten by a Lizard*, of which several versions survive. The boy's expression of pain and horror reappears on the face of Medusa, whose decapitated head Caravaggio painted as if reflected on a shield – the hero having to rely on this reflection in combatting the gorgon since her gaze will turn men to stone.[2] Allusion to phallic hardness is difficult to resist if we follow psychoanalytical equation of head and vagina, the gorgon's serpent-hair hinting at pubic venom. Perseus avoids this danger by regarding image in place of reality, intricate reminder that the spectator, looking at the image on the convex surface, sees not a reflection in a shield but paint on canvas. The parallel with the *Boy Bitten by a Lizard* might encourage us to find a sword-wielding hero impicit here too. But in this case we seem to see the entire drama as the creature, which has been lurking amongst the fruit, now attaches itself to the boy's finger. Shakespeare, in *2 Henry VI* III.ii.325, uses the comparison 'as smart as lizard's sting'; but the Italian saying, '*come il Ramarro*', alludes to the lizard's tenacity, refusing to let go once it has bitten – its metaphorical aptness confirmed by Dekker's comment, in *1 Honest Whore* (1604) II.i.356, on the way that 'the French . . . sticks to you'.[3] But the real equivalents, in a country where lizards are not part of the domestic scene as they are in Italy, are those used by Matthew Parker of whoremongers 'stung with yᵉ Turnbull-street Bees' or 'bitten with Turnbull-street Fleas'.[4]

Bronzino, too, in that *Allegory* in London's National Gallery discussed in the last chapter, uses a reptilian figure to assert the virtually inescapable link between illicit sex and syphilis. Behind his protagonists, Venus and Cupid, is Deceit with an angel's face but a serpent's tail. The serpents of popular belief all sting with their tails, just like women.[5] So with one hand she offers a honeycomb while clutching the poisonous sting in her tail with the other. Bronzino's image resembles that used by Shakespeare's Timon:

> This fell whore of thine
> Hath in her more destruction than thy sword,
> For all her cherubin look.
>
> (IV.iii.61)

He refers to one of a pair of whores accompanying Alcibiades in his invasion of Athens. Women have a minimal part in *Timon*, which helps to register their Act IV appearance as a kind of counterpart to that '*masque of Ladies as Amazons*' which has entertained Timon and his dinner company in Act I. This floor-show offers considerable scope on stage, and Apemantus's mordant counterpoint to the frivolities of these 'madwomen', as he calls them, strengthens further their relationship to the camp-followers:

> We make ourselves fools to disport ourselves,
> And spend our flatteries to drink those men

Upon whose age we void it up again
With poisonous spite and envy.

He here develops his earlier avowal that 'I eat not lords' (I.i.208),
capping Timon's facetious reply, 'An thou shouldst, thou'dst anger
ladies', with a pregnancy gibe: 'O, they eat lords. So they come by
great bellies'. This earlier exchange alerts us to a latent sexuality
in the present speech, further helping to align these masquing
'madwomen' with the camp-followers – sisters to that harlot in
the Dekker passage quoted above who 'Swallowes both English,
Spanish, fulsome Dutch'.[6] Nor are the masquers kept aloof from
pox, a disease which figures obsessively in Timon's later speeches.
Here, when one of the ladies acknowledges Timon's praise – 'you
take us even at the best' (I.ii.148), Apemantus glosses: 'for the
worst is filthy, and would not hold taking'. This taking becomes
sexual possession, made intolerable by the presence of 'some filthy
disease', as Harman styles venereal infection.[7]

Cupid serves as Master of Ceremonies at the masque, as he
implicitly does for the activities of the camp-followers. The
link between Cupid and Death, if not between Cupid and the
dissemination of pox, is an ancient one. Wind notes how 'The
Renaissance identified him with Death itself, in its painful no
less than its joyous aspect'.[8] Barnfield, in *The Affectionate Shepherd*
(1594), absorbs continental influence in relating how, following
drunken revelry, 'Loue tooke vp Deaths dart, / And Death tooke
vp Loues Arrow'.[9] But Jean Lemaire, in *De Cupido et d'Atropos*
(1525), entangles this same fable with another that is seminal for
the age of syphilis. When Death's arrows are thrown into the moat
of Love's castle, the water becomes full of death and serpentine
poison. Those drinking it soon develop all the symptoms of pox
(*mal serpentino*, as Ruy Diaz de Isla calls it in his 1539 *Tractado*).
This provides the basis for *Le Triumphe de Dame Verolle* (1539),
where Dame Verolle claims to be 'queen and princess of the
well of love'. Most people, she says, honour her (i.e. are poxed),
having drunk of this well which is stinking and blackened with
infection.[10] The same myth lurks behind Shakespeare's Sonnet
153, where 'Cupid laid by his brand and fell asleep'. He is
discovered by 'A maid of Dian's' who steeps that phallic brand[11]
in a fountain – a 'well' according to Sonnet 154 – which 'grew

a seething bath', providing 'Against strange maladies a sovereign cure'. But the fountain of love which becomes 'a seething bath' is more ambiguous, recalling that vernacular blurring of pox with consequent salivation through double-application terms like stewing and boiling.[12]

Timon draws together myths of syphilis and its socio-medical reality when exhorting one of Alcibiades's camp-followers to 'Be a whore still'. In this key speech he is interested in the spread of the disease rather than its containment, but inevitably includes a picture of hospitalized lovers:

> Make use of thy salt hours: season the slaves
> For tubs and baths, bring down rose-cheeked youth
> To the tub-fast and the diet.
>
> (IV.iii.86)

OED glosses 'tub-fast' as 'abstinence during treatment in the sweating tub', although Bucknill observes that he has never 'found that the old surgeons recommended fasting during the treatment, and therefore cannot explain the word'. However, Ulrich von Hutten makes it plain that the sweat treatment with guaiacum works properly on 'not such as be full, but onely those that are emptye, . . . and truly the stronglyer a man abideth to hunger, the better and more quickely he shall be healed'.[13] Timon recalls the astrological explanation[14] of syphilis when he invites the whores to

> Be as a planetary plague when Jove
> Will o'er some high-viced city hang his poison
> In the sick air.
>
> (IV.iii.109)

But the main thrust of his thought is far more immediate. He plans nothing less than to launch the two whores into Athens as weapons of germ warfare. The idea might well seem monstrous to Shakespeare's contemporaries, as it does to one of the women; but it would not be unheard of. No more than a year before *Timon* was written, Caesalpino published one version of a story tying the dissemination of pox to the Siege of Naples in 1495. This tells how wine was left secretly by night for Charles VIII's besieging Frenchmen; it had been infected with blood taken from inmates of the lazar hospital, causing the soldiers to contract what consequently became known as *morbus Gallicus*. But during the 1550s, the renowned anatomist Fallopius had provided a much more apposite account, wherein the besieged Spaniards at Naples, including some who had returned from Columbus's first voyage to the New World, drove out unvalued citizens because of the shortage of supplies. But they cunningly included amongst those expelled certain beautiful but infected harlots, who were eagerly received amongst the French troops. The unbridled sexual activity which followed soon infected the entire army.[15]

Timon is totally undiscriminating in his desire to see the Athenians, 'Men, woemen, children, perish by the sword' – as the anonymous *Timon* has it (V.ii.2233).[16] Where military violence stops short he would have sexual contagion take over; and fantasies of lust evidently play their part in Timon's imaginings. The very babes should be put to the sword since, assumed to be bastards, they speak eloquently of lecherous encounters. But there is a particular virulency about the way in which every seemingly honest matron is considered bawdy and every virgin treacherous, her

> milk paps
> That through the window-bars bore at men's eyes
>
> (IV.iii.117)

being credited with an active malevolence. A note of antifeminism rises above the general stridency of his utterances. Perhaps the feeling has its roots in the anonymous play where Timon discovers that his sexual attraction is geared to his financial status.[17] Indeed he complains at I.ii.164 that '*Venus* / was not a Freind to my Nativitie'. But in Shakespeare such explanations reduce to the idea that he has been a toy of the harlot-goddess Fortune, and now seems to usurp her function. He offers gold as a stimulus not only to Mars but to Venus, and turns the camp-following whores into parody Danaës:

> Hold up, you sluts,
> Your aprons mountant.
>
> (IV.iii.135)

Behind Shakespeare's heraldic irony is such interpretation of the whore's favourite apron-garb as Barnfield provides: 'White is the Ensigne of each common Woman'.[18] The whores are invited to raise their clothes to receive not a lover but sterile gold. They are adjured to

> Be whores still,
> And he whose pious breath seeks to convert you,
> Be strong in whore, allure him, burn him up.
> Let your close fire predominate his smoke.
>
> (IV.iii.140)

The implication is that they will have no trouble in destroying this preacher with their 'close fire' – sexual heat acquiring a pox overtone here – since his 'pious breath' is mere 'smoke' or empty vapouring. Athens is full of canting hypocrites. But Timon looks for a kind of honesty in these whores, who must keep the faith 'And be no turncoats'. Even so, the idea of conversion persists in his next words, for a whore's hazardous profession may find her laid up for as long as she is active:

> yet may your pains six months
> Be quite contrary.

If this folio reading is correct, the thought follows the contours of a speech in Fletcher's *Thierry and Theoderet* II.iii.83: 'Go get you to your foyning worke at Court, / And learne to sweate again. and eate dry mutton' – a cycle of whoring and doctoring.[19] But if there is anything in the Wells-Taylor alteration of 'pains six' to 'pain-sick', we might risk further speculation that a turned letter conceals 'mouths' as 'months'; then what is contrary to the preacher's breathing smoke would be the vaginal mouth's 'close fire'.[20]

Either way, honesty in whores has its limits, and Timon accepts the deceptions of the trade as furthering his designs:

> thatch your poor thin roofs
> With burdens of the dead – some that were hanged,
> No matter. Wear them, betray with them; whore still;
> Paint till a horse may mire upon your face.
>
> (IV.iii.145)

This anticipates Apemantus's comment on Athenian flatterers who enjoy a sybaritic life and 'Hug their diseased perfumes' (IV.iii.208). The ravages of disease have to be concealed with cosmetics thick enough to bog down a horse, while mercury treatment if not pox itself renders the sufferer bald. Hence the fashion of wearing wigs; and the process came full circle when hair lost to the disease was used by the wigmakers: 'whoremongers and adulterers thatch their empty noddles with whole thickets of whore's-hair'.[21]

The whores' consciences are readily eased by Timon's gold. They encourage him by declaring that they will 'do anything for gold' (1.150), and he warms to his theme:

> Consumptions sow
> In hollow bones of man, strike their sharp shins,
> And mar men's spurring. Crack the lawyer's voice,
> That he may never more false title plead, . . .

(IV.iii.151)

Motteux, in his translation of Rabelais (1694), alludes to 'the new consumption, I mean the Pox'.[22] This is late euphemism, but the relationship implicit in Shakespeare is spelt out by Pepys in a diary entry for 14 July 1667, where he records how a clerk 'looks like a dying man, with a consumption got . . . by the pox'.[23] Hollowness suggests the way that pox destroys the marrow; but that shins were subject to still worse damage is indicated by William Clowes, describing a case of one beset for five years, whose 'shin bones, were with the malice of this sicknesse corrupted and eaten very deeply in certaine places, so that they were for the most part taken away'.[24] This is the process which will 'mar men's spurring', the symbolism being noted by Middleton in *Your Five Gallants* (1604–7) II.i.28, when Mrs Newcut gives a man money for the purchase of 'silver spurs': 'a pretty emblem! . . . all her gifts are about riding'.[25] Few of pox's depredations are overlooked by Timon. It badly affected speech since it attacked both the gristle of the nose and the palate, artificial replacements being available for both.[26]

There is a terrible literalness about Timon. He envisages the lawyer literally prevented from following his corrupt court practices by the loss of his voice, or the hypocritical priest more generally incapacitated: 'Hoar the flamen', leprous whiteness carrying a pun on 'whore' (1.157). He would have 'the unscarred braggarts of the war / Derive some pain from' these whores (1.161), recalling how the *miles gloriosus* had acquired an added dimension of burlesque through his whoremongering campaigns in the 'Low Countries' (*DSL*). Finally he gets to the root of the matter: their activity will 'defeat and quell / The source of all erection', destroying the very means of continuity. This resonates with terrible power in a post-Augustinian world which had accepted Aristotle's idea, as packaged by Averroës, of time as an infinite continuum – an endless cycle of birth, copulation, death.[27] It is no accident that the thirteenth-century recovery of Aristotle via the Arabs was quickly followed by the innovation of the mechanical clock. The medieval notion of life being bound up with the eternal, while time symbolized death, had shifted decisively. Now time was invested with ethical value as the symbol of life, of endless duration. The repercussions were profound, showing up in scientific development and economic revolution – indeed, in all that political, social and religious unrest which marks the late Middle Ages. Time is an issue throughout Shakespeare, being, like everything else, confusingly dependent on perception. In *Julius Caesar*, the sleepless conspirators anxiously looking for signs of dawn in the sky, are mocked by the sound of a clock striking three (II.i.192); but the next scene finds Caesar's time running out, for the clock is 'strucken eight' (II.ii.114).

That central image of the clock in Poe's *Masque of the Red Death* would have been well appreciated by Shakespeare's contemporaries. But the story has other features worth recalling in relation to *Timon*. It is centrally concerned with the impact of colonialism on America's indigenes, and Poe shows himself alert to the colonial issue in *The Tempest*. It is Prince Prospero and his court who shut themselves away from pestilent reality in a world of empty pleasure not unlike that inhabited by Timon in Act I. But the festivities are disturbed by the hourly striking of the clock, which prepares for the arrival of the masquer Death. Edwin Fussell takes Prospero to be 'a typically ironic allegorical name for the United States, and the Red Death a somewhat more complicated emblematic equivalent for the Indian – or for American maltreatment of the Indian, together with Indian reprisal'.[28]

It is difficult not to associate Poe's Red Death with syphilis, which as early as 1518 had been noted by the Salzburg physician Leonard Schmaus to be endemic amongst the natives of the Americas. He recommends the wood guaiacum 'which the Indians use against pox' according to first-hand reports made by European traders (Ulrich von Hutten says the Indians first revealed it to 'A certayne noble man of Spayne' who had acquired the disease amongst them).[29] The American origin of European syphilis is a vexed issue. J. Johnston Abraham mentions paragraphs in the manuscript of Ruy Diaz de Isla's *Tractado contra el Mal Serpentino* (1539) omitted from the printed text, one of which concerns a pilot, Pinzon of Palos, who accompanied Columbus on his first American voyage and returned with pox.[30] In the 1542 edition of his book, Diaz records how he treated some of the infected personnel from that voyage. The many attempts to discredit him must stem from a desire to preserve the idea of America as a refuge from European corruption: what the Romantics came to recognize as the beginning of a new stage in Europe's moral understanding. This would be effectively subverted by the idea that transatlantic traffic brought a particularly virulent plague back from the New World. But John Alden regretfully concedes that

> the appearance in Europe of syphilis at the end of the 15th century seems, all too inexorably, due to its transmission from Hispaniola, beginning with Columbus and his men: modern diagnostic techniques and paleobiologic investigations lend little support to the contention that syphilis was known in Europe prior to the year 1493.[31]

Oviedo, in his *Historia de las Indias* (1535) II.14, comments wryly: 'In Italy I often laughed at the Italians calling it the French disease whilst the French called it the disease of Naples. Indeed they would have been nearer the mark had they called it the disease of the Indies'. But these favourite names embody European antagonisms. As Guicciardini intimates, for the Italians newly introduced by the French to the horrors of total war, *male franzese* represented an amalgam of military and venereal plague.[32] But European politics had by no means obscured the terminological link between New World and new disease. Cotgrave's *Dictionarie* records 'Ameriquain . . . *The Neapolitane, or French disease; called so, because it first came from America*'; and Cornwallis includes 'the *Indian Sarampion or tetter*' in a series of names for pox.[33] In Webster's *Devil's Law-Case* (1610–19) III.iii.228, a merchant cynically proposes to get rid of trial witnesses to the East Indies, reflecting that 'the Scurvy, or the Indian Pox . . . / Will take order for their comming backe'.[34] There is some confusion of Indies here, but not in *Comedy of Errors* III.ii.136, which shows that the American link was firmly in Shakespeare's mind. When the mock-blazon of a kitchen maid locates 'America, the Indies' in her nose, it is credited with recognized pox tokens, a formidable crop of 'rubies, carbuncles, sapphires, declining their rich aspect to the hot breath of Spain'.[35]

So the riches of the New World are hardly distinct from its paramount disease. What promised to be a recovered Golden Age which might be expressed in a new celebration of the body was undercut by the advent of syphilis. Indeed, the golden reality proved as pernicious as pox and might be more truly taken to be Montezuma's revenge. The scholar–diplomat Languet, replying to Sidney's letter about Frobisher's supposed discovery of vast gold deposits, passionately denounces this 'great incitement to evil'. Then, by an interesting association of ideas, he suggests that pursuit of these fabulous riches will be as disastrous to England as her policy of enclosure.[36] Internal land policy as well as such notable external factors as the opening up of the New World had a powerful impact on Britain's economy. The latter had given Britain a 'new geographical position as the entrepôt between Europe and America', and did much to bring about that rapid social transformation which forms the thematic core of *Timon*.[37] By the time that Elizabeth came to the throne, Spain had shipped some 100 tons of gold across the Atlantic, and during her reign 68 times as much silver (doubling the stock of silver existing in pre-discovery Europe).[38] From the pressures of sixteenth–century European inflation was formed the counters of modern world finance: 'The medieval silver penny and the four-penny piece or groat had given way to a system based on the dollar or crown' (écu).[39] These new coins both provide a pox pun in *Measure for Measure* I.ii.43, when Lucio declares of a bawd that 'I have purchased as many diseases under her roof as come to ——', and his companion waggishly supplies a figure: 'To three thousand dolours a year'. But Lucio caps this with 'A French crown more', the grim joke depending on the way the disease 'crowns the Patient with a Diadem of Rubies about the forehead'.[40]

Timon's attitude, shaped by a confusion of gold with pox, agrees with that of Spenser in Book II of *The Faerie Queene*, where it emerges as a base metal, capable of debasing. By contrast, Columbus's response to the gold of the New World, which he takes to be 'the earthly Paradise',[41] is both rhapsodic and mystical: 'Gold is most excellent. Gold constitutes treasure, and anyone who has it can do whatever he likes in the world. With it he can succeed in bringing souls to Paradise'.[42] That latter phrase alludes to ordering masses for the dead. But it acquires sombre irony from the fate of the Indian, whose nakedness suggested a prelapsarian state but whose position outside the Christian orbit could be readily finessed into subhumanity – making butchery or exploitation easy options. This is the ambiguity explored through the character of Caliban.

Montaigne recognizes that the indigenous culture of the New World has been devastated along with much of the population. For the Indian, gold threatened no instability since its value was aesthetic rather than material. But for the European, 'gold is employed in commerce and trafficke betweene man and man. Wee mince and alter it into a thousand formes: wee spend, we scatter and dispense the same' a thousand ways. He sees how a money economy cannot allow gold to lie idle; instead it must be used ceaselessly to engender more. This goes beyond a simple contrast of barter and money economies. He is pointing to the spirit of usury which has become the norm, causing the profit motive to override all other considerations. Caliban fits Montaigne's perception of the Indian in his contempt for paltry plunder when Trinculo proposes stealing clothes hung out to dry.[43] The ignoble savage and Timon's loyal servant Flaminius have this much in common, the latter contemptuously hurling a golden bribe back at the giver, ascribing to it the malignancy of pox as well as perdition. His words,

May these add to the number that may scald thee.
Let molten coin be thy damnation,
Thou disease of a friend, . . .

(III.i.50)

recall the punishment traditionally reserved in Hell for the usurer, who 'Is forced to sup whole draughts of molten gold'.[44] The strand of latent sexuality is exposed when Timon suggests that Apemantus would have 'melted down thy youth / In different beds of lust' (IV.iii.257). But already Flaminius's speech serves to gloss the fool's words in the preceding scene. This fool serves a bawd, and vents his wit on 'three usurers' men'. He claims that his mistress too is a usurer, since bourse and brothel are alike workshops for the 'two usuries' (*Measure for Measure*, III.i.275). He warns that she is 'e'en setting on water to scald such chickens as you are' (II.ii.68), punning on a familiar term for poxing.[45] The scene is closely recalled in Heywood's *The Royall King, and the Loyall Subject* III, where a bawd exclaims: 'get you from my doore you beggerly companions, or I'le wash you hence with hot scalding water', a clown commenting: 'Nay I warrant her wenches can afford her that at all times'.[46] Soon after, as the configuration of the Prodigal Son amongst the whores is evoked by the bawd: 'will you get out of my doores, or shall wee scolde you hence?', Heywood recycles the 'scald' joke: 'That you shall never by thrusting them out of doores'.[47] In this play, it is a prodigal who has secretly restored his fortunes in the wars who puts his 'trencher-friends' to the test. He accuses whores of bedding the most pox-riddled client for gold:

> Have he no Nose, be all his body stung
> With the French Fly, with the *Serpego* dry'd:[48]

(cf. Thersites's 'dry serpigo', *Troilus* II.iii.73). But the moralizing chimes with Timon's horrified recognition that gold makes palatable one 'whom the spittle house and ulcerous sores / Would cast the gorge at' (IV.iii.40).

As Heywood's bawd says, 'They be Rascalls that have no money; those be Gentlemen that have Crownes';[49] but the sentiment had already been voiced by an aristocrat: 'They are noble that have nobles; gentle they / That appeare such'.[50] Such is the crisis of Mannerism, where distinctions between appearance and reality waver as the nature of reality itself falls under scrutiny. Columbus's celebration of gold is an unwitting challenge to the fundamentals of medieval socio-political order. His discovery of the New World did much to precipitate social change as its mineral wealth poured across the Atlantic to blur the edges of class division. As Anthony Pagden observes, the conquistador Pizarro was 'an illegitimate, illiterate orphan on one side and a Marquis on the other'.[51]

But Europe too was turning into a land of opportunity for the social climber, Timon recognizing how gold will

> place thieves,
> And give them title, knee, and approbation
> With senators on the bench.

> (IV.iii.36)

His associates in Athens all wear figurative masks, which might find quibbling emphasis on stage when they join in the masquing entertainment. The mask is the very emblem of Mannerist art, raising the question of whether it conceals a reality or just another deceptive face. For, whether the play acknowledges it or not, nobility presents another mask. It is not innate, a fact which the nobility henceforth could only conceal by hanging on to that wealth which had become the true source of difference, of power. Timon is out of step with new developments, being doggedly wedded to an aristocratic ethic which despises that very usury which had acquired such a commanding place in his (and Shakespeare's) society.[52] To that extent he is aligned with Aristotle, whose view of usury as the unnatural generation 'of money from money' was seminal.[53] That Aristotle focused opposition to the new money culture is acknowledged in the frequently sensualized language of condemnation, the Greek τοκος (offspring or childbirth) also meaning interest. Hence Francis Meres's resounding comparison: 'As *Paederastice* is vnlawfull, because it is against kinde: so vsurie and encrease by gold and siluer is vnlawful, because against nature; nature hath made them sterill and barren, and vsurie makes them procreatiue'.[54]

Such reassertions of traditional doctrine, as Tawney well observes,[55] acquire 'an almost tragic intensity' at this time not because usury was any new thing, but because it had finally won open acceptance. This makes Timon a legitimate target for the entrepreneurial spirits of his changing world. For him, gold is not to be bred like cattle, but has value only as it permits the virtue and pleasure of largesse. Such an attitude is clearly irreconcilable with that of the new rich, who will simply exploit it until the well runs dry. He does things in an impulsive, expansive way, which puts him as out of step with his Athenian peers as the Antony of *Antony and Cleopatra* is with the new Roman power. His bounty, like Antony's, has 'no winter in't'; and his attempt to obtain help without collateral is as futile as Antony's challenging Caesar to meet him in single combat. Plutarch, of course, compares Antony in retirement to Timon, and in May's *Cleopatra* (1626), Antony adopts a Shakespearean updating of Timon's misanthropy:

I'll sett no gallowses or gibbets upp
As I entended once for men to come
And hang themselves, I'll keep a bawdy house.[56]

May has perhaps noticed that Shakespeare gives them several features in common, Timon too being a warrior who has placed 'sword and fortune' at the service of the state (IV.iii.96). It is he to whom the Athenian capitalists turn for protection from the invader in the last act; but by then a hermit's solitude has more charm than the Athenian rat-race.

Timon is caught up in an early capitalist crisis which had been a long time brewing. Tawney (p. 79) notes how the discovery of the New World was the result of pressure which had steadily built up over the previous century. It was pressure which had already resulted in the development of the printing press. Concern with profit motivated early readers just as it did Columbus's westward voyage after the Turk had blocked the eastward trade route to the Indies. Both navigation and print involve exploration, and the two modes persistently interact. Timon is not exactly a victim of print-culture. But he has fallen foul of those demands which had been met by printers as well as navigators. So the irony of being approached to subsidize publication of a poet's work is not unlike that of his bounty being poured on those who aim to replace him as the new power base in Athenian society.

The link between print and the opening up of the Americas is close. As Lewis Hanke notes, coincidentally in 1492 the scholar Antonio de Nebrija justified his Spanish *Gramática*, 'the first grammar of a European modern language ever written', with the claim that language is the 'instrument of empire'.[57] But the imperialists themselves, in language and thought, were profoundly affected by the discovery of the New World. Cartographical revision was the least of it. Moral, emotional and intellectual life were all challenged and changed by the effort of accommodating a New World beside the Old. In Spenser's terms, Duessa had triumphed over Una since that idea of oneness – stemming from the oneness of God – had yielded to a new pluralism. Indeed that pluralist outlook, a necessary preliminary before the likes of Montaigne could take imaginative hold of the New World's implications, coursed through Europe on a river of print. Casualties of this process were long-standing intellectual assumptions and habits of mind, matters which exercised Guicciardini as he worked on his *History* shortly before his death in 1540. The authority of the ancients was thrown open to question as the voyagers' discoveries revealed their knowledge of the world to be seriously defective; and not ancient learning merely but the authority of holy scripture itself was giving 'some anxiety to its interpreters'.[58]

Guicciardini observes how, with the discovery of the Americas, the dispute of the ancients about the existence of those 'whom they called the antipodes' has been resolved. Shakespeare never mentions the antipodes in the play, since he focuses on those who pursue a domestic El Dorado in their new-style acquisitive society. But references run through the anonymous *Timon*, where a lying traveller cozens a city heir with tales of the antipodes, where

> the earthe brings forth
> Among the wheate eares of gold & siluer.

> (IV.ii.1687)

Perhaps recalling one of the numerous narratives of New World exploration, where food often enough proved more precious than the precious metal sought, Shakespeare develops the collocation differently as Timon's search for sustaining roots results in the discovery of sterile gold. He has been made painfully aware that his former social existence had depended on the free flow of wealth; so now he can put his new fortune to no better use than to turn it on itself – as a means towards the destruction of a gold-orientated society. If gold as corrupter is associated with New World wealth by Shakespeare's contemporaries, there is a sense in which Timon sets up an alliance between two curses of the Americas, gold and pox – the latter too ironically transformed in his mind into a cleanser rather than a defiler. But he recognizes that time – or the time – is against him, that there is no way of turning the clock back. While he sets gold against gold it is no more than a reminder that this dog-eat-dog world has the power to resist everything save its own self-destructive processes.

PART III
The Sexual Reformation

Introduction

As we have seen, the Elizabethans' culture heroes and villains are frequently borrowed from classical sources, just as for much of the twentieth century they have derived from the cinema. In the Middle Ages, church frescoes would have vied with oral tale as imaginative stimulus, but now print was the great provider. And in Britain, unlike Germany or Italy, print meant above all language rather than visual image. Winds of change had blown through social organizations in Chaucer's day; his *Canterbury Tales* bear witness to attempts at rethinking the place of marriage and women in his society. Behind such rethinking was the growing appeal of the temporal over the eternal, summed up by Chaucer's host who takes a Lollard line in favour of the manly monk being allowed 'To parfourne al thy lust in engendrure'.[1] Such views acquired a new urgency and fresh embodiments through the power of print. But in fact one major push towards the emergence of the printing press in the next century came from the activity of social and religious reformers like the Lollards. Another began with the spread of court culture from Avignon, its passage via Paris to London being assisted by Richard II's marriage into the French royal house. The new cultivation made literacy fashionable; court ladies and favourites, often without Latin, became the new readers, with a decisive impact on what was being written. Imitation of the new court fad by the non-élite may be gauged from the number of papers, like the Paston Letters, which they have left from the fifteenth century. But the demands of a growing middle-class readership could only be met by the introduction of a technology to supersede scribes and parchment. This conjunction of forces, one court initiated and the other consciously subversive, helped bring about a print revolution which in its turn would rapidly transform traditional practices and outlook in every sphere throughout Europe, besides generating a new global awareness.

This new print age was one of redefinition, and theories about sexual rôles and behaviour and about family structures poured off the presses. Humanists, Reformers, and Counter-Reformers all weighed in; and the debate conducted through the medium of moral conduct books spilled over into ballad and play. Castiglione's *Il Cortegiano* insisted 'that without women no contentation or delite can be felt in all this life of ours'.[2] Rendered widely accessible through an English translation available from 1561, it left its mark on all the aristocratic characters of Sidney, Spenser, and Shakespeare. Another key humanist text, Erasmus's *Matrimonii Encomium*, was translated in 1536 and further popularized through its inclusion in Wilson's *Art of Rhetorique*, which went through many editions from 1553, and was still in print for Shakespeare to use in composing *Love's Labour's Lost*.

Development in marriage portraiture provides a rough index to the changes occurring in the relationship. An anonymous painting of an aristocratic Ferrarese family in the Alte Pinakothek, Munich, dating from the 1480s, shows the wife with her hands resting on her young son's shoulders. Her husband stands to one side holding a peregrine falcon on a gloved fist while his other hand rests proprietorially on his wife's shoulder. The relationship between falcon and wife is decoded by Petruchio in *The Taming of the Shrew*, who is determined 'to man my haggard' (tame my wild wife):

> My falcon now is sharp and passing empty,
> And till she stoop she must not be full-gorged,
> For then she never looks upon her lure.

(IV.i.176)

Wolf-Dieter Dube comments of the painting that 'The figures' feelings for one another convince . . . through reticence and restraint';[3] and proprietary attitudes are not incompatible with love. But there is no ignoring the power structure within this family. It was Lorenzo Lotto who took this stiffness out of Italian marriage portraits, introducing the psychological intimacy of the northern painters. But the Flemish artists ventured lower down the social scale, Quentin Matsys painting a half-length portrait of *The Moneylender and his Wife* (1514; Louvre). There is a touch of satire in the way that the wife is distracted from her book of hours by the glitter of the gold which her husband weighs. But in the post-Reformation versions by his pupil Marinus van Reymerswael, a highly significant change has taken place, one mirroring the shift from a medieval culture, international and Latin, to that of the Renaissance, national and vernacular. So the wife's handsome *atelier* product has become a modest vernacular manuscript, probably containing accounts: this is a partnership where business and domesticity interact.

Renaissance humanist and medieval schoolman were as far apart in outlook as these two pictures of a bourgeois marriage. The schoolman's study fitted him for contemplation of the divine; the humanist's was an end in itself, or rather an endless drive to master knowledge. Hans Baron shows how these differences reflect a shift from static feudal values to the ceaseless enterprise of an industrial society. The morality of the market place is taken up by the scholar, whose precious commodity is time: Baron notes how a Florentine humanist recommended equipping libraries with clocks 'to remind scholars of the passing of the precious time'.[4] This is reflected in *Love's Labour's Lost*, where the rules of the academy characteristically begrudge time spent in eating and sleeping – and of course sex, that greatest of time-wasters; though there is a powerful anti-humanist protest from Biron, who iterates that illumination is to be found in the eyes of a lovely woman rather than in library learning.

It was the high value placed on time which made the Protestant wary of reading anything but the Bible. Although non-Catholics had their attitudes towards whores affected by Counter-Reformation propaganda (a matter for consideration in Chapter 13), it was naturally the Reformation which had most to do with remoulding sexual attitudes in northern Europe. This was achieved not merely through Heinrich Bullinger's seminal *Christen State of Matrimonye*, but still more because of the fillip which the Reformation gave to Bible translation. This undermined the older pattern of formal mediation, which gave people not information upon which they could test their own thinking but instruction on how to think. New conditions enfranchised ordinary folk and accelerated psychological change. Renaissance concern with sifting the evidence, the basis of modern scholarship as well as jurisprudence, had its reflex amongst readers of the vernacular Bible.

Explicating the text to their own satisfaction became the surest guide to the Christian life. This approach resulted in precisely that breakdown of uniformity which the medieval Church had fought to prevent. This new individualism is epitomized by Hercules at the Crossroads, an early modern figure not a medieval one.[5]

Print had acquired an authority which could vie with that of parents and the community of wise elders. But it brought with it the first shockwave of cultural pluralism. For the Elizabethan this threatens anarchy, and a notably loaded warning is sounded in Dickenson's *Greene in Conceipt* (1598), where a gossip persuades a young wife to adultery on the word of '*Licurgus* the Spartane . . . that a vigorous man knowing an able woman matcht with an husband impotent through yeares or some naturall defect, might lawfully demaund and no lesse lawfully vse her companie to raise vp issue in the others behalfe' (p. 19). If this is a negative example of that web of emotional and practical support which women provide for each other in the writing of the time, some of the more positive aspects feature among the concerns of the next chapter.

10

The Education of Women:
Textual Authority or Sexual Licence

The present chapter looks at aspects of women's education, both formal and informal, as well as ways in which that education equips them to address social and marital problems. Notable in this respect is a play about which Philip King has reservations. How absurd, he suggests, to assume 'that the condition of all our *English* women may be drawn out of *Shakespeers* merry wifes of *Windsor*'. Is he doubtful about the portraiture or about the women's collective ability to cope with the men in their lives? Either way, Margaret Cavendish, whose eccentricity tends to overshadow her sober grasp of reality (the reality of war, for instance), is altogether more positive. She is impressed by Shakespeare's understanding of women's behaviour, asking rhetorically: 'who could Describe *Cleopatra* Better than he hath done, and many other Females of his own Creating, as *Nan Page*, Mrs. *Page*, Mrs. *Ford*, the Doctors Maid, *Bettrice*, Mrs. *Quickly*, *Doll Tearsheet*, and others, too many to Relate?'.[1] These 'Females of his own Creating' will all demand space in the remaining chapters, several of them in the present one. If the weight of discussion favours the women rather than the men, that is because the problem of sexuality tends, in Elizabethan society, to be easier for men to resolve. A youth may express his masculinity either through a display of sexual prowess, or by rationalizing that fear of being swallowed up by woman – by the engulfing vagina – as resistance to such an effeminizing process. Since sexual involvement was widely held to be a threat to maleness – 'O sweet Juliet, / Thy beauty hath made me effeminate', complains Romeo (III.i.113) – theoretically either approach might be expected to preserve the masculine image intact. But the contradictions are exploitable, as the jailer's daughter recognizes in *Two Noble Kinsmen*:

                    Let him do
What he will with me – so he use me kindly.
For use me, so he shall, or I'll proclaim him,
And to his face, no man.

(II.vi.28)

The problem is more acute for a woman. To affirm her identity, her womanhood as Angelo puts it in sugaring the pill of rape (*Measure for Measure* II.iv.135), she must find sexual fulfilment. There is no comfortable, socially acceptable alternative within the Elizabethan Protestant ethos. This is further complicated by that double pull exerted on women: fulfilment through sex, but also through childbearing. It is the latter which causes the trouble, since it gets to the economic root of things. For the poor, unsanctioned pregnancy means a demand on community resources to support the child. Hence the stigma attached. Juliet, in *Measure for Measure* (II.iii.12), is said to have 'blistered her report' – with a glance at the swelling of pregnancy. She is 'a gentlewoman', reminding that economics dictate moral attitudes at all social levels. Breeding is the patina worn by the old rich which distinguishes it from the new. It is metaphor for, as well as manifestation of a family's continuing grip on power. It will not be compromised except by the pressure of economic necessity; but then willingly enough as the old bloodline weds itself to new money. With so much at stake and paternity in the end the woman's secret – 'It is a wise father that knows his own child' (*Merchant of Venice* II.ii.72), it is hardly surprising that powerful efforts are made to control her sexual activity.

But it is not only the economic factors, together with their moral wrappings, which made childbearing a problem area. Women's role in the reproductive process, from menstrual cycle to birth, formed part of a private world into which Renaissance men ordinarily never penetrated. Romantically, this might help to promote the idea of women as 'mystick books', linked to Venus as the 'sovereign queen of secrets'.[2] But in reality it invited real tension since male involvement was conventionally denied at a point which had serious practical as well as emotional consequences. Mystery is fruitful soil for the growth of anxiety, and it is a sombre fact that midwives featured significantly in witchcraft accusations.[3]

This central mystery of woman helped to sustain those conflicting paradigms supplied by the Bible: woman as Eve and woman
as Mary. The former was buttressed by Aristotle, whose recovery
had achieved a profound reorientation in European thought and
assumptions from eternity to the temporal. His insistence that
'there will be no end to time and the world is eternal' began a
process which may be conveniently summed up as the change from
a medieval to a modern world.[4] By Shakespeare's day, to think of
the workings of the universe in terms of a clock mechanism had
become commonplace; but the new prestige attached to things
temporal, including earthly fame, gave Aristotle himself canonical
status. Like Shakespeare later on, he was lifted outside history as
one who spoke for all time. This idea continued strong even
when Renaissance exploration proved him wrong in claiming that
human life was not to be found beyond the temperate zones.[5] In
fact, discovery of America caused him to be challenged on another
count. His view that some men are born to rule and others to
subjection was invoked to justify enslaving the American Indian.
To oppose the weight of Aristotle was no mean undertaking,
particularly as one 'whose ideas had prepared the philosophical
substratum of Catholicism'.[6] But this was done, and successfully;
and his parallel thinking on the relations of the sexes provoked
similar divergences of opinion, as we see in Castiglione's highly
influential *Book of the Courtier*, where the pro-feminist Lord Julian
is given the last word (III, p. 197). Aristotle claims that the female
in most animals, but especially man, is softer and more emotional,
less aggressive but more cunning and impulsive. He favours oppositional thought patterns, so that if the male is perfect it follows that
the female, in her difference, must be imperfect. Hence once again
he takes a hierarchical line, rejecting the Platonic view of moral
equality: 'the courage of a man is shown in commanding, of a
woman in obeying'. He follows up with the proverbial 'Silence
is a woman's glory', though in borrowing a Sophoclean form he
provides the model for that way with Shakespeare of tearing
a line out of dramatic context and offering it as a nugget of
unanswerable wisdom.[7] However, in this case Shakespeare himself
has undermined the absolute position, when Enobarbus (*Antony
and Cleopatra* II.vi.122) observes that the newly wed 'Octavia is
of a holy, cold and still conversation'. And to the joking 'Who
would not have his wife so?', he answers soberly: 'Not he that

himself is not so'. Aristotle and St Paul (1 Timothy 2:11) form a powerful combination on the silent woman theme. But the extent to which Elizabethan moralists harp on this as an ideal makes it seem as wistfully remote as the Golden Age.

Besides, as that exchange in *Antony and Cleopatra* intimates, there was no single pattern of feminine virtue. Marston, whose *Dutch Courtesan* (1603–4) provides too stark a contrast between vice (Franceschina) and virtue, none the less presents two distinct models for the latter. There is the demure and dutiful Beatrice, but there is also her sister Crispinella whom she fears speaks 'too broad' (III.i; see Marston, II, p. 98). Crispinella dares 'as boldly speak venery, as think venery', and her 'honest freenes' is presented for our approval. She declares without contradiction that 'I love no prohibited things', though explaining that she 'would have nothing prohibited by policy but by vertue, for as . . . those bookes that are cald in, are most in sale and request, so in nature those actions that are most prohibited, are most desired'. Her spikiness contrasts with her sister's passive virtue. But she is no less chaste for bringing a critical intelligence to bear, one indebted to the intellectual stimulus of Montaigne.

Set in this context, the anxieties found in current criticism about Desdemona's engagement in mildly bawdy banter with Iago seem odd. Women needed to exercise their wit in such games since it was required for more serious engagements. When Chaucer makes Criseyde resolve 'ful sleighly for to pleie' (II.462), he makes it clear that this is a necessary response to social patterns and pressures. Those readers who prefer to see it as an inherent, Aristotelian trait are unlikely to be well disposed towards Helen in *All's Well*. Her counterpart Bertram embarks on foreign wars to prove himself; but it is her struggle for fulfilment, endangering no one but herself, which is often found disagreeably tricky. When she meets with Paroles he asks if she is 'meditating on virginity' (I.i.109). She admits as much, and raises a question which for her has serious implications, though she expects no serious answer: 'Man is enemy to virginity: how may we barricado it against him?'. Paroles conceives the virgin as a walled city, threatened by man as a besieging army: 'Man, setting down before you, will undermine you and blow you up'. At least part of the sense of 'blowing up' here involves the rounding of pregnancy. Helen would be spared 'from underminers and blowers-up', and wonders 'how virgins might blow up men'. Now Paroles turns this blowing up and down to mean erection and detumescence, together with a glance at orgasm. But to reach that stage, the girl must achieve her own explosion, thus confirming her womanly status: 'Virginity being blown down, man will quicklier be blown up. Marry, in blowing him down again, with the breach yourselves made you lose your city'. Behind the humour, there is the difference between male and female perspectives. For Paroles, the broad banter has added piquancy since it is exchanged with a respectable young woman. But for Helen it touches on the woman's dilemma of combining healthy sex with reputation.

The dilemma is by no means resolved by the strikingly unAristotelian view of women as both practical (competent household managers) and devout (influencing men of their household towards piety). Judith Brown notes how Italians as far apart as St Bernardino of Siena and Lodovico Dolce saw woman's capacity to lie in these directions.[8] Nor are these attitudes too culturally remote to have meaning for Elizabethan society. They formed the basis for popular British attitudes into the twentieth century. Hence men's avoidance of 'strong' language in the company of women; and, more interestingly, the weekly working-class ritual of the breadwinning male, head of the household, presenting his unopened wage-packet to his wife. Both the domestic responsibility and piety became fixed as part of the woman's image through the assertions of Protestant Reformers. Against the Aristotelian view, women were often represented as of finer quality than men, Maria in Fletcher's *Womans Prize* (1604 or later) I.iii.243 claiming them to be creatures 'for men to wonder at, / But too divine to handle'.[9] However, this does tend to make them vulnerably innocent – with perhaps the analogy of the easily ruptured hymen in mind – rather than robustly virtuous. It is the fragility of reputation which Greene points to in *Perimedes the Blacke-Smith* (1588): 'men in their loues haue liberties, that soare they neuer so high nor stoope they neuer so lowe, yet their choice is little noted: but women are more glorious obiects, and therfore haue all mens eyes attentiuelye bent vpon them'.[10]

Aristotle seems to return by the back door with fragility attaching to both moral and physical images of women. But there is a degree of complexity to the figure of the woman scrambling fearfully on to a chair at the appearance of a mouse. It is gratifying to the man to be welcomed, however absurdly, as courageous protector. But the dependence has a double movement, satisfying a need in both parties. Of course this particular rôle is no longer sustainable if the town girl becomes a farmer's wife, a point overlooked during the Second World War controversy over recruiting of women as fire-watchers since, confronted by an unexploded bomb, they were expected to faint. Necessity is the enemy of luxury, including that of being terrified by mice.

But the idea that women need protecting from the harsher, coarser aspects of life does raise the question of how, where such a view prevailed, they were to become educated in the cruder realities. Vives suggests two ways in which the deficiency might have been supplied: 'I maruayle that wyse fathers wyll suffre theyr daughters / or that husbandes wyll suffre their wyues, . . . to rede wantonnes'. Quite possibly he envisages the kind of reading to which Crispinella has patently been exposed, since hers is not the first female generation emancipated by print. But the older means is oral, and he would welcome legislation against the predominantly 'foule & fylthy songes' heard in the city, which 'songes seme to haue none other purpose / but to corrupt the maners of yonge folkes'.[11] The new orientation towards city life, where the sexual-seasonal rhythms are less marked, will sometimes produce discord out of harmony. Even the fescennine rituals enacted at marriages are decried by Bullinger, wedded couples finding no rest from 'vnmanerly and restlesse people [who approach] theyre chambre dore / and there syng vycious and naughtie balates that the deuell maye haue his whole tryumphe now to the vttermost' (*Christen State of Matrimonye*, sig. G6). And the problem continues active during Shakespeare's theatrical life: William Burton, in *The Rowsing of the Sluggard* (1595) p. 95, sermonizing against those who 'goe vp and downe the streetes with such filthie songs, oathes and ribaldries in their mouthes'. That Ophelia has benefited from such instruction seems highly likely. But, product of that court culture which popularized the book of hours as a means of private devotions, she is armed by her father with just such a book for the 'seduction' of Hamlet (III.i.46). This is to foist upon her an iconic role which proves all too transparent. From Carolingian times, representations of the Annunciation show the Virgin interrupted in her reading by the angel, the Immaculate Conception symbolized in this preference for contemplation over action.[12] This scheme became almost obligatory from Duccio's day, and by the 1430s the Master of Flémalle made it fashionable to include a book in Madonna and Child pictures.[13] Once established there, this reading habit migrates to other virgin saints as well as to the repentant Magdalene, marking her shift from sexual activity to the contemplation of divine love. But for Hamlet, Ophelia is no Magdalene – or at least no repentant one. She has become a political whore, one whom he would consign ironically to a 'nunnery' (III.i.123). He understands the ostensible meaning of her book, but registers only dissimulation. As an echo of his own appearance reading a book, it has equally problematic connotations. He no more represents thereby the studious graduate of Wittenburg than she the contemplative saint. Fake piety was not the only negative signal which might be received when a character wandered on stage reading. That it might warn of mental upset makes the prince's doctor in Ford's *Lover's Melancholy* (1628) expostulate:

A book! is this the early exercise
I did prescribe?[14]

(II.i)

For a young man to prefer a book to healthy outdoor activities is again a source of anxiety in Fletcher's *Elder Brother* (1625?), where Brisac declares of his 'book-worme' son: 'I will not trust my land to one so sotted, / So growne like a disease unto his studie' (II.i.78).[15]

Such anxieties about reading, reminiscent of those aroused by the early popularity of television, emphasize that for the Elizabethans the novelty of print had still not worn off. Ophelia herself, as her fund of folksongs indicates, is poised between two worlds. But whereas her book is associated with deception, the reality of her love emerges by that quite other route, the older, oral tradition of balladry. When she enters according to quarto 1, '*playing on a Lute, and her haire downe singing*', the loose hair may signal a disordered mind; but it was also a style affected by the virgin available for marriage or the prostitute available for sex. So the relationship between mental disorder and physical need is confirmed by this single emblem. The first verse she sings deals with love and pilgrimage. Both of her male supports,

Hamlet and her father, have gone on a journey. Her father's is final, as her next snatch on death and graves recalls. But the way that sex and death entangle shows in the corpse's shroud, white 'as the mountain snow' (IV.v.35), which has been Hamlet's 'dowry' of enforced virginity (III.i.138). Her preoccupation with this irksome state shows in her most fully rendered song. It is of the 'night-visit' type, but is unusual in describing not a lover's knocking on the woman's door, but a young maid appearing at his window on St Valentine's eve. She uses the song both to express her sense of burdensome virginity and of sexual betrayal. She has been betrayed into keeping her virginity not into relinquishing it; but her predicament parallels that of the Valentine, who loses her chance to wed by being too free with her body:

> Young men will do't if they come to't,
>   By Cock, they are to blame.
> Quoth she 'Before you tumbled me,
> You promised me to wed.'
> So would I 'a' done, by yonder sun,
>   An thou hadst not come to my bed.

> (IV.v.60)

'By Cock' is a softening of 'By God', but also a reminder of the traditional cockcrow parting, signal of dawn and orgasm.

Lawrence Babb claims that Ophelia's madness 'is due principally not to disappointment in love, but to grief for her father's death'.[16] But under the cloak of mental disorder, she is able to give vent to her frustrations. The neat eloquence with which Rosemary Harris played the part in 1963, 'convinces us that underneath the court costume an animal was always yearning to be undressed'.[17] Probably no reviewer would write like that in the present hyper-sensitive climate. In terms of performance, this climate inhibits subtle indirection (which might be misconstrued) in favour of such underscoring as Helena Bonham-Carter supplies during the mad scene in Franco Zeffirelli's 1990 film version. As she sings of the pilgrim's 'cockle hat', she flips off a sentry's helmet. He seeks to remain stiffly indifferent during her lament on man's infidelity, though her fingers trace the curve of his breastplate before lifting his dangling belt-strap on the words 'By Cock'.

'I must lose my maidenhead by cocklight', says the jailer's daughter in *Two Noble Kinsmen* (IV.i.112). Like Ophelia she has her little flower rituals, and sings a Willow song like Desdemona (IV.i.80). The same mood of fragile romantic melancholy serves wife and virgin. But the surprise conclusion of Desdemona's song, 'If I court more women, you'll couch with more men' (*Othello* IV.iii.55), speaking of an undiminished need despite the pain accompanying the transports, also hints at sexual complications unconsidered by the jailer's daughter. However, the latter combines several factors of present interest. She has a more accommodating father than Desdemona, who asks her wooer: 'have you a full promise of her? When that shall be seen, I tender my consent' (II.i.13). This squares with a good deal of contemporary thought which had relaxed the pattern set by Heinrich Bullinger. Protestant teaching rejected the sacramental nature of marriage, removing the limitation which that had placed on parental authority. Hence Bullinger laid much weight on filial obedience, though he also spoke of marriage as a 'yokynge together of one man and one woman with the good consent of them both'.[18] The back-swing of the pendulum shows in Charles Gibbon's *Work Worth the Reading* (1591), where St Paul is cunningly enlisted to the cause of liberalism:

> shall the maide increase in sin for want of her desire, because her father wil not yeeld his consent, vnlesse it bee to her disliking? I say no. The Apostle telleth vs, *It is better to marrie than burne*, and yet she shall keepe her within the bounds of obedience, because she doth it not of purpose in contempt of her parents, but in regarde of Gods glory to auoyd the occasion of euill. (p.14)

But the problem for the jailer's daughter, as she well understands, is that her affections cross social barriers. They cross plot-lines too, since she has settled on one of the main-plot lovers derived from Chaucer's *Knight's Tale*. Her clear choice between the two princes allows her to provide the same refreshing contrast to Emilia's artificial dilemma as the juxtaposed *Miller's Tale* does in the original. That it was the latter *Tale* which furnished the dramatists' inspiration is suggested by her echo of Chaucer's wry social comment that his heroine is one 'For any lord to leggen in his bedde, / Or yet for any good yeman to wedde' (1.3269). The daughter's choice is a prince and she is 'base': 'To marry him is hopeless, / To be his whore is witless' (II.iv.2). This blend of sex and class distinctions surfaces again when she distractedly fancies herself in Hell, listening to 'a proud lady and a proud city wife'. First 'one cries, O that ever I did it behind the arras!, and then howls – th'other curses a suing fellow and her garden-house' (IV.iii.48). But, like Ophelia, she is also strangely preoccupied with sexual betrayal: 'Lords and courtiers that have got maids with child – they are in this place. They shall stand in fire up to the navel and in ice up to th' heart, and there th'offending part burns and the deceiving part freezes' (IV.iii.38).

Thoughts of Hell have been triggered when she sees herself gathering flowers beside Proserpine (IV.iii.24). It was while the latter was so engaged that she was raped by Pluto, sexual violence and death crowding together. Similar subliminal patterns lie behind the daughter's proverbial wish 'for a prick now, like a nightingale' (III.iv.25), to keep herself awake. The nightingale as ravished Philomel assists this unwitting betrayal of need. Fortunately, her instinctive sense of the remedy for 'livers perished, cracked to pieces with love' (IV.iii.22) accords with medical theory. There is the wooer at hand to play the prince; and the doctor advises him to 'do anything – / Lie with her if she ask you' (V.iv.18). He must

> Please her appetite,
> And do it home – it cures her, *ipso facto*,
> The melancholy humour that infects her.
>
> (V.iv.36)

The Elizabethans understood the illness in psychological terms, whereas the medievals followed the ancient view that it was physical. This shift was facilitated by changing attitudes towards madness, formerly seen as a meeting point between human and transcendent but now entering the sphere of medicine and psychology. Either way, however, methods of coping with this love madness remained much the same. It had long been considered chiefly an affliction of virgins and widows through an abundance of unreleased seed. This could turn poisonous and result in madness as in the present case. The favoured cures were marriage or masturbation, the latter recommended by Galen. That the doctor's prescription follows the current orthodoxies is demonstrated by the royal physician Andreas Laurentius, who asserts that 'this rage and furie of erotike loue, may be staied by the inioying of the thing beloued'.[19]

Young virgins would have been allowed only a narrow range of emotional expression. It is illness which truly unfetters Ophelia and the jailer's daughter, like the lady in Pope's *Rape of the Lock* who takes to her sick-bed to show off a new nightgown. Songs provide a useful displacement, though they are just one of the routes by which sexual folklore comes to intersect with the adolescent's awareness of bodily change. In *Romeo and Juliet* (II.i.35), Mercutio refers to 'that kind of fruit / As maids call medlars when they laugh alone', pointing to those single-sex gatherings where demureness may be dropped. Juliet would be well furnished with bawdy humour, having been instructed from a tender age. She was less than three when, falling on her face, the nurse's husband had joked: 'Thou wilt fall backward when thou hast more wit' (I.iii.44). And the nurse herself, though her bawdry is often unintentional, loves to talk of how 'women grow by men' (I.iii.97), 'bear the burden' (II.iv.76), and happily lose their 'rest' through men's night-attentions (IV.iv.36). Her vicarious relish for youthful sexuality would have ensured enthusiastic tutelage for Juliet. Mercutio calls her 'A bawd' (II.iii.121), and her antecedents are Ovidian: Myrrha's nurse in *Metamorphoses* X.419, and that cynical old woman in *Amores* I.8, who passes on her experience to the new generation. Shakespearean imitations occur through most of the seventeenth century, from Marston's *Antonio's Revenge* (1599–1601) to Otway's *Caius Marius* (1679). In the former, Nutriche (nurse) claims to instruct on the basis of four husbands as well as having 'red *Aristotles Problemes*, . . . Go to, to bed, lye on your backe, dream not on *Piero*. I say no more: to morrowe is your wedding' (III.iv).[20]

The comic, ribald old wife is a type familiar from Chaucer. Women's gatherings offer a variation, though topics of conversation remain fairly constant. *A Talk of Ten Wives on their Husbands' Ware* (c.1460)[21] is an ancestor of Samuel Rowlands's *Tis Merrie when Gossips Meete* (1602) and *A Whole Crew of Kind Gossips* (1609). Its comic sub-text is woman's insatiability, whereas Rowlands's crew of six wives reveal themselves to be shrewish, bullying, and generally unruly. In an appendix, 'Six honest Husbands giue their Wiues the lye', an arrangement which eschews dialogue since that would imply a relationship where none exists. This is the reflex misogyny of the potboiler, with marriage offering no more than an excuse for grumbling. But his earlier piece, reporting 'a Merrie meeting heere in *London,* betweene a *Wife,* a *Widdow,* and a *Mayde*', includes an educational feature, the maid being coached in hard drinking and a cynical view of sex.[22] This too is caricature, but fleshed out as domestic friction has tended to be on the music-hall stage.

Dunbar's 'Tua Mariit Wemen and the Wedo' (*c*.1508) is a notably complex version, where the dubious morality of the male voyeur supplies a certain justification for the women's unscrupulous sex-war tactics; and one of the jokes turned against him is woman's superior sexual staying power. It might have been Dunbar's widow haunting Sir Thomas Monson's Jacobean household in the shape of Mrs Turner, 'a very lewd and infamous woman who revelled in the servingman Simon's gifts of musicianship and 'a Catzo of an immense length and bigness'. His instrument served to beat time to the music by which 'the young Ladies . . . dance ever after Supper; the old Lady . . . could scarce sit for laughing; and it was beleeved, that some of them danced after that Pipe without the Tabor'.[23] Clearly old Mrs Turner is an encourager of such youthful diversions. These gossips are viewed with uniform displeasure in bourgeois fiction, whether they seduce young wives into a culture of garden-house sex or into misguided meddling with domestic arrangements.[24]

Such instruction is at odds with the more sober kind dispensed in the home. The latter is reflected in the cult of St Anne, which gained momentum during the fifteenth century, the *Gospel of Pseudo-Matthew*[25] declaring that than the child Mary there was 'no one more learned in the wisdom of the law of God'. In the early 1420s Masaccio painted her enthroned, uniting her with Mary and the Christ child in a Holy Maternal Trinity. Later in the century, this form became very popular with northern painters, who even earlier than Masaccio had given Anne the book attribute of the Virgin Mary whom she was instructing to read.[26] In fact, medieval legend gave her three daughters; and a triptych by the Master of the Family of St Anne shows the educational role continuing as one of them, Mary Cleophas, appears teaching her four children to read,[27] That fourteenth-century court culture and the print revolution which followed inspired such representations cannot be doubted. The domestication of Mary is the work of a sensibility far removed from that of the twelfth century which introduced both Mariolatry and courtoisie on the same idealized plan. In the apocryphal *Protevangelium of James*,[28] Anne does no more than teach Mary to walk, determining that the child's first steps shall be her last contact with the ground until she enters the temple. Like the lady of romance, 'Her feet were much too dainty for such tread'; though Dumaine explodes the convention: 'Then as she goes, what upward lies / The street should see as she walked overhead' (*Love's Labour's Lost* IV.iii.276). It is a different bringing down to earth which these paintings of Anne achieve, anticipating Luther's more theoretical advocacy of women's formal education. He argues for 'the establishment everywhere of the very best schools for both boys and girls', producing 'men able to rule well over land and people, women able to manage the household and train children and servants aright'.[29] The key factor here is not Luther's ideas about the division of labour but his wholehearted espousal of women's education.

Brian Morris identifies the theme of education as the most important one in *The Taming of The Shrew*.[30] A servant amiably suggests that the rigours of Aristotle need balancing with the delights of Ovid (I.i.32), and his master professes to court ladies out of the *Ars Amatoria* (IV.ii.8) – no supplier of smooth phrases but a cynical guide to seduction. But Baptista, although ready to sell off Bianca to the highest bidder, yet accepts the principle of educating daughters; though his efforts are vitiated since the tutors he hires are suitors in disguise. However, the central educational move is made by Petruchio to refashion the shrewish Kate along more socially approved lines, abandoning the book in favour of psychological strategies which are rooted in the tradition of husbandly power. Peter Berek, while disliking the play's sexism, argues 'that Shakespeare was less sexist than his contemporaries'. But that is to ignore the way that a revival prompted Fletcher's rebuttal, *The Woman's Prize*, which, taking its cue from that line in *The Shrew* "'Tis thought your deer does hold you at a bay' (V.ii.58), allows Petruchio's second wife to tame the tamer. It also ignores the relationship of *The Taming of A Shrew*, which Morris understands to be an inferior version of Shakespeare's play. While the taming procedure is more rawly undertaken in this version, which might suggest that it was appealing to a more hard-line audience than *The Shrew*, recent editors point out that, since the Sly framework is insistently present, it enables the audience to acquire a self-conscious metadramatic awareness of the illusion being offered by the "taming" play'.[31]

The last word on the relationship between *A* and *The Shrew* has not been uttered. Morris accepts that the former is not simply 'a memorial reconstruction of *The Shrew*', but involves 'a good deal of conscious originality' (p. 32). Thus some of that patchwork of 'Marlovian passages', which might be taken as signs of a hack's desperation to eke out his recollections to play-length, are identified by Holderness and Loughrey as a 'series of running gags referring to Marlowe's *Dr Faustus*' (p. 91). Whether this places it in the same parodic relationship as Fletcher's *Woman's Prize* is hard to say in view of the problem posed by that partial framework surviving in (or added to) the folio text. However, whereas that folio text concludes with congratulations on the taming of 'a curst shrew', Kate's final 'duty' speech in *A Shrew* is capped by her sister Emilia:

> POLIDOR. I say thou art a shrew.
> EMILIA. Thats better then a sheepe.

                                                        (p.88)

So as it stands, the folio text is more deeply conservative than *A Shrew*. Especially hard to view ironically is that ugly detail in Petruchio's scheme when he turns Kate on other recalcitrant wives; she has become a prefect in his 'taming-school'. During a session of supposedly formal education, Bianca has pointed out that she is 'no breeching scholar' (III.i.18). But in this other mode of education she has become subject to the rod. At the outset, Kate has shown a willingness to bind and beat her sister; now she may follow her impulses at her husband's behest and with social approval (V.ii.108).

Clearly Luther's aims in promoting the formal education of girls is to shape them along socially approved lines. But his approach is fundamentally at odds with Petruchio's. Luther wants universal literacy whereas Petruchio eschews the book. For all the ideological weighting of Luther-style education, it contains the seeds of subversion. Literacy is a form of freedom, and there is no guarantee that extra-curricular reading will follow approved lines. *The Shrew* rejects book culture just as decisively as *Love's Labour's Lost*. But in the latter, the unstated élitism of *The Shrew* is disclosed when the king of Navarre observes of Biron's anti-intellectual stance, 'How well he's read, to reason against reading' (I.i.94).

Shakespeare seems less than easy with the book culture which he was busily exploiting; and indeed that figure of St Anne reading to her daughter finds parodic restatement in the instructional role of bawd or witch. The former mode, most perfectly set forth in Aretino's *I Ragionamenti*, takes root in English writing only from the mid-seventeenth century, though Shakespeare (in *Pericles*) presents the bawd coaching a novice whore. Aretino's treatment is amiable enough, but Charles Zika detects a more sinister manifestation in German illustrations of witches during the early sixteenth century. He examines prints of 'The sociability of women at table', where 'the older woman often adopts an instructional pose'. For him such portrayals suggest 'a separate female culture', and in the general run of witch prints, 'the threats which they represent, the fears which inspire their representation, are surely related to their rejection of male sexuality'.[32]

But the relationship sought by feminists between Renaissance perceptions of witches and an assertion of women's independence,[33] is problematic since the idea of organized covens was the fantasy of a Church eager to identify an enemy in its own likeness. A ritual was fabricated in which women had connection with the Devil, and the frenzied reaction expressed itself in the great European witch-hunt. Cohn, demonstrating how attitudes were no longer local, peasant-led, but rapidly and uniformly disseminated from the centre, concludes that the key requirement is literacy. Those implementing at local level 'were often themselves of peasant origin; but they were literate, which meant that a view of witchcraft which was enshrined above all in written texts was current amongst them'.[34] This is a striking instance of how the Church sought to maintain thought control through the press. Dominicans and Franciscans, those two most dynamic orders of the period, were responsible for two-fifths of all incunabula;[35] and the former were heavily involved in the witch-hunt. Dunbar's 'Off Februar the fyiftene nycht' supplies dogs' names for the Dominican and Franciscan arrived in Hell, recalling the *Domini canes* pun: dogs of the Lord, sniffing out heretics. Pope Innocent VIII, in that notorious Bull of 9 December 1484 which presented witches as an international organization, gave full powers to two leading Dominicans, Heinrich Kramer and James Sprenger, to act as Inquisitors in Northern Germany and the Rhineland. A couple of years later this pair produced *Malleus Maleficarum*, one of the most depraved and influential books ever published. Why was this book, awesomely powered by fear and hatred yet plainly the work of morbid imaginations, so influential? The later fifteenth century was an anxious time; but anxiety falls well short of the sick fancy which would be hospitable to such a book. It has the weight of Rome behind it; but still more the printed word was coming to have a terrible authority: 'Shall we not beleeve bookes in Print?', asks a servant in Fletcher's *Night Walker* (1611?).[36] And in *The Winter's Tale* (IV.iv.258), when Mopsa declares: 'I love a ballad in print, alife, for then we are sure they are true', this amiable folly of a shepherdess conceals the dangerous fetish of the sophisticated. The real *maleficium* lay in the printed word: first the book, then the mass burnings. Heine, in *Almansor*,[37] saw it differently: 'Where one burns books, one ends by burning people'. Either way, the power of the book is indisputable; and it is noteworthy that in England and Wales, where the witch problem continued to be local rather than centralized, Continental theory remained untranslated and unpublished until the 1570s. Even then, it took more violent root in Scotland than in England.

'All witchcraft comes from carnal lust, which is in women insatiable', trumpet Kramer and Sprenger.[38] And Shakespeare, who shows little enough interest in the subject prior to the Union of the Crowns, gives witchcraft a characteristically sexual turn in *Macbeth*. 'Titty, Tiffin, keep it stiff in', croons one of Hecate's troop as they plan the seduction of a 'younker' (IV.i.46). Nicholas Brooke, noting this scene to be the result of revision, finds no trace of its 'specifically bawdy' tone in the earlier witch-scenes.[39] But this overlooks the first witch's irritation at a sailor's wife, and her grim tutorial on vengeful sex. The wife is disparaged as a 'rump-fed runnion' (I.iii.5), presumably a gibe at that sexual servicing for which her husband will be unfitted when the witch has overtaken him at Aleppo. She will travel like those witches who 'went by Sea each one in a Riddle or Ciue' before gathering to plot mischief against King James.[40] This account by Agnis Tompson is surely the inspiration behind Shakespeare's speech, Agnis's bid to kill the king at sea being evoked in the lines about the seaman: 'Though his barque cannot be lost, / Yet it shall be tempest-tossed' (I.iii.23). The seaman's doom seems more certain than James's, since the witch promises that when she has caught up with him, her only spell will be her femininity: 'like a rat without a tail / I'll do, I'll do, and I'll do' (I.iii.8). The rat's tail indicates phallic potency, as in Dekker's *1 Honest Whore* (1604) 2.1.417, where – mindful of the constabulary's habit of taking sexual bribes from prostitutes – the whore imagines 'euery Rat / A long tayld Officer'. But absence of phallic tail in *Macbeth* implies that far greater power which is at the witch's command. When the seaman is confronted with this, it will 'drain him dry as hay' (I.iii.17).

In calling the wife a 'runnion' (a prick: *DSL*), the witch adopts the form of insult directed at Falstaff in *Merry Wives*, when he is disguised as an old gossip: 'you witch, you rag, you baggage, you polecat, you runnion' (IV.ii.171). Ironically, he is mistaken for one of those troublesome old women who lead wives astray, and treated accordingly by the outraged husband. The original is the aunt of Mistress Ford's maid, who must have been no stranger to the household since she has left spare clothes there. According to Ford she dabbles in fortune-telling and the occult (IV.ii.161), and in the 1602 text of this scene she is called '*Gillian* of *Brainford*', associating her with Copland's scurrilous, scatological creation of *c.*1525. But the Brentford locale is common to quarto and folio versions, and no doubt meaningful as a notorious resort for dirty weekends.[41] Hence Ford calls her not only 'witch' but 'an old, cozening quean' (IV.ii.158); and in the bourgeois tradition it is inevitable that he will have forbidden her the house.

Falstaff's earlier ignominious experience has a different sexual resonance. Wilson Knight notices how Shakespeare uses the traditional link between stagnant pools and sexual vice, and this includes 'The lascivious Falstaff', who is ducked 'in flowing water, certainly, but the dirty-linen basket supplies the rest'.[42] At the reprise of the buck-basket episode, as Ford shamelessly scatters the soiled clothing in search of Falstaff, Parson Evans slips into innuendo: 'Will you take up your wife's clothes? Come, away' (IV.ii.129). It suggests the degree of seamy intimacy which is the best that Falstaff could manage. Ford has been quick to draw the cuckoldry hint from the buck-basket: 'Buck? I would I could wash my self of the buck!' (III.iii.150); and he sees himself well-antlered ('of the season'). But it is finally Falstaff who is equipped with horns in Windsor Forest, sign of that erotic folly which makes cuckold and cuckold-maker two sides of the same coin.[43] Ford and Falstaff have been acting out these roles, each of them 'an ass . . . and an ox, too' – ox horns being a sexually specific version of the ass's ears. So when Ford removes

Falstaff's horns, making reference to the buck-basket as he does so (V.v.111), it is a release for both of them; and the party can 'laugh this sport o'er by a country fire, / Sir John and all' (l.234). The threat of the titled outsider to this tight-knit bourgeois community has been neutralized so effectively that he can be absorbed, at least temporarily, into the Windsor social framework.

These episodes show the women as educators, working on both Falstaff and the jealous husband: 'I know not which pleases me better: that my husband is deceived, or Sir John', muses Mrs Ford (III.iii.168). The men are no match for the women, who combine with practised ease to offset male prejudice, folly and dissimulation. Ford is very conscious of the two women's close relationship: 'I think if your husbands were dead you two would marry' (III.ii.12). But Mistress Page's answer – 'Be sure of that – two other husbands' – shows that he has overlooked the compatibility of this friendship with marriage. The women's solidarity is no substitute for a marital relationship, but it enables them to hold their own within that relationship. Mistress Page's merry anger at the receipt of Falstaff's love letter makes her talk of exhibiting 'a bill in the Parliament for the putting down of men' (II.i.27). This is not to be construed crudely as a salvo in some kind of sex war, since she enjoys a very satisfactory relationship with her husband. But it does point to the growing confidence of Parliament in Elizabeth's later years and to a species of humour which found shape in an anonymous pamphlet, *The Parlament of Women* (1640), and several imitators. Parliament is involved with bourgeois aspiration, as is the women's concern with education. This is subject for satire in Middleton's *Chaste Maid in Cheapside* (1611–13), where sending a boy to Oxford or possessing 'a close-stool of tawny velvet' (V.i.164) both serve as status symbols.[44] However, the Pages' concern that their 'son profits nothing in the world at his book' (IV.i.13) is subjected to more gentle mockery. The lad declines the Latin '*hic*' with indifferent success, forgetting the accusative and being tricked by the vocative. But his parroting of Lily's *Grammar* impresses his mother: 'He is a better scholar than I thought he was' (l.74); and Parson Evans encourages her optimism. Evans is a less than perfect teacher. Some of his speech mannerisms, like failing to pronounce the first letter of a word – especially the 'w' of 'woman' – survived in South Wales mining communities until their recent demise. But his idiomatic English is less confusing to the boy than his imprecision when he fails to specify that he wants to have the *interrogative* pronouns declined (l.68). Presumably English is his third language behind Latin and Welsh;[45] a flurry of 'which' clauses when he talks of 'Anne Page which is daughter to Master George Page, which is pretty virginity', suggests that he thinks in Latin (I.i.41).[46]

While this viva-scene may be an addition to the script as originally devised (see. p. 36), it fits neatly into the thematic texture. Whereas Latin is a desirable acquisition for the social climber, awkwardness with English marks the outsider. The French physician Dr Caius is said to abuse 'the King's English' (I.iv.5), while Evans is 'one that makes fritters of English' (V.v.142). But Evans at least has been pretty well absorbed into the local community as parson and schoolteacher; and it is the 'outsider' Falstaff who criticizes his speech. Mistress Quickly, with no social aspirations, is suspicious of Latin, interpreting it in terms of English homonymic approximations. Since these are often bawdy, she is concerned for the moral welfare of the young who are instructed in the language. Her views on their corruptibility have already been expressed: ''tis not good that children should know any wickedness. Old folks, you know, have discretion, as they say, and know the world' (II.ii.124). So now she scolds the parson: 'You do ill to teach the child such words. He teaches him to hick and to hack, which they'll do fast enough of themselves, and to call whorum. Fie upon you!' (IV.i.59).[47] Lying behind her nonsense is perhaps a more informed worry that this instruction gives access to Martial and Juvenal, and all those indiscretions of the Roman authors which Loeb translators carefully conceal in Greek.

What the play marks are the beginnings of cultural separation. Impetus for this is provided by the class aspect of education, as espoused by the Pages. Mistress Page is clearly without Latin, so has no direct access to the Roman writers. But it is precisely these education-conscious middle classes who created the demand for the many reprints of Golding's Ovid, a demand which continued until his translation of the *Metamorphoses* was superseded by that of Sandys in the 1620s. Mistress Page's response to the discovery that she and her friend have received identical amorous propositions from Falstaff is shaped by this print factor:

I warrant he hath a thousand of these letters, writ with blank
space for different names – sure, more, and these are of the
second edition. He will print them, out of doubt – for he cares
not what he puts into the press when he would put us two. I
had rather be a giantess, and lie under Mount Pelion.

(II.i.71)

T.W. Craik finds this classicized allusion to Falstaff's bulk incon-
sistent with what we know of Mistress Page's education.[48] But
he underestimates the amount of reading likely to have been
undertaken by someone in her position. She need have progressed
no farther than Golding's Ovid I.55 for the necessary information;
and the fall of the Titans figures division (echoed thematically in the
play) as well as that Mannerist preoccupation with punishment and
expiation. Servants in *The Taming of the Shrew* talk easily of 'Adonis
painted by a running brook, / And Cytherea all in sedges hid, . . .
/ Or Daphne roaming through a thorny wood' (Induction 2, 49).
This visual art penetrates beyond the limits of literacy, as does the
theatre. The latter especially shows socially mixed audiences still
responding to the same culture heroes, many of them (as we have
seen) drawn from the classical world. But the underpinnings are
a book culture which the likes of Mistress Page were helping to
shape into an instrument for change. That she has plenty of leisure
for reading is attested by Mistress Quickly (II.ii.114); and she would
be in that major consumer-group flatteringly wooed as 'right
courteous gentlewomen' by authors of popular fiction. Barnaby
Rich's *Farewell to Militarie Profession* (1581), source of *Twelfth Night*,
appeals throughout to its 'gentlewomen' readers. This had its fourth
edition in 1606; and George Pettie's *Petite Pallace* (1576), drawing
chiefly on classical stories, was still more popular, being reprinted
until 1613. Robert Greene, whose bestseller status was based on
an acute ear for current tastes and trends, targeted women readers
while loading his fiction with the fruits of that university education
which he proclaimed on his title-pages.

Merry Wives offers genial pictures of social difference, preoccupation with insider–outsider status reflecting that oppositional
mode of thinking which has its roots in Aristotelian logic. This
is a buoyantly self-confident middle class which considers itself
markedly superior to dissolute and down-at-heel courtiers. So the
class terms in which self-defining takes place are subtle and fluid.

Money is a major factor, but a Latin education adds the polish required for true insider status. For people in this society, the ultimate form of self-expression is not sexual but social identity. Hence the clash between love and parental control when nubile Anne Page settles her affection on Fenton. He is thought by her father to have as little character as he has cash, and 'shall not knit a knot in his fortunes with the finger of my substance' (III.ii.68). But Anne devastatingly exposes her father's match-making criteria:

> O, what a world of vile ill-favoured faults
> Looks handsome in three hundred pounds a year!
>
> (III.iv.31)

Mistress Page opposes her husband's choice: 'That Slender, though well landed, is an idiot' (IV.iv.84). But her own candidate, Dr Caius, has only come into the reckoning because he 'is well moneyed, and his friends / Potent at court' (l.86). Fenton himself confesses to having first looked on Anne with the eyes of a fortune-hunter, before falling in love with her (III.iv.13). And even Falstaff's adulterous designs are motivated more by 'thrift' than sex (I.iii.38). If the two things fuse in his punning comment that Mistress Page 'bears the purse', his priorities become clear when he adds that 'She is a region in Guiana, all gold and bounty. I will be cheaters to them both, and they shall be exchequers to me' (l.61).

But whereas the wives are more than a match for a would-be adulterer and a jealous husband, both Mistress Page and her husband are foiled by Anne's determination to marry the man she loves: though in this cash-driven world her woman's wit is aptly supplemented by the promise of £100 to a helpful innkeeper (IV.vi.4). But if sex and finance work in unison here, all too often they conflict. As Mistress Quickly asserts, young folk lack their elders' sober appreciation of things. Assumptions are shared by the latter, men and women alike. It is not a matter of women's being caught up in their men's ideological preferences, but of both sexes being conditioned by a culture which makes social advancement its supreme goal. It makes good sense to use their children to help things along, though the sexual urgency of the young proves a frequent stumbling block.[49] Sex has its own rules, and the worry is that, besides thwarting alliances, its disruptive influence will show even in the confines of marriage. Indeed, the link between arranged marriages and infidelity was often remarked: 'for money many men are horned. For when maids are forced to love where they like not, it makes them lie where they should not'.[50] Although it hardly follows that husbands who are cash-orientated will be cuckolded, in the drama they usually have that anxiety. Hence Ford, like the husbands of those other merry wives in Dekker and Webster's *Westward Ho* (1604), is only with difficulty persuaded that 'Wives may be merry, and yet honest, too' (IV.ii.95). The play's affirmation of the point is timely since Ford's suspicions are symptomatic of the post-print social change which the play abundantly represents. They lightheartedly register a new concern with spouse-breaking as northern and southern Europe were brought closer through the first of the mass media. Darker manifestations of this concern will be the subject of the next chapter.

11
Othello, Cuckoldry, and the Doctrine of Generality

In May 1416, Poggio wrote from Baden where he had travelled to treat his rheumatism in the baths.[1] Arrived there he had been amazed to find a kind of Eden or garden of love in the shape of the public baths. He observed the common people bathing naked, men and women together, wondering 'at the simplicity of these people who do not stare, suspect evil, or speak it'. As an Italian humanist, he can only contrast what he sees with that outrageous jealousy 'which weighs upon nearly all our husbands at home'. That the Germans neither suffer from nor 'even have a name for this ailment' is perceptively linked to the fact that theirs is not an acquisitive society, whereas the Italians are ever eager 'to make a fortune, content with no gain, appeased by no money'. This is early notice of something to be considered further: that sexual jealousy in an acute form spread northwards along with protocapitalism. In the north, where the upper classes generally had the protection of primogeniture, it was to become the hallmark of the bourgeois. But in Italy, where all noblemen's children inherited title and property, it was first of all an aristocratic phenomenon. So Poggio is taken aback to find that in the select baths as well as the common ones 'Men watched their wives being handled by strangers and were not disturbed by it; they paid no attention and took it all in the best possible spirit'. He responds to the 'gaiety'; yet, belonging to a culture which produces paintings of the Feast of Herod in which Herodias always eats apart from the men, he is bewildered that 'men are usually present' during picnics in the water. Likewise, he fails to notice women playing voyeuristic games, his account placing only men on the gallery to ogle the bathing women and throw pennies to those who ask 'in fun for alms'. Possibly the voyeurism is only his Italian overlay, since it is hardly an issue even in Beham's moralistic attack of *c.*1536, where his Fountain of Love recalls the Baden arrangement of outside and interior baths.[2]

But by Beham's day some of the bath-houses, and much of that easy-going state of mind on which they depended, had disappeared. A significant factor in the decline of this bath-house culture was apprehension over the spread of syphilis; the ban on public bathing at Nuremberg in 1496 was motivated by this.[3] But as we have noticed in discussing *Timon*, momentous changes had taken place in Europe during the course of that century, amongst which the discovery of the New World and the advent of pox were effect rather than cause. The tenser feelings characterizing marital relations in Italy had spread north along with the new commercialism. A rough guide to the former process is provided by the growing popularity of the cuckold's horns, a figure already in Italian use by Boccaccio's time.[4] A Florentine engraving, *The King of the Goats* (*c.*1470–90)[5] represents a horned and hoofed king on a horn throne, surrounded by horned courtiers, one of whom is having the excrescences sawn off. A naked woman symbolizes the source of the problem, and part of the inscription claims that horns are as inevitable as death. Sixteenth-century German print clings tenaciously to the pattern of that seminal fool-book, Brant's *Narrenschiff* (1494), where the erotic is just one amongst many styles of folly. But the broader symbolism of the ass's ears yields to the specificity of the horned cuckold earlier in English culture than in German. It shows up from Lydgate's day, though it was not until the later sixteenth century that it took firm root.[6] What Chapman facetiously dubs 'the *horned age*' is his own time and that of Shakespeare, the latter credited with the first use of the proverbial 'horn-mad' in that cuckold sense which soon became dominant.[7] And by 1604, Dekker could give 'as madde as an English cuckolde' a proverbial ring.[8]

The process by which southern European paranoia became naturalized in Britain is traceable through the printed record. But print has a dynamic as well as a recording function, instrument of sexual as well as other aspects of socio-economic change. Mediterranean-style jealousy merged easily with bourgeois anxieties over wives' sexual morality, rendered acute by the non-aristocratic custom of partible inheritance. The complexities of sex and marriage, hitherto given ecclesiastical definition, had been opened up to secular debate through the agency of print. The shift from agrarian to urban economy parallels that from the celibate ideal to a newly valued marital state. Marriage, giving rational shape to the irrational sex drive, was of key importance to the bourgeoisie, committed to order and stability. So adultery posed a major threat, making wives the focus of male vulnerability. Heywood's Vulcan – an undoubted authority – might assert that wives' 'guilt 'tis better to suspect then know'.[9] But Jonson, in *Every Man in His Humour* (1601), offers a powerful demonstration to the contrary, the unfortunate Thorello being battered into final awareness that '*Hornes in the minde, are worse then on the head*' (V.iii.417).[10]

Patterns of deception and self-deception interweave. The Spanish humanist Vives, a strong champion of marriage, cautions the wife: 'If thou be good / and haue a ieolious husbande / yet mayste thou hope that he wylle put awaye that vnquietnes of mynde. But and thou be nought / be sure that that fantasye shall neuer go from him / but rather increase dayly'.[11] The translator's word 'fantasye' hints at factual knowledge spiralling into delusion. Husbands like Cornelio in Chapman's *All Fools* or Don Zuccone in Marston's *Fawne* (1604–6) affect gross suspicions even while believing in their wives' honesty. The latter – like Camillo in Webster's *White Devil* – has long avoided his wife's bed, so prurient fantasy becomes a substitute for conjugal pleasure. Presumably Ford, in *Merry Wives*, does actually believe in his wife's infidelity. But Shakespeare shows him taking perverse pleasure in his 'fantastical humours and jealousies' as he pursues his own self-exposure: 'Up, gentlemen! You shall see sport anon. Follow me, gentlemen' (III.iii.160). These fantasies of supposed wifely guilt are so common that Webster can effectively turn matters around in *A Cure for a Cuckold* (*c.*1625) with a fantasy of wifely innocence. A sailor home from a long voyage to find his wife with a young baby insists that seafarers 'send Windes from sea, to do our commendations to our wives' (IV.iii.101).[12]

Notions of the actual had become unusually fluid with the transition from a religious to a more scientific system of belief, a transition which escalated problems of witchcraft and morbid jealousy and produced the stigmata of cuckolds' horns and witches' marks. The workings of the melancholy imagination take an apt form in Barten Holyday's Τεκνογαμια (1618, sig. K), given as part of a Shrovetide entertainment at Robert Burton's college in 1618 to which the anatomist himself contributed. The jealous husband hammers his supposed horns against the wall until he has literally bled off the troublesome humour; whereupon, as Holyday slily remarks, his wife 'became as honest a woman . . . as any in Europe'. The incident is very close to one recounted by Reginald Scot in his *Discoverie of Witchcraft* (1584), where once again the distinctions between literal and figurative are eroded. This time a man imagines 'that his nose was as big as a house; insomuch as no freend nor physician could deliuer him from this conceipt'.[13] Eventually a wiser physician pretends to operate on the nose and bleed it extensively, whereupon the man is cured. The condition is proverbially a sign of sexual jealousy: 'the Conveniency of *Concubines* was used in the very Primitive Ages: And the good Wives were in those Golden days so obedient and well Condition'd, as not to . . . have their Noses Swell at it'.[14] But such Griseldas had long been in short supply, and in *Westward for Smelts* (1620), as a fishwife hears a *Cymbeline*-like tale of a patiently loving wife, she comments: 'I like her as a garment out of fashion: shee shewed well in that innocent time when women had not the wit to know their owne libertie: but if she lived now, she would shew as vild as a paire of Yorkshire sleeves in a goldsmithes shop'.[15]

Wife-testing is a favourite plot-element in early seventeenth-century theatre, prompted by the 'Blacke Iaundeys' of jealousy. Matters are taken to an extraordinary length in Sharpham's *Cupid's Whirligig* (1607), where – borrowing an old jest-book property – a knight has himself castrated to prove his wife's infidelity.[16] Cuckoldry itself is a psychological castration. Barry speaks for his culture in setting against the Pauline hierarchical notion that 'The husband is the wiues head', the purely rhetorical question: 'Where should the hornes stand but vpon the head'.[17] Power entails responsibility, so the husband who cannot control his wife must expect to have a terrible disgrace fastened on him. Thus it makes more sense than William Heale allows, that frequently 'husbands are punished only for the faults of their wiues'.[18] Heale, of course, is preaching sexual revolution. As he well appreciates, to question the stigma of horns or the justice of the skimmington is to attack the creed of masculine superiority.

But whereas the duped male is subject to informal castigation, it is unsurprising that the full rigour of Deuteronomic law is avoided for adultery. Vives had adopted a double standard which remained orthodox in Shakespeare's day: 'the man is nat so moche bounde as the woman to kepe chastite / at leaste wayes by the lawes of the worlde / for by godis lawe both be bounde in lyke'. And specifically on adultery he commends

> Tertia Emylia / wife vnto Affricane the fyrste [who] knewe well inough / that she was the wyfe & the lady of the house / whether so euer her husbande went. And if she shulde beare any grutch / that her husbande shulde lye with other women that were but a fantasye of bodely pleasure / and nat of loue.[19]

Short of endorsing such flagrant injustice as that found amongst southern Europeans and Turks, where 'it is counted a capitall crime in the wife to tread awry, but in the husband it is vsuall and veniall',[20] the British judiciary could only fudge in the manner of a present-day driver-magistrate faced with a speeding motorist. Moralists like Gouge might urge equality of guilt, while acknowledging that 'more inconueniences may follow vpon the womans default then vpon the mans'.[21] Clearly the real issue is not one of biological difference, but of that self-interest which the powerful maintained until 1650 when Cromwell's Parliament introduced the death penalty for adultery. It is a measure of the concern over adultery that at the same time ordinary fornication incurred the relatively mild penalty of three months' imprisonment for a first offence.[22]

Shakespeare's interest in the death penalty for sexual offences shows in *Measure for Measure*. But marital disloyalty is a recurrent feature, along with the mocking of cuckolds (real or imagined). Notably sour treatment is meted out to the cuckold-archetype Menelaus in *Troilus*, where Thersites, Patroclus, Ulysses, even the chivalrous Hector, all deride him (pp. 106–7, 112 above). For Thersites he is 'the bull, the primitive statue and oblique memorial of cuckolds, a thrifty shoeing-horn in a chain, hanging at his brother's leg' (V.i.51) – the latter emblemizing subordination as well as cuckoldry. To be 'a herring without a roe', adds Thersites, would be preferable to being Menelaus; and here it is worth recalling how Romeo is thought to be 'Without his roe, like a dried herring', after a draining session with Rosalind (II.iii.35).

In view of the intense preoccupation with adultery, it is hardly surprising that Shakespeare based several of his major Jacobean plays on the subject of unfounded suspicions. In *The Winter's Tale*, Leontes's symbolic wounding in the loins, rendering his land infertile, is ironically self-inflicted. The play is a resonant iteration of the idea that suspicion of cuckoldry is as damaging as the reality. And it is surely no accident – more an allegory – when in *Cymbeline* the Englishman's sturdy faith in his spouse is undermined by a Renaissance Italian. It is the dire topicality of the theme which helped to make *Othello* the most admired and imitated of English-language tragedies during the seventeenth century (see p. 12). Jealousy prompts much anxious discussion in the moral conduct books of the day; and in 1615 Robert Tofte thought it worth translating Benedetto Varchi's Italian treatise, *The Blazon of Jealousie*.[23] As an aspect of the cuckoldry paranoia, jealousy had come to be regarded as an enemy of love, a monstrous perversion of it. An attraction of Spenser's temple of Venus is that lovers there are 'free from feare and jealosye' (*Faerie Queene* IV.x.28). This was a huge shift, a more traditional view being represented by Andreas Capellanus, whose second rule of love, that 'He who is not jealous cannot love', is reinforced by rule 21: 'Real jealousy always increases the feeling of love'.[24] Jealousy takes various forms, that exhibited by Othello being far removed from Iago's envy. In Othello it is inseparable from his love, giving an attractively dangerous edge to the tender gratitude which is an element in that love. It excites Desdemona, but is released against her by Iago's machinations. For if the latter cannot comprehend the love, he knows how to work on the accompanying jealousy. When he stimulates Othello's hurt or outrage it is not at the prospect of losing face, but at being shut off from the finer reaches of love by what appears to be a woman's gross and transient desire. There is more than hysterical disillusionment in those 'horned men' colloquies in IV.i, more than puritanic revulsion from a libidinous world in Othello's horrified view of Desdemona – his very life – as 'a cistern for foul toads / To knot and gender in' (IV.ii.63).

Edward Snow sees this brothel scene as a demonstration of Othello's 'deeply-rooted misogyny' where 'he is compulsively acting out under the pretext of irony a latent sense of his own marriage as an adulterous affair, a matter between a whore and her client'.[25] Othello the bigot is in danger of replacing Othello the primitive savage. But there is no more powerful or terrible proof of his love for Desdemona than this scene. It is because seamy sex is so outside his experience with her, making it impossible to reconcile that experience with the idea of a betraying Desdemona, that he must resort to this piece of play-acting. Emilia becomes door-keeping bawd – 'Cough or cry 'Hem' if anybody come'[26] – as he envisages himself in a brothel. Only by putting himself as well as Desdemona through this terrible ordeal can he hope to grasp something of what he fears to be the unthinkable truth about her. His need to get at this truth is worse than the rapist's compulsion; it is jealousy-impelled, no longer the positive jealousy of tradition but a new strain which has spread through northern Europe like a more virulent pox.[27] This is what traps Othello rather than that sex-shame nexus which is part of the Judaeo-Christian heritage. Accommodations reached with the latter were now being over-turned by epidemic cuckoldry-phobia. Because Othello's jealousy is so bound up with his love, Iago's trick is to turn the power of that love destructively upon itself. There is even the sense that he has conferred a benefit on Othello in stripping away the illusions of romantic love with which fools embellish a brief span of fleshly delight. And this view seems to prevail as the act of love becomes an act of butchery; or not even butchery since Iago's fervid proposal to 'Strangle her in her bed, even the bed she hath contaminated' finds approval (IV.i.202). Earlier, Othello has exclaimed: 'when I love thee not, / Chaos is come again (III.iii.92), and Iago has striven hard for recognition that Chaos is indeed the condition in which these characters move. But Othello provides a final affirmation that, for all the terrible circumstances, love has survived. He has kissed Desdemona ere he killed her; and now his way is in 'Killing myself, to die upon a kiss' (V.ii.368).

Othello dies in no mood of facile optimism; but he aims deliberately at a fleeting reunion in death as he collapses beside his wife's corpse on the marriage bed. Michael Neill demonstrates the continuing fascination exerted by this scene when Othello, convinced that their bed has been violated, is moved to his own appalling violation. But there is no need to follow Neill in his suspicion that the play's earliest commentator, Henry Jackson (1610), suppresses anxiety over miscegenation when remarking the power exerted by the dead Desdemona *'lying in her bed'*.[28] Nor would I care to draw any similar conclusion from the fact that none of the seventeenth-century echoes of the play, a number of them noted in Chapter 1, seems to take up the colour issue. Dread of cuckolding is more of an obsession than colour. Not that there can be any question about the racial dimension of the play. Indeed, it will be the purpose of what follows to explore the way in which Shakespeare resorts to the stereotypes of African, of soldier, and of unfaithful wife in working out his tragedy. G.M. Matthews, who provides a key assessment of colour in the play, draws attention to the way 'that Shakespeare forced his audience to see Othello first with the bodily eye of Iago'.[29] But Iago, in spite of himself, reveals his own untrustworthiness rather than anything damaging about Othello. Indeed, the first thing we learn is that the latter chose not to ingratiate himself with those 'Three great ones of the city' (I.i.8) who allegedly applied pressure on Iago's behalf. Nor, apart from folio's strengthening of quarto's 'his Worships Ancient' to 'his Moorship's' (I.i.33), is there any sign of racism in Iago's opening complaints. Perhaps this is why to Neill it seems 'as if racism were just something that Iago, drawing in his improvisational way on a gallimaufry of quite unsystematic prejudices and superstitions, made up as he went along' (p. 295). But Iago is like the Nazis in having nothing fresh in his box of tricks beyond an eager knack for deadly combinations. So whereas, at the outset, it is Roderigo who sneers at 'the thick-lips', it is Iago's bounding zest which inflames Brabanzio against his daughter's secret match:

> Even now, now, very now, an old black ram
> Is tupping your white ewe.
>
> (I.i.88)

Roderigo lacks the furious excitement felt by Iago when turning tenderness to grossness: 'you'll have your daughter covered with a Barbary horse, you'll have your nephews neigh to you' (l.113). Neighing is a recognized sign of lust, and Shakespeare may have taken it from source – Jeremiah 5:8, a much-cited allusion to Jewish lasciviousness. The term recurs at 13:27, just a few verses after that proverbial expression of incorrigibility, 'Can the Ethiopian change his skin,..?'. So there is biblical precedent for telescoping black and Jew, the latter associated with *Luxuria* as well as *Avaritia* in Bible commentary. Iago has already joined black with diabolism as well as brutishness: Brabanzio must hasten or 'the devil will make a grandsire of you'. And this voodoo notion sticks with Brabanzio, who imagines that only 'foul charms' can explain Desdemona's shunning 'The wealthy curlèd darlings of our nation' for Othello's 'sooty bosom' (I.ii.69). But Othello brings the senate to realize that love has been his only 'witchcraft' (I.iii.170), aided by his tales of marvels. The duke imagines that they might have won his daughter too, though some critics have been less impressed, considering the rhetoric overblown and underfelt. But surely not even honest Othello can be expected to divulge the whole truth when answering charges before his chiefs. He handles a trying situation with aplomb, though later Iago's tactics produce not only self-doubt but a despair that not to share the dominant culture is to lack culture. He must have lost Desdemona because

> I am black,
> And have not those soft parts of conversation
> That chamberers have.

> (III.iii.267)

Iago never doubts Othello's skill as wordspinner, but believes that words will fail to hold Desdemona – a woman and therefore inconstant as well as lascivious: 'with what violence she first loved the Moor, but for bragging and telling her fantastical lies' (II.i.223). His tall tales sufficed to prompt the first urgencies of lust; but now 'Her eye must be fed, and what delight shall she have to look on the devil?'. Rather, she will 'begin to heave the gorge' as 'Very nature will instruct'.

In the last act, Emilia goes half way with her husband, her perception of an angelic Desdemona making Othello seem 'the blacker devil' (V.ii.140). Of course, she speaks in shock at the appalling murder of an innocent woman, one with whom she was on close terms. And at this point Othello too, as he has done before under stress, applies racially compromising language to himself. He, 'Like the base Indian, threw a pearl away';[30] and the comparison is odious since the Indian appears to be reckoned base only for not sharing European materialist values. But a further layer accompanies Othello's suicidal blow as he recalls his encounter with 'a malignant and a turbaned Turk' in Aleppo: 'I took by th' throat the circumcisèd dog / And smote him thus' (V.ii.364). 'Why is a matter of head-dress apparently pejorative?', asks Ridley, as if a rational explanation is required.[31] Like circumcision it marks difference, and that is enough. But here there is a confusion about who is the outsider: Othello has become both 'the circumcisèd dog' and the avenger of an affront to God and state.

Certainly the Venetian lords do not seem disposed towards racist responses in this case. Matthews, allowing that they have need of Othello's military skills in the Act I emergency, points out that finally 'there is strong sympathy for him, and some reluctance to condemn'.[32] That racist explanations, all too easy and consoling, are not adduced by the Venetian lords recalls the duke's Act I linking of his daughter with Othello. Although this was a formula for cutting short the elopement debate, it is surely one which no crypto-racist would slip into. If *Othello* is a reasonable reflection of early seventeenth-century society, then that society seems to be one where colour prejudice has not grown too corrosive. C.J. Sisson discovers evidence of sympathy amongst the crews of British ships used in the expulsion of Moors from Spain to Africa in 1598 and 1609. But at the same time, recession made Elizabeth anxious to get rid of those living in Britain.[33] Her concern, first voiced in 1596, was repeated in 1601, the year which saw a Moorish embassage leave London after a six-month stay to discuss an anti-Spanish alliance. The visitors had become 'unpopular on all sides', but it is the fate of allies to arouse British dislike.[34] Ned Ward waxes sarcastic in 'The Dutch-Guards Farewel to England' (1699), verse celebrating the departure of troops who had come over in the service of William of Orange;[35] and the Americans swarming over Second World War Britain were said to have just three drawbacks: they were 'overpaid, oversexed, and over here'. So Shakespeare, intent on holding up racism for his audience's inspection, has judiciously chosen an area of prejudice which, while active enough, is likely to avoid the closed mindedness which Jew or Turk would provoke.

But the African himself is subject to more than local prejudices, often being typed as beast of burden or natural slave. Even Bartolomé de las Casas, champion of the Indian and of human rights, had in 1518 supported the enslavement of blacks to relieve the Indians.[36] Othello relates how he had once been 'sold to slavery' (I.iii.137), though emerging from that darkness into the warmth of Venetian favour. So he offers a different paradigm, that of rags to riches, one that would have struck a chord with the Jacobean bourgeois. By contrast, it is the investigation of difference conducted in *The Tempest* which takes some account of the slave system. Everything hinges on the nature of Caliban, obscurely animal-like in appearance yet teasingly human in behaviour. Contemporary responses are summed up by the way that for Trinculo a dead Indian is as much of a freak as this 'strange fish' Caliban, while Sebastian talks in the same breath of four-legged monsters and 'men of Ind' (II.ii.27). Othello himself slips into this manner, talking of adventures amongst 'the Cannibals, . . . / The Anthropophagi, and men whose heads / Do grow beneath their shoulders' (I.iii.142). Confusion over whether Othello's cannibals or Shakespeare's Caliban are to be regarded as human exactly reflects the dilemma facing Renaissance explorers, their conscience strained by conflict of interest. The problem at bottom is always economic, a question of protectionism or rapacity. So the Inca Garcilaso de la Vega aptly sums up the conquest of the New World: 'by means of it Castilians have won temporal riches and Indians spiritual ones'.[37] He orders events advisedly since it is as an infidel that the Indian was denied property rights.

But the heathen or outsider serves an important psychological function in having a group's deepest anxieties projected on to him. So the patterns of vilification, following predictable lines, always include charges of sexual excess. *Sir Thomas More*, a play in which Shakespeare collaborated, dramatizes friction between Londoners and certain Frenchmen living in their midst. Although the real issue is economic, the play opens with a Frenchman's attempted rape on a citizen's wife. Later she appeals to Elizabethan xenophobia by declaring that

So long as I an Englishman can see,
Nor French nor Dutche shall get a kisse of me.

(III.i.132)[38]

The non-European is set apart still more decisively. Prospero, alive to the way that youthful ardour may outrun discretion, anticipates no such human lapses from Caliban. When the latter shows himself all too human, Prospero can still attribute his action to an incapacity to learn human ways. Failing to meet expectations of innocent simplicity, these denizens of remote places become black or red devils, insatiable in their sexual appetites. Roderigo's 'lascivious Moor' (I.i.126) is such a cliché response, as is Iago's suspicion that 'the lustful Moor / Has leaped into my seat' (II.i.290). Earlier he suggests that it is familiar talk 'that 'twixt my sheets / He's done my office' (I.iii.385).[39] Sexual habits calculated to disgust are regularly alleged against those whose culture is marked for destruction. William Cuningham apparently translates from Vespucci's fabrications in alleging that, amongst the Indians, 'There is no law or order obserued of wedlocke, for it is lawful to haue so many wemen as they affect, and to put them away with out any daunger. They be filthy at meate, and in all secrete acts of nature, comparable to brute beastes'.[40] Vespucci has a still more lurid account of how Indian 'women, being very libidinous, make the penis of their husbands swell to such a size as to appear deformed; and this is accomplished by a certain artifice, being the bite of some poisonous animal'.[41] The porter in *Henry VIII* V.iii.33, whose folkloric lumber includes 'some strange Indian with the great tool', would readily give credence to such tales. Bernal Díaz has another preoccupation. He begins with the discovery of temple pottery representing 'Indians committing sodomy with one another',[42] and thereafter his account of the invasion of Mexico is punctuated with references to this habit, seemingly as widespread as idolatry and cannibalism. He claims that Montezuma was persuaded against the latter practice by Cortez. As for sodomy, while stressing the absolute secrecy surrounding arrangements in the royal harem, Díaz feels able to affirm that Montezuma was 'quite free' of it.[43]

Clearly kings, even heathen kings, are above such practices. This is in accordance with what is sometimes called the doctrine of generality. Sidney amuses himself with it in a scene of Arcadian tournament when declaring of a lady whose honour was being fought over that 'she was a queen, and therefore beautiful'.[44] And it is a cornerstone of Rymer's attack on *Othello*. In his *Tragedies of the Last Age* (1678), he questions 'whether in Poetry a King can be an accessary to a crime'; and in *A Short View of Tragedy* (1693), he similarly objects that Othello's 'Love and his Jealousie are no part of a Souldiers Character, unless for Comedy'.[45] Presumably the tradition of Caesar as bald lecher renders lust appropriate to the barrack-room,[46] making Iago acceptable thus far. But in every other way he offends Rymer's notion of the soldierly far more than Othello: 'He is no Blackamoor Souldier, so we may be sure

he should be like other Souldiers of our acquaintance; yet . . .
against common sense and Nature [Shakespeare] would pass upon
us a close, dissembling, false, insinuating rascal instead of an open-
hearted, frank, plain-dealing Souldier, a character consistently worn
by them for some thousands of years'.[47] Criticism in the days of
Shakespeare and Rymer was as doctrinaire and authoritarian as it is
in ours. Shakespeare pays little attention on the whole, being more
given to the eclectic and empirical than to systems. But in *Othello*,
as Rymer disparagingly notes, he acknowledges the system only to
subvert it: 'In this very Play he pronounces:

If thou dost deliver more or less than Truth,
Thou art no Souldier.'[48]

But Rymer's notions of decorum have so blurred with class and
race prejudice − 'With us a Black-amoor might rise to be a
Trumpeter; . . . might marry some little drab or Small-coal
Wench'[49] − that his distaste prevents him from appreciating
Shakespeare's method.

For Shakespeare neither ignores the stereotype nor does he
adopt it as a convenient shorthand. Instead, he plays it off against
another. If a soldier is of an open nature, and an Italian is subtle and
devious, how will an Italian soldier be? In fact, the contradiction
is resolved deftly enough. Those about Iago see what they expect
to see − a free and open nature reflecting that of his superior.
So acknowledgment is made of the one convention while the
other is satisfied through the seething discontent which manifests
itself in devious plotting. Soldier or not, Iago is a Machiavel. But
Italianate qualities are unstressed in the other Italians, a matter
neatly complicated at the very outset when Cassio is noted as 'a
Florentine': evidently Machiavelli's home town can produce open,
guileless people too. And the irony is consolidated later in Cassio's
expression of gratitude to Iago: 'I never knew a Florentine more
kind and honest' (III.i.39).

Iago, a sinister conjurer dedicated to collapsing distinctions
between appearance and reality, serves ironically to confirm
those distinctions − a strident warning against basing conclusions
about people's moral worth on their colour, class, creed or sex.
Specifically, he supplies a point of reference to both the moral
ambiguities playing about Othello's blackness and to facile notions
about faithless wives. His attitude has something in common with

Rymer's. The famous sarcasm about 'Maidens of Quality' who 'run away with Blackamoors'[50] embraces Desdemona as well as Othello. Robert Heilman, in a perceptive account of Iago, traces the workings of his 'erotic imagination', the 'drooling relish' with which he lingers over thoughts of Desdemona naked and abed, 'snatching vicariously at the unattainable'. Noting how 'lust and malice' combine, Heilman concludes that 'Voyeurism may spring from different kinds of hopelessness'.[51]

Iago resembles the sardonic clown who often plays voyeur to point out the vices and absurdities of life. But another aspect of the clown is that genital orientation noted by Heilman and betrayed in the leering distaste of 'she repeals him for her body's lust' (II.iii.348). Iago shows just how determined he is to refashion love as a foul imposture through that fiction in which Cassio talks in his sleep. His picture of hot adultery blends torment of Othello with self-titillation: for Cassio is Iago's surrogate as he is imagined in Desdemona's embrace. But he becomes something else as the fantasy takes a homosexual turn, cultural condemnation adding to the piquancy:

> And then, sir, would he grip and wring my hand,
> Cry 'O, sweet creature!', then kiss me hard,
> As if he plucked up kisses by the roots,
> That grew upon my lips, lay his leg o'er my thigh
> And sigh, and kiss.
>
> (III.iii.429)

For Iago, Desdemona is 'a guinea-hen' (I.iii.315), 'a land-carrack' (I.ii.50).[52] The latter is a trading galleon, a rich prize, so it anticipates Brabanzio's idea of the elopement as a theft (I.ii.63). Possibly Beaumont and Fletcher's *Coxcomb* (1609–10) I.i contains a vague recollection, where women are said to 'venture further for their lading, than a Merchant, and through as many stormes, but theyle bee fraughted; they are made like Carracks, only strength and stowage'. Here too an elopement is conceived as a privateering venture, the lover's helpers vainly hoping for 'shares in her, like lawfull prize'.

The contrast in sensitivity between Iago's public comments on Desdemona and Cassio's is apparent during that first night in Cyprus. For Iago 'she is sport for Jove' and for Cassio 'a most exquisite lady', to which Iago adds: 'And I'll warrant her full of game' (II.iii.16). Earlier, Cassio awaits Othello's safe arrival with the words:

> Great Jove, Othello guard,
> And swell his sail with thine own powerful breath,
> That he may bless this bay with his tall ship
> And swiftly come to *Desdemona*'s armes.

(II.i.78)

That last line is from the 1622 quarto, folio substituting 'Make love's quick pants in Desdemona's arms'. That 'fertility-feeling' noted by Matthews[53] in these lines is clear without this change, which loses Cassio's habitual delicacy when speaking of Desdemona. It sounds Shakespearean enough, resembling Antony's invitation for Cleopatra to leap 'Through proof of harness to my heart, and there / Ride on the pants triumphing' (IV.ix.15), but may be owed to a reviser who has missed the careful character-nuancing. In this same scene Cassio has greeted Emilia on her arrival with a kiss, and some commentators detect both a lingual and a cunnilingual quip in Iago's response:

> Sir, would she give you so much of her lips
> As of her tongue she oft bestows on me,
> You would have enough.

(II.i.103)

He can afford to let the rankness flow in an aside as Cassio kisses his fingers to Desdemona: 'yet again your fingers to your lips? Would they were clyster-pipes for your sake' (l.178). Such pipes were used anally, but also genitally by pox-sufferers; confusion of the two is achieved through a joke which Shakespeare would have encountered in the anonymous *Timon*, if not elsewhere:

> [wives] will be sicke
> Then comes the Doctor with his Clister pipe
> And makes them well, their husbands heades ake still.

(II.iv.890)

But Iago is a malign joker here, his hatred of Cassio due to more than a coveted promotion. He has contempt for Cassio the 'arithmetician', one versed in 'the bookish theoric' but with no practical experience: contrast Cassio's goodnatured chaff that Desdemona 'may relish [Iago] more in the soldier than in the scholar' (II.i.168). But this professional grievance at the new system of values introduced by print is symptomatic of vaster problems accompanying socio-religious upheaval which has left the Iagos of a changing world adrift without values. Heilman points to a conspicuous feature of this Mannerist villain: 'his tactics flow from his convictions: reality is either relative or meaninglessly undifferentiated, and appearance is fluid and controllable'. All Iago's lies are desperate efforts to expose the sham which people mistake for a moral system; his manipulations are aimed at misleading Othello into a realization of how things truly are. Such a state of mind is conventionally blamed on the 'Italian air', said in Chapman's *Widow's Tears* (coeval with *Othello*) to have so corrupted Tharsalio that everything 'is to your fancy represented as foul and tainted, which in itself, perhaps, is spotless'. But he claims that, on the contrary, 'it hath refined my senses, and made me see with clear eyes, and to judge of objects as they truly are, not as they seem, and through their mask to discern the true face of things'.[54]

Heilman[55] glimpses how Iago, aware that Desdemona is not adulterous, is excitedly bent on convincing himself as much as others of her falseness. His belief, passionately held, works like a slewed version of Original Sin to affirm her guilt. He has affinities with both Thersites and Timon. But the former does have a way of cutting to the heart of the matter; and his flow of bile is too brazenly uttered to be lethal. Closer is the demented Timon's desire to have his perception of the Athenian world confirmed by the collapse of all her spurious 'Degrees, observances, customs, and laws' (IV.i.19). Like Iago, he will intervene to make the world conform to the image he has of it.

Iago relies on more than glib notions of woman's frailty. He is able to insinuate that, as a Venetian, Desdemona must surely be sexually promiscuous: 'In Venice they do let God see the pranks / They dare not show their husbands' (III.iii.206). Venice has been ready made for Shakespeare's purpose not only through its custom of picking foreigners as military leaders, but because of social conditions which make the city a breeding ground for adultery enacted or suspected. As William Thomas observes, in the leading families it is customary for only one brother to wed, to limit 'the numbre of gentilmen ...: wherfore the rest of the brethern dooe kepe Courtisanes, to the entent they maie haue no lauful children'.[56] And while Venice had an unmatched reputation for its courtesans, younger brothers must have been quite apt to find solace amongst the married women of their circle.

The practice, not confined to Venice, results from aristo-cratic systems of inheritance. But Desdemona's 'scorn of fortunes' (I.iii.249) deprives her father of his chief means of control: the prospect of disinheritance will not deter her from a love match. Inheritance, though sometimes involving economic survival, is more commonly bound up with a sense of status. But, as Carol Neely says, Desdemona shows no class consciousness.[57] She is friendly and outgoing: 'my wife is fair, feeds well, loves company, / Is free of speech, sings, plays, and dances well' (III.iii.188). Othello can take pleasure in her extroversion since, thus far, he has no prompting 'To follow still the changes of the moon / With fresh suspicions' (l.181).[58] He sees her more accurately than Brabanzio, who has invented a daughter to accord with his wishes: 'A maiden never bold of spirit, / So still and quiet, that her motion / Blush'd at her self' (I.iii.94). But however much he dislikes the thought, Brabanzio comes to recognize that Desdemona has been 'half the wooer' (I.iii.176), though Othello is not so unversed in gallantry that he misses her hint (l.166). This needs stressing since too many critics are apt to view Othello as a sexual novice, a superannuated Leander. Nor should the tonal contrast in the speeches made by Desdemona and Othello on the subject of whether she is to join him in Cyprus be read in this light. Her youthful ardour is plain, though it is an ardour which embraces the whole rich range of sensual and spiritual love. She insists that she 'did love the Moor, to live with him', yet 'saw Othello's visage in his mind' (I.iii.248); and in a controversial line, she pleads against being left behind, whereby 'The rites for which I love him are bereft me'. However, as Heilman justly remarks, 'Rites may mean the whole experience of living together, even of sharing life at the front; but it is difficult to exclude from it the sexual meaning'.[59] Since her urgent desire is phrased with delicacy, there is no wincing response from the senators. But Othello, equally eager to have her join him in Cyprus, swiftly offers a politic qualification, stressing that there will be no uxoriousness to damage the state's interest. After such an asseveration, he can hardly do other than greet with zeal the news that he must set off that very night. Under these circumstances, he can spare Desdemona 'but an hour', though love takes precedence

in his thoughts for that hour. Just what we are to understand by this
is not made clearer when he says, on their reunion in Cyprus,

> The purchase made, the fruits are to ensue,
> The profit's yet to come 'twixt me and you.

(II.iii.9)

But perhaps the emphasis should be that supplied by Iago when
he confides that Othello 'hath not yet made wanton the night
with her' (l.15). A quick consummation would hardly constitute
a bridal night.

Some of the terms of Othello's joyful reunion with Desdemona,
when 'If it were now to die / 'Twere now to be most happy', are
opposed by her:

> The heavens forbid
> But that our loves and comforts should increase
> Even as our days do grow.

(II.i.190)

The exchange has been taken to indicate Othello's sense of the
threat posed by marriage and consummation, assuming that the
marriage has not yet been consummated.[60] But this ignores
Othello's happy acquiescence, 'Amen to that', followed by his
eager kisses. The 'greedy ear' with which Desdemona has devoured
Othello's exotic tales has also been interpreted as betraying 'a
masculine fear of a cultural femininity which is envisioned as a
greedy mouth, never satisfied'.[61] But some stage Othellos might
allow the phrase to show how flattered and excited they have
been by the avidity of Desdemona's response. The physicality of
the expression hardly needs confirming with Cleopatra's 'Ram
thou thy fruitful tidings in mine ears' (II.v.24). However, Thomas
Wright shows how 'wise men' absorb reason through their ears,
while 'common people, . . . more persuaded with passions in
the speakers', use their eyes to catch rhetorical expression and
gesture.[62] According to a current school of thought, Desdemona
is doomed for listening too hard and talking too much. But this
is to ascribe too much influence to Paul's enjoining of woman
to silence (1 Tim. 2:11). That the silent woman – portrayed
as headless – was a joke does not guarantee easy laughter; but
there is no reason to suppose its relation to actuality was closer
than in the case of children being seen and not heard. This is

urged on children precisely because they are noisy; most parents would be anxious about the health of a child who began to live up to this pseudo-ideal. According to Newman, 'Both Rymer and Cinthio reveal how Desdemona is punished for her desire', since it 'threatens a white male hegemony in which women cannot be desiring subjects'.[63] Rymer had quoted Desdemona's despairing words where she fears becoming an example against marrying 'a man whose nature, heaven, and our mode of life separate from us'. But this is hardly Cinthio's moral; rather an expression of distress and bewilderment as the Moor becomes unaccountably estranged from her. 'Cinthio affirms that *She was not overcome by a Womanish Appetite, but by the Vertue of the Moor*', concedes Rymer, adding sourly that 'It must be a good-natur'd Reader that takes *Cinthio's* word in this case'.[64] Cinthio is at pains to represent the marriage as idyllic until the ensign's poison begins to work, using his fictional audience to give further pointers. The latter unqualifiedly laments Disdemona's fate and marvels at the ensign's villainy, while attaching some blame to Disdemona's father for giving her a name of ill omen and to the Moor for his credulity.

It is ironic that this play about stereotypes should have fostered such stereotyping of Elizabethan marital roles amongst its critics. As a corrective, it is worth recalling Marston's *Insatiate Countess* (*c*.1610), where two young husbands seek revenge on each other by means of cuckoldry. But their wives, uncommitted to the double standard, foil them by swapping beds, and in the process demonstrate that chastity and strong sensuality are perfectly compatible. For in exchanging notes they delight in their 'deceived' husbands' virility and their own orgasmic capacity. Their wit and initiative easily rivals that of Desdemona, and their sexual outspokenness far surpasses that of one who hesitates to pronounce 'whore' (IV.ii.121); yet there is never a breath of condemnation attaching to them. Indeed, the surface nature of even virginal diffidence is suggested in Webster's *White Devil* (1609–12), describing

> Brides at wedding dinners, with their looks turn'd
> From the least wanton jests, their puling stomacks
> Sicke of the modesty, when their thoughts are loose . . .
> Even acting of those hot and lustfull sports
> Are to ensue about midnight.
>
> (IV.iii.147)

Notably this coyness serves as a simile for the cunning exercise of power.

It is a moot point whether recent use of Desdemona as a character *à thèse* is more sophisticated than Auden's rationalizings of his dislike for her. His main criticisms are that she nags her husband over Cassio, and fails to trust him sufficiently to tell him the truth about the handkerchief. He takes that abstracted reference to Lodovico during the willow-song scene as proof that she is regretting the absence from her bed of 'someone of her own class and colour'.[65] One of the strangenesses of this 'filthy sort of Pastoral Scene', as Rymer calls it,[66] is the way that it might be a bridal preparation. Indeed the wedding sheets have been laid on the bed and Desdemona requests Emilia:

> If I do die before thee, prithee shroud me
> In one of these same sheets.
>
> (IV.iii.23)

Then she sings her song, a popular item doctored to resonate with her own situation: a technique well known to modern showbiz. That altered conclusion to her song says more than it should:

> 'I called my love false love, but what said he then? . . .
> If I court more women, you'll couch with more men.'
>
> (IV.iii.53)

Ernest Brennecke sees it as evidence 'that she is inwardly and explicitly aware of the cause of Othello's passion'; and the way she immediately raises the seemingly naïve question of whether 'there be women do abuse their husbands / In such gross kind' provides confirmation. This might appear to be innocence, but innocence is too inert a state to describe Desdemona. In fact, there is something of a correspondence with Othello's attitude in the brothel scene: she is unable to correlate infidelity with that harmony which she and Othello have enjoyed until recently. Her exchange with Iago when they await Othello's ship has earned considerable adverse comment. But Granville Barker sees it aright, her anxiety emphasized 'in a bout of artificially comic distraction'.[67] Her fears are betrayed at the outset, and the hint of guilt at seeming merry is of a kind experienced by those suffering bereavement when surprised into a smile. Iago's gibe at woman's shifting nature, ending with the paradox 'Players in your housewifery, and housewives in your beds' (II.i.115), takes the form of a proverb current through much of Europe.[68] Its proverbial shape is both a cover and an indication that his thoughts on the subject run on thoroughly clichéd lines. Beneath the fun of his theming game lurks a similarly reductive view of women. His bawdy extemporising on the woman who is 'black and witty' supplies another dimension of the play's colour symbolism:

> If she be black and thereto have a wit,
> She'll find a white that shall her blackness hit.

> (II.i.132)

If the last word is quarto's 'hit' rather than folio's 'fit', the figure is from archery, a pun on 'wight' linking bowman's target with vaginal black (literally pubic hair).[69] The hint in this 'blackness' joke that Iago's distaste is as much for women as for Moors is affirmed by his soliloquy at the end of the scene. He professes to suspect the Moor (and parenthetically Cassio too) with his wife, 'the thought whereof / Doth, like a poisonous mineral, gnaw my inwards'. Hence he loves Desdemona 'Not out of absolute lust, . . . / But partly led to diet my revenge' (II.i.291).

But Desdemona, not seeing behind his clown-mask, has taken his wit in good part. In this she conforms with the ideal prescribed by Castiglione, where the woman must not be 'squeimish and make wise to abhorre both the company and the talke (though somewhat of the wantonest)', which will only make her seem hypocritical.[70] She is as balanced as the princesses in Sidney's *Arcadia*, who react with 'merry anger' on finding that they have been secretly observed bathing.[71] The genial paradox indicates that, confident in their beauty and virtue, they leave any feelings of guilt or shame to the voyeur. But Desdemona's balance eludes her when Othello casts her in the role of brothel whore. All three of the women in the play are touched by the whore's mark: the handling is free rather than schematic, but the broad outline is plain to see. Besides this wife whose vibrant virtue is no protection from fatal accusation, there is Bianca, a whore in deed, and Emilia a whore in talk.[72] The latter is somewhat like Crispinella in Marston's *Dutch Courtesan* (1603–4), whose sister, less robust than Desdemona, is shocked by her advanced views. Emilia edges towards a concept of relativity in response to Desdemona's protest that she would not commit adultery 'For the whole world': 'Why, the wrong is but a wrong i'th' world, and having the world for your labour, 'tis a wrong in your own world, and you might quickly make it right'. She argues for parity. Having identified the factors prompting male adultery, she asks: 'have not we affections, / Desires for sport, and frailty, as men have?' (IV.iii.78). But there is a strand in her playfulness which mildly resembles Iago's in taking its form from her jaundiced view of men and marriage. Living with Iago has presumably nurtured cynicism. Even if it has not driven her to the act of adultery as either weapon or escape, she delights in the vicarious role of adulteress. But the wide gap between her humour and that of her husband shows when she is stung by his obscene slur, which he smoothly translates into a different kind of insult:

> EMILIA. Do not you chide. I have a thing for you.
> IAGO. You have a thing for me? It is a common thing.
> EMILIA. Ha?
> IAGO. To have a foolish wife.
>
> (III.iii.305)

But whatever the provocation, she introduces yet another example of stereotyping with her proposal that men

> are all but stomachs, and we all but food.
> They eat us hungrily, and when they are full,
> They belch us.
>
> (III,iv.102)

How some of these stereotypes are print-impelled will be amongst the concerns of the next chapter.

12

Class and Courtship Ritual in Much Ado

Othello is Shakespeare's only tragedy of a husband's unfounded suspicions, but he returned to the subject in both *Cymbeline* and *The Winter's Tale*. Apart from his unique foray into city comedy with *The Merry Wives of Windsor*, Shakespeare explores his subject in high society settings. *Much Ado About Nothing* takes place in the court of Messina, where the Florentine Claudio and Paduan Benedick merge easily through the aristocratic freemasonry into a society where the lower orders are more or less invisible. It is a scurrilous suggestion that Dogberry and his followers have the effect 'of widening the social range'.[1] Comparison with *The Partiall Law*, an anonymous play dramatizing the same story, highlights how little attention is given to those outside court circles. Indeed the anonymous author offers a theatrical critique of Shakespeare's play through his stress on class, sex, and the class implications of sex. The class issue comes to the fore in the opening discourse between two gentlemen of the court. the conservative spokesman getting sharp reactions to his dismissal of the hero as 'but a private gentleman' and conviction that 'A Prince / Should be more than a man'.[2] This is taken further when the princess tells the hero Bellamour that she would 'rather begge / With thee than feast it with the greatest Prince alive' (I.iv). But her avowal loses weight when we hear that if they elope, her 'Jewells, Cash, and other things' will keep them in her accustomed style (I.iv).[3] That love transcends class is a moral drawn from Ariosto, though it is finally vitiated here when Bellamour is revealed as prince of Cyprus. However, the play goes further than Ariosto in portraying a world where princes are above the law – Philocres declares his princely immunity from torture – and the poor in some measure below it. Thus they are unaffected by the sexual law of the title, which operates only where property is involved: though this brings even (or especially) princesses into its orbit. (In reality, Elizabethan sexual legislation was aimed particularly at the poor, since parishes were concerned at the prospect of bastards needing upkeep.) A visual image of the class structure occurs when the king's party watches tilting from an upper window while common folk have a vantage point beneath. One of the women wonders 'who were those that talk't over our heads?' (I.v)[4] and, hearing it was the king, declares that she 'had rather than a groat have seene his sweet face, 'tis a sweet face, I warrant you, is it not? I never saw him in all my life'. When the tilt is paralleled later by another aristocratic blood-sport, the princess's intended execution, the women come for the entertainment without any idea of the form it is to take. Hearing that the princess is to lose her head, they wonder why, and are told: 'For that, which had you all your dues, I am afraid your's would not sit long upon your shoulders: for loosing of her mayden-head' (V.i). That this law 'does contend 'gainst nature' (IV.iv)[5] is emphasized by one of the princess's waiting women, whose sympathy is not based on any faith in her mistress's innocence: 'though she be a Lady, / She is compos'd of the same flesh as we / Her servants are' (IV.iii).[6] But it is made clear that special factors produce lower-class readiness to seize pleasure where it offers: 'though some vertue went from me last night, 'twas no vertuous act my neighbour's daughter and I were employed in' (III.iii).[7] The quibbling is ironic, virtue making little impact at this distance from court sophistication and hypocrisy. As Greene versifies, in his *Groatsworth of Wit* (1592), the hungry poor have no time for finesse in sexual matters.[8] These people value the quick fun of holiday pairing since their holy days offer the only remission from otherwise endless toil. For all the play's limitations, the interspersion of low-life comedy – with its Dogberrian malapropism – offers not parody of the main action but valuable perspective on it.

Shakespeare provides quick perspective through that reference to battle-costs at the start of *Much Ado*:

LEONATO. How many gentlemen have you lost in this action.
MESSENGER. But few of any sort, and none of name.

(I.i.5)

This is even better than that Agincourt tally – they were written within months of each other – which includes just four, 'None else of name' (*Henry V* IV.viii.105). There is a circularity about the

Arden editor's attempt to counter charges of heartlessness by reference to the 'Generous affection' characterizing this play-world.[9] They would be better met by a demonstration of irony, which is easier in the case of *Henry V* than *Much Ado*.[10] At least the horror of war is brought home in *Henry V* by reference to the appalling casualties on the French side. Although it is a standard propagandist ploy to exaggerate enemy losses and play down one's own, it is at least possible to see *Henry V* turning from the romantic image of war towards *Troilus and Cressida*-style disenchantment. The latter reflects what had become for the sixteenth century the new reality of war, devastatingly visualized by Bruegel. *Much Ado* stays with the old-fashioned kind where a freemasonry of aristocrats demonstrates its prowess at the risk of a ransom while an expendable cannon-fodder foots the bill of mortality. It is as heartless as it is customary for this latter side of the equation to be ignored; though, when required, justification could be found in the old myth that the plebs descends from Cain and continues to pay the price of that biblical fratricide.

Romance, by definition, avoids critical engagement with social structures. It ignores the reality of a middle class bent on self-definition, on distinguishing itself (up to a point) from a raffish upper class and (absolutely) from an uncouth lower. Middle-class ideals were those of order and sobriety, entailing a distaste for sexual passion as much as for war. The former was tamed by the institution of marriage, though the latter – the ultimate form of disorder – remained a more problematic threat to prosperity. For the moment support was forthcoming for the new humanist concern over war's inhumanity, though attitudes would change decisively as war became recognized as a boost to trade, a contest for larger markets, even a tool of bourgeois revolution. But one aspect of sixteenth-century change was a withdrawal from alliance with the poor, whose expressions of discontent increasingly jarred with the interests of those who were experimenting with financial leverage.

Disorder was seen as the normal condition for the lower classes, while the upper, with a very different power-base from the bourgeois – landed estate rather than money – could accommodate change and even thrive upon it. If they became impoverished, they could withdraw to their estates, the natural resources of which would provide a comfortable existence. The traditional means of recovering their fortunes was by participation in a foreign war or a coup d'état at home. So war, something they were trained for, was to them a normal part of existence, its motivations veiled in the rituals of manliness and honour.

The male protagonists Claudio and Benedick, like Bertram in *All's Well*, fit smoothly into this pattern. Claudio has been successfully blooded in the late campaign, about which we learn nothing because nothing signifies beyond the exploits of a few champions. Claudio and Benedick having distinguished themselves in battle, those in power would help them to favourable marriages. Out of obstacles to this matchmaking arises the drama.

Aristocratic and romance values coincide when Claudio thinks himself deceived by his bride-to-be. He seeks to wipe out the affront to his honour in a savage, open denunciation at what was to be the nuptial ceremony. This is Sicily, where a slur upon a woman's good name is tantamount to proof of guilt. But shadowing this harsh, aristocratic environment, giving it immediacy, is that of the Elizabethan burgher who has his own cuckoldry anxieties. So the excluded middle class makes its ghostly appearance through the sexual mores of this Sicilian court.

As noted in the previous chapter, styles of sexual jealousy were amongst the many Italian importations into Elizabethan culture through the agency of print. Even Dogberry, who has trouble enough with spoken language, is aware of another mysterious language belonging to the literate, which buys them power inaccessible to himself: 'To be a well-favoured man is the gift of fortune, but to write and read comes by nature' (III.iii.13). But it is Benedick, while still declaring himself an enemy of marriage, who draws print and cuckolding into witty conjunction. First, he insists that he will not 'have a recheat winded in my forehead, or hang my bugle in an invisible baldric' (I.i.225); and that 'invisible baldric' blurs cuckold's with phallic horn by evoking the vaginal (torrid) zone utilized by Fletcher in *Beggars' Bush* (*c*.1615–22) IV.v.6: 'I would my clapper / Hung in his baldricke'. This is followed up by a declaration that those finding him lapse into love may 'pick out mine eyes with a ballad-maker's pen and hang me up at the door of a brothel house for the sign of blind Cupid'. Allusion is dense: blind Cupid has an extensive iconography, while the idea of being hung up as a sign of lechery was something of a catchphrase.[11] The 'horn' displacement in the first quotation is followed up here by the familiar disguise of castration as blinding.[12] Love and marriage would not only make of Benedick a figure of erotic folly but would involve a symbolic emasculation through cuckoldry. Even though he would not sound the horn of his own disgrace, he is keenly aware of the ballad-makers' trading on the misfortunes of their married neighbours. Broadside ballads are an extension of the mocking fingers pointed at the cuckold; and he fears the potency of their derision as much as Cleopatra does (V.ii.211).

But once committed to matrimony, Benedick is ready to brave the mocks of street satire: 'Shall quips and sentences and those paper bullets of the brain awe a man from the career of his humour?' (II.iii.227). Against his new maturity it appears like children's projectiles of masticated paper, at worst producing only superficial stings. This passage is evidently one of the several recollections of *Much Ado* in Glapthorne's *Wit in a Constable* (1636–8), a 'booke-worme' in Act I being declared 'Fit only to devour more paper then . . . a legion of boyes in pellets to their elderne gunnes'.[13] The very experience of love is literary; the lover constructs a world of language, a world derived from the romancers and Petrarchans. As Don Pedro tells Claudio,

> Thou wilt be like a lover presently,
> And tire the hearer with a book of words.
>
> (I.i.289)

For Benedick, observing how Claudio 'was wont to speak plain and to the purpose, like an honest man and a soldier, and now is he turned orthography' (II.iii.18), his friend has become the epitome not of fine speech but of fine writing. In just this style, Armado in *Love's Labour's Lost* I.ii.174 declares that he has changed from soldier to lover, crying: 'Assist me, some extemporal god of rhyme, for I am sure I shall turn sonnet'. If the link between experiencing love poetry and love itself seems strangely tight, that is because, in the present century, the power of the book has been eroded first by the cinema and thereafter by other non-literary entertainments. The fashionable lover of yore would compose verse to his mistress or, like the one described by Aretino, would court her with a volume of Petrarch for inspiration. Indeed, it was possible to draw from the sonneteers more than just a few seduction ploys or a spurious reputation for wit. Their anatomies of love were the most subtle and penetrating handbooks of sexual psychology then available, so there is a distinctly practical side to it. Nor does literary heightening necessarily preclude the reality of sweat and semen, as Astrophil makes clear: 'Let *Vertue* have that Stella's selfe; yet . . . that body graunt to us'.[14] But Claudio's is something of an adolescent passion where, although the pen hardly substitutes for the penis, the relationship between romantic idealism and physical sex is awkward and uncertain. This explains, without excusing, his harshly self-righteous treatment of Hero:

> I never tempted her with word too large,
> But as a brother to his sister showed
> Bashful sincerity and comely love.
>
> (IV.i.52)

From certain styles of critic this is apt to trigger a gush of sub-Freudian speculation about incest. But neither repressed incest nor the traumas associated with wet-nursing are required to explain Claudio's hesitancies and need for reassurance as he first ventures into the unexplored terrain of adult sexuality. His behaviour is not especially remarkable: there is no difficulty in finding present-day counterparts. Shakespeare seems intrigued by this development out of puerility, but is not usually very good at portraying it. Romeo is perhaps his best effort, but Adonis and Bertram are even less interesting than Claudio, who additionally focuses Shakespeare's concern with sexual jealousy and its capacity to destroy people as well as relationships. It is this bitter quality which Beatrice registers when declaring Claudio to be 'civil as an orange, and something of that jealous complexion' (II.i.275); and he gives the figure an indecent turn when rejecting Hero as a 'rotten orange' (IV.i.32).[15] He seems to have met the exigencies of the battlefield more effectively than those of the boudoir, having been 'unblowne, unhardend' like Fletcher's warrior-novices, yet displaying 'virgin valour'.[16] But that he continues encumbered by a second virginity is plain enough, making redundant Janice Hays's complaint that no questions are asked about *his* 'sexual purity or lack of it'.[17] After all, there is no broad questioning of Hero's chastity either, but a specific accusation. And the behaviour of which she is accused, fornicating with one person on the eve of espousal to another, might seem, even to those with no solemn views on chastity, a serious failure of tact.

Even so, that attitudes on marital fidelity put forward here and elsewhere in Shakespeare appeared a trifle stodgy to the next generation is suggested by Glapthorne's play, where Shakespeare's girl-cousins reappear in city attire as hard-boiled versions of Beatrice. One of them offers matrimonial terms which would stop Claudio or Benedick in their tracks:

> And if you chance, as fooles will oft be peeping
> To spye us coupling, with respective silence,
> You shall depart, . . .
>   [happy] that you have wives
> That are in so much credit, as to have
> Persons of quality, take the paines to get you
> Heires to your large revenewes.
>
> (Act IV)[18]

In this play, the constable's fifth-act instructions to the watch are direct borrowings from Dogberry. But if Dogberry's stumbling into sense only reinforces the impression that wit is the property of the upper classes, this is wryly undercut by Glapthorne's constable, ironically insistent about being 'a Citizen, and by my charter, . . . not allowed much wit' (Act V).[19]

Wit is a court affectation at Messina. Those who lack it must rely on borrowed material like the 'empty wit' characterized by Earle, who adapts his epigrams out of Martial just as the lover drew his amorous effusions from Petrarch or *Venus and Adonis*.[20] The compiling of commonplace books provided saws for all occasions; and inevitably in a bustling age printed versions became available to save people a lot of laborious reading.[21] Bookshops supplied not only a lover's eulogies but also 'all the railing Bookes and Ballads / That Malice hath invented against women', the latter ordered by a disgusting magistrate in Fletcher's *Night Walker* (1611?), II.v.19.[22] Beatrice is alleged to draw her 'good wit out of the Hundred Merry Tales' (II.i.119), making it not only second hand but decidedly stale since this jestbook dates originally from 1526. She self-deprecatingly claims to have been 'born to speak all mirth and no matter' (II.i.308), and Leonato recalls hearing that 'she hath often dreamt of unhappiness and waked herself with laughing' (l.323). The hint here, as in the reference to her mother's crying in child-bed (l.313), that the jester's mask covers pain, seems not to have registered with Leonato, who adds (again with no insight) that 'She mocks all her wooers out of suit'. He takes her at face value, recalling the advice supplied, when Helena Faucit first assumed the role, to 'give way to natural joyousness'.[23] But neither this nor a more recent tendency to load Beatrice with bitter hostility towards the opposite sex satisfy like the quick glimpses through these lines of the character's vulnerability.

Leonato has chaffed Beatrice earlier about finding a husband, though she deflects with a proverb, preferring to die an old maid and lead 'apes into hell' (II.i.35; Tilley M37). But she fantasizes that the devil will meet her at the gate, 'like an old cuckold with horns on his head', and direct her to heaven, where there is a special place for the unwed. The association of the devil's horns with those of the cuckold predates Shakespeare's use.[24] But here Beatrice's quip takes its place in the play's thick texture of references to marital infidelity. Hints of a fractured relationship between Beatrice and Benedick surface from time to time, which help to explain her preoccupation with infidelity and the elaborate wit-defences which she throws up against him. She concedes that he 'lent' her his heart for 'a while', but claims that he won hers 'with false dice' (II.i.260). When her wit is accounted to have put Benedick down, she instantly retorts: 'So I would not he should do me, . . . lest I should prove the mother of fools' (l.266) – a seeming allusion to the folklore that 'maidenheads paired produce a fool'.[25] On the other hand, she may simply mean that a foolish father begets foolish offspring, since her own gibe at Benedick as 'a good soldier to a lady' (I.i.52), and Leonato's banter about being indeed father to his daughter since Benedick at the time was but 'a child' (l.102), suggest that the latter may be reputed a womanizer. Benedick's boast to Beatrice that he is 'loved of all ladies, only you excepted' (I.i.119), provides no clue since he merely seeks to redress the balance of her disdain. So Shakespeare withholds confirmation that Benedick is a rover just as he does details of a pre-play relationship between him and Beatrice, knowing that a few scattered hints are more teasingly effective.

Enough emerges not to explain but to suggest that an explanation exists for Beatrice's edge of insecurity. Her practised aggression towards Benedick skates over undisclosed depths of isolation and loneliness, even downright frustration. Leonato sees only 'a kind of merry war' (I.i.58) such as Benedick conducts with Margaret. But that, too, broadens into revelation after a bawdy exchange. Margaret playfully requests that in payment for bringing Beatrice to him, he write 'a sonnet in praise of my beauty' (V.ii.3). But when he talks of composing 'In so high a style, . . . that no man living shall come over it', she pretends dismay that she will 'have no man come over me'. In the ensuing duel of wit he proverbially yields her 'the bucklers', but this only prompts a further response: 'Give us the swords. We have bucklers of our own'. Benedick caps this in terms which have caused misunderstanding in the Arden edition: 'If you use them, Margaret, you must put in the pikes with a vice – and they are dangerous weapons for maids'. *Vice* allegedly makes 'bawdy allusion to thighs closed in intercourse'. This is such nonsense that we should perhaps pause to set the matter right: 'vice' is used in the old sense of 'screw', alluding to the buckler's 'central spike which was sometimes as much as ten inches long and could be unscrewed and carried in a pocket in the deerskin lining'.[26] Although written record of a coital meaning for 'screw' may not pre-date 1661, the idea is clearly present here. That the sexual image of grinding ('To work into . . . by means of pressure or friction': OED, v. 9) provides further reinforcement is indicated by Beaumont and Fletcher's *Cupid's Revenge* (c.1608) IV.iii.6: 'Take downe my Buckler, and sweepe the Copwebs off: and grinde the picke ont'.[27]

But as Margaret leaves on her errand, it is her request for a poem which stays in Benedick's mind. Although not the literary lover that Claudio is, he ironically identifies with some of the doom-laden heroes of romance, 'Leander the good swimmer, Troilus the first employer of panders, and a whole book full of these quondam carpet-mongers' (V.ii.29). Nashe, in his *Unfortunate Traveller* (1594), suggests that 'a curious carpet knight . . . is, by interpretation, a fine close leacher', shifting terms to '*carpetmunger*' in *Lenten Stuffe* (1599), a date which makes it impossible to determine whether he or Shakespeare has precedence in the latter's use.[28] Benedick too is mindful of love's seamy side. Reference to 'panders' probably suggests 'mongers', just as his attempt to find rhymes begins with an unsatisfactory 'lady' and 'baby', then '"scorn" "horn", a hard rhyme', and finally '"school" "fool", a babbling rhyme', the school presumably that of Venus graduating erotic fools. The cuckold's horn, as earlier, is a displacement from below to above, and the babbling of the fool also glances at the phallic bable. But the real subliminal link is marriage, a species of folly leading with folkloric inexorability to (suspect) offspring and cuckoldry.

Clearly the security and fulfilment promised by marriage may have
a less welcome resonance for the man – detecting overtones of
entrapment in security – than the woman, since their frequently
differing patterns of premarital experience come into play. Even
in the ironic context of Chaucer's Patient Griselda tale, marriage
is viewed apprehensively as a source of servitude for husbands.
Whereas the Elizabethan woman is likely to have welcomed the
exchange of parental control for that of a husband, Benedick is
fairly typical of his sex in having qualms about this irrevocable shift
from carefree youth to adult responsibility.

Beatrice is impatient and unrelenting as she goads him towards
commitment. Her style is to twist every 'word out of his right
sense' as she continually wrong-foots her opponent (V.ii.50).
Trying to draw out a declaration of love from each other,
they quibble on the problem of getting bad and 'good part to
intermingle'. Eventually, Benedick admits to suffering love, 'for I
love thee against my will' – though here again he undercuts the
painful admission with a bawdy pun.[29] Beatrice's tartness is still
firmly in place here, despite her earlier notion of 'Taming my wild
heart to [Benedick's] loving hand' (III.i.112). It has been suggested
that Shakespeare introduced that speech to neutralize those traits
in Beatrice calculated to unnerve fragile Elizabethan males.[30] But
what she is really concerned to drop is her 'maiden pride' (l.109),
the defensive aspect of her raillery. It is unthinkable that she will
shut up once wed to Benedick; that kiss with which he stops her
mouth (V.iv.97) is a temporary expedient. Even so, there is no
need to assume with Leonato that 'if they were but a week married
they would talk themselves mad' (II.i.330).

The tendency for Beatrice and Benedick to upstage the main-
plot pair is marked in the earliest traces of stage history. It is
not simply that their compulsive sparring, opening up fissures
of uncertainty, provides the play's real centre of energy. Hero
can never match her cousin's ebullience, but nor is she the
pallid creature described by Helena Faucit.[31] The problem is
that the more the actress fleshes out the character, the more
problematically callous does the behaviour of Claudio and his
circle appear following her supposed death. Claudio sees things
in harsh contrasts, of course, his view of her swinging from a
chaste 'Dian in her orb' to a man-eating Venus, 'more intemperate'
than 'those pampered animals / That rage in savage sensuality'

(IV.i.57). His horrified response to her supposed infidelity is both like and unlike that of the lover in Swift's 'Lady's Dressing Room', which mercilessly explodes the illusions of romantic love. The lady being absent, the lover's distracted eye is allowed to prowl over a staggering array of powders, unguents and other beauty aids. The poem works by compromising our smiles at the lover's naïveté with a shared recoil from the disclosures. For no noisome detail or implication is spared until, climactically, the lady's close stool is discovered and her angel-image destroyed for ever. By contrast, once the slander is exposed, Claudio's illusions are restored; and they survive no matter how successfully the actress contrives to make Hero human as well as decent. Faucit's thought that Hero's 'prospect of lasting happiness with the credulous and vacillating Claudio is somewhat doubtful'[32] might almost have been planted by the dramatist. At any rate, directors feel constrained to stifle it by whisking up the whole business into a froth of inconsequence: much ado about nothing. But it is precisely the way that the physically inconsequent is loaded with cultural significance which powers the main plot. As the play's title ironically acknowledges, both virginity and vagina are characterized as a nothing in the wit of the period.[33] But according to the virginity cult, this nothing is the something which must only be surrendered in marriage. The title's nothing, of course, is not only this pretty figment but the non-event, since Hero has given no thought to defying the cult with premarital adventures. And herein lies a further problem, since it would be impossible to credit Faucit's 'characterless and over-gentle' heroine with any such capacity. So it behoves the actress to forget Faucit and go with the script, even though it must alienate the Claudio crowd.

This is not the only problem in the script, though the others – we are frequently told – are inconsistencies which pass unnoticed in the theatre. But the present one is glaringly obvious, since it is hard to deny Hero a distinctive presence amongst her women friends in the play. Faucit herself is unable to sustain her reductive view when considering Hero's 'powers of witty and somewhat merciless sarcasm' in the plot against Beatrice.[34] Something of the same quality has already emerged when she fences with Don Pedro during the masked ball (II.i.78–89). Had this been an open confrontation, she would never have allowed herself such freedom. But one might almost suppose that Claudio had spotted something beneath the demure surface, or even he could never have given such quick credence to the accusations made against her. This lends plausibility to report of her joking over Beatrice's letter where, 'reading it over, she found Benedick and Beatrice between the sheet' (II.iii.134) – a joke spawned by the new literacy.[35] And indeed it becomes clear that she can hold her own amongst the sprightly women of her circle. She is sensitive – or mock-sensitive – about her own imminent transformation to womanhood when Margaret quips on her heavy heart that "Twill be heavier soon by the weight of a man', exclaiming 'Fie upon thee, art not ashamed?' (III.iv.25). But this is all part of the game, and Margaret smoothly extricates herself, claiming that she spoke honourably since marriage is honourable: for if 'bad thinking do not wrest true speaking, I'll offend nobody'. She well understands the technique of allowing her stage audience – like the real one – to construct its own meanings from utterances which she insists are wholly innocent. But she continues irrepressibly: 'Is there any harm in "the heavier for a husband"? None, I think, an it be the right husband and the right wife – otherwise 'tis light and not heavy'.

The latter pun is developed as Beatrice enters looking unwell. To cheer herself up she is advised to sing 'Light o' love' – a hint about the nature of her indisposition – while Margaret dances it. But Beatrice can still rally with a playful accusation of infidelity: 'Ye light o' love with your heels. Then if your husband have stables enough, you'll see he shall lack no barns' (bairns; *stables* = erections, firm-standing). An 'illegitimate construction' indeed; but Margaret gets her chance when Beatrice complains that she is 'stuffed' and 'cannot smell': 'A maid, and stuffed! There's goodly catching of cold'. (Margaret is probably the first recorded user of 'stuff' as sexual verb, and of 'catch cold' meaning to suffer mishap – here loss of virginity, or perhaps pregnancy.)[36] She recommends holy thistle, a general panacea, conveniently latinized as '*carduus benedictus*', which Beatrice must lay to her 'heart. It is the only thing for a qualm'. That Benedick is the cordial remedy which she needs is further focused by Hero's contribution: 'There thou prickest her with a thistle', demonstrating that the genital pun holds no terrors for her. While she might avoid unequivocal use of the word 'prick', her innuendo reflects the response which the theatre itself was constrained to make in dodging social controls. The pleasure attaching to such circumventions is demonstrated by

Gloria Wandrous, heroine of John O' Hara's *Butterfield 8* (1935), who, reading of the bad reputation of the Fokker 29 since Knute Rockne's crash, crows gleefully: 'I can use Fokker in a sentence'. But Shakespeare himself, writing *Henry V* within months of *Much Ado*, shows Catherine's joy in discovering that English language lessons provide an excuse for saying rude French words (III.iv.48).

A new awareness of linguistic uncertainty both facilitates the pun and the verbal deceptions practised in the play for sexual ends. The perfect emblem is the masked ball, with its mistaken identities and motives including Don Pedro's wooing of Hero in the guise of Claudio. Benedick, deceived about Beatrice's feelings for him, scrutinizes her words for double meanings, translating scorn and sarcasm into veiled protestations of love. It is said that what Benedick's 'heart thinks his tongue speaks' (III.ii.13); yet when asked for his opinion of Hero he hesitates between honest reply and antifeminist flippancy (I.i.158). Linguistic forms enshrine the most irrational prejudices, as even Dogberry concedes: 'Write down Prince John a villain. Why, this is flat perjury, to call a prince's brother villain' (IV.ii.39). And Dogberry's fumbling misuse of 'perjury' short-circuits to that point where Hero's one grace is said to be that, by her silence, she avoids perjury (IV.i.173). In this context, Don John represents himself as the more honest for being 'not of many words' (I.i.150). He is no 'flattering honest man' but 'a plain-dealing villain' (I.iii.29), his paradoxes revealing a kinship with Iago as he brutally hacks his way to a word-eschewing integrity.

This is an attack on wit, part of that upper-class veneer of elegance which, as reference to *A Hundred Merry Tales* reminds, was available at second hand to all social levels. But refinement or extravagance of dress, especially when backed by Tudor sumptuary laws, seems a more certain guide to social status. Benedick is teased for his fanciful garb, appearing as 'a Dutchman today, a Frenchman tomorrow, or in the shape of two countries at once, as a German from the waist downward, all slops, and a Spaniard from the hip upward, no doublet' (III.ii.31). This is an aspect of that national stereotyping which was such a feature of popular print. Print accelerated the shift from internationalism to nationalism. The pulpit, the one mass medium of the Middle Ages, preached uniformity; the new mass medium produced a Tower of Babel. And Benedick seems to be a walking emblem of this. So the signals are not as unambiguous as they might appear, and it is hardly surprising if Don John should exploit them just as he does ambiguities inherent in verbal signs. Bent on undermining faith in Hero, he gives genital shading to his proposal that if Claudio 'Go but with me tonight, you shall see her chamber window entered' (III.ii.102). Although the window assignation does not occur on stage, and there has been no reference thus far to Margaret's dressing in Hero's clothes to further the plot as her equivalent does in Ariosto's version, it is hard to explain Borachio's animadversions on fashion unless this trickery is assumed. He prefaces details of his part in the deception by pondering 'what a deformed thief this fashion is' (III.iii.120), tending always to dissimulation or instability. Reference to 'the shaven Hercules in the smirched, worm-eaten tapestry, where his codpiece seems as massy as his club' (l.131), suggests how dress encodes sexual as well as social status. It recalls Benedick's fantasies of a gelding Beatrice, an Omphale who 'would have made Hercules have turned spit, yea, and have cleft his club to make the fire, too' (II.i.237). For Borachio, club and codpiece blur, since the latter is a sartorial detail which proclaims rather than conceals. It was already out of fashion, but even forty years on, when Cavendish wrote *The Varietie*, there was amused recollection of how tight-fitting Tudor breeches necessitated the codpiece since even pocketing of 'halfe a crowne, looks like a poltisse, or a swelling in the groine' (ed. 1649, III.i). And Herbert of Cherbury recognizes that women's gowns too, elaborately modest as they purport to be, use the taper of the bodice towards the groin to signpost the same genital target: 'Her Waste's an envers'd Pyramis, / Upon whose Cone Love's Trophee is'.[37]

Emphasis on dress is an emphasis on body rather than spirit, though the play offers no moral reproof along those lines. Instead, for all the evident dangers, there is acknowledgment that dress, like wit, provides a screen which is as often defensive as deceptive: fallen creatures being ever mindful of their nakedness and vulnerability. Indeed, it is self-deception which is the principal hazard, for as Benedick's blind Cupid sign hints, neither verbal nor visual communication can be trusted. No resolution gets beyond that attempted by Benedick himself, when he finally settles matters with a kiss. Touch, we may suppose, is more reliable than sight, and lips more than tongue.

13

Honest Whores, or the State as Brothel

Shakespeare in *Much Ado* borrows chiefly from Bandello's version of the story rather than that found in Ariosto's *Orlando Furioso*. Hence he omits the issue of capital punishment for sexual offences which forms such a conspicuous part of *The Partiall Law*. But he deals with this in *Measure for Measure*, where it becomes a vehicle for exploring the way that hypocrisy and undeclared – even unrecognized – emotions shape the thinking of those responsible for law and order. The pattern informs Sir John Davies's epigram 33 (*c.*1599) about the man who, coming 'to sollace with his whoore, . . . sends for rods and strips himselfe stark naked', and concluding with Davies (or his poetic persona) wishing he 'had the powre, / To make my selfe his wench but one halfe houre'.[1] Such punitive zeal betrays too much excitement; it resembles current advocacy of the birch to meet the rise in violent crime, enquiry into causes having less appeal than a response rooted in sexual fantasies powered by public school education. Shakespeare touches on it when Lear envisages a Bridewell beadle:

> Why dost thou lash that whore? Strip thine own back.
> Thy blood as hotly lusts to use her in that kind
> For which thou whip'st her.

> (xx.155)

This same tangle of legal power and sexual disorder is right at the heart of *Measure for Measure*, which is notable too as Shakespeare's contribution to a debate on prostitution fuelled by Counter-Reformation print. But first I wish to look at two other plays which offer highly contrasted pictures of the brothel. In the first of these, *Henry IV, Part 2*, prostitution features in that collision between law and disorder chiefly embodied in Falstaff and the Lord Chief Justice. For all the superficial morality-play structure, with Falstaff cast as Vice against the judge's rectitude, the contest between them for moral control of Hal is spurious. Even the hostess's picture of Falstaff as brothel rowdy, as she seeks to have him arrested for debt, is drastically modified later. Her own relationship with the law is strained. Falstaff accuses her of 'suffering flesh to be eaten in thy house' (II.iv.348). But her evasion fastens on to seasonal prohibition while still suggesting the carnal trade at which Falstaff hints: 'All victuallers do so. What's a joint of mutton or two in a whole Lent?'. Likewise, she reveals more than she intends earlier, stumbling from one innuendo to another in warning the officers that Falstaff 'stabbed me in mine own house, most beastly' (II.i.15). This and her legal-vaginal lapse as she protests her 'case so openly known' (l.30) frame her remark that Falstaff comes 'continuantly to Pie Corner . . . to buy a saddle'. Being adjacent to the Smithfield horse-market where Falstaff does business, there would have been no shortage of saddlers' shops. But it is also the corner of Cock Lane which, along with Southwark, had been designated a brothel area since 1393.[2] That saddles of 'mutton' as well as pork pies were still to be had there is plain from court records: in 1586 a parson committed 'carnall copulation . . . twyce in one Theals house a cook by Pye Corner'; and in 1608, a woman was seen 'occupied in a stable at Pye Corner'.[3] So there is scant doubt of what Falstaff's pursuit of 'Py-corner merchandize' has entailed.[4]

That in truth the hostess regards Falstaff as both 'a man-queller, and a woman-queller' is apparent when she undertakes to supply the whore Doll Tearsheet 'at supper' (l.166). But it is Pistol who assumes the role of swaggering brothel 'captain', one whose best claim to that title is 'For tearing a poor whore's ruff in a bawdy-house' (II.iv.140). He is said to live 'upon mouldy stewed prunes and dried cakes', both favoured in brothels as pox-diet.[5] The genital implications of his name are underscored when he threatens to 'discharge upon' the hostess 'with two bullets' (II.iv.111). But when he brandishes his sword, his playhouse fustian, 'Have we not Hiren here?' (l.156), puns on iron and a Greek concubine of the Great Turk. So his weapon is bisexual, suggesting that the equivocal imagery attached to the bayonet in the Great War has a long history.[6]

This scene has begun with Falstaff and Doll emerging from their private supper-room, which has grown 'too hot'. Falstaff is buoyant, though Doll has been 'Sick of a qualm' (l.35);[7] and it is unclear whether her *tête-à-tête* with Falstaff has caused this or dispelled it. It is the relationship between the two which requires attention, its harmony threatened by Falstaff's determination to probe the paradox that when whores 'be once in a calm, they are sick' – a lack of clients being the smooth sea which produces sickness. But Doll's attempt to divert the predictable course of this banter is unsuccessful. When she claims that a client like Falstaff 'catches' the poor whore's chains and jewels, he translates into 'brooches, pearls, and ouches' (l.47). The ouch is a sore as fiery red as the precious stone. Such brooches – including the pearl – are part of the disfigurement undergone by the pox-sufferer, badges of the brothel-warrior's courage.[8] And since Falstaff is destined for the war, the rake's passage from quean to quack is figured with special aptness as a move from field of battle to field dressing station: 'for to serve bravely is to come halting off, you know; to come off the breach with his pike bent bravely, and to surgery bravely'. He talks of venturing 'upon the charged chambers bravely', alluding to that part of a gun's bore in which the charge is placed – but charged here with pox, not powder.

Doll erupts on hearing this dubious reference to her 'chamber'.[9] But the hostess points to their exchange as a ritual sparring: 'You two never meet but you fall to some discord' (l.53). No doubt they enjoy it, and Doll turns easily to praise of Falstaff's valour in helping to eject the disruptive Pistol. 'I will toss the rogue in a blanket', threatens Falstaff; and Doll promises as reward to 'canvas thee between a pair of sheets' (l.223). But she knows his limitations: 'Thou whoreson little tidy Bartholomew boar-pig, when wilt thou leave fighting o'days, and foining o'nights, and begin to patch up thine old body for heaven?' (l.232). This is at once humorous gloss on his visits to the Pie Corner district, scene of the great Bartholomew Fair, and a compassionate regard for a tired and sick old man whose lifestyle uncomfortably parodies youthful exuberance. Noisy aggression has given way to a scene of peace as Doll settles comfortably on Falstaff's lap and Bardolph and the hostess nod off to the soft strains of newly entered musicians. The moment is one of deep feeling, of tenderness unmatched by anything else in the play. But already it is threatened by the surreptitious arrival of Hal and Poins.

Beyond the immediate contrast of the Pistol episode and the

moment when the prince reveals his presence, there is a political framing of this brothel scene. It presents two other sick old men, their sickness caused by less innocent debaucheries than Falstaff's. Immediately before, Northumberland determines to sell out his fellow rebels; and afterwards the king uses more oblique rationalizing to ease his own battered conscience. The brothel scene powerfully restates Falstaff's awareness of the inhumanity of war and politics. The crudity of the latter seeps into this scene through Hal's insensitive commentary: thus Doll's loving attentions show as 'the withered elder' having 'his poll clawed like a parrot' (l.260). Although it is not Hal but Falstaff himself who finds it necessary to break the poignant mood, it is not lust but loneliness and a heavy sense of mortality which resonate through his phrases. He calls for 'A merry song! Come, it grows late; we'll to bed. Thou'lt forget me when I am gone'. That it is not Falstaff who threatens to corrupt Hal but Hal who reanimates Falstaff's corrupt nature is suggested by the way that the prince's assertive presence destroys innocence. Doll is abruptly transformed from companion to commodity, a thing of 'light flesh and corrupt blood' (l.291 – folio punctuation). Soon Falstaff is back to his old style of banter, seeing Doll and the hostess in terms of those 'two usuries', harlotry and moneylending: 'For one of them, she's in hell already, and burns poor souls. For th'other, I owe her money, and whether she be damned for that I know not' (l.342). That venereal disease gave a foretaste of hell-fire is a hurtful commonplace. None the less, Doll weeps for him as he leaves for war; no one sheds a tear for Hal.

Our last glimpse of Doll and the hostess finds them being manhandled to punishment by callous agents of the law. It is a problematic scene, since their alleged offence is murder: 'the man is dead that you and Pistol beat amongst you' (V.iv.16). Tavern-brothels provided a frequent setting for bloodshed, though it was bad for business and generally unpleasant for those running the establishments. The hostess, upset by Pistol's violent antics, has been ready to 'forswear keeping house afore I'll be in these tirrits and frights!' (II.iv.203); and Doll is represented as an equally unlikely accomplice of the man. Besides, if they are seriously implicated in a capital offence, why has the constabulary handed them over to the beadles instead of having them brought before 'a justice' as Doll desires? The beadles punish non-felonious crimes, and it is apparent that the women are heading for Bridewell correction.

This seems to be part of a royal tidying up of those embarrassing Eastcheap acquaintances who, in Prince John's words – and the rebels have learnt how much store to place on what he says – 'Shall all be very well provided for' (V.v.97). This is to highlight a scene which, as Giorgio Melchiori observes, is 'frequently cut in performance'.[10] But either approach is an acknowledgment that the scene will not play neutrally. Immediately before, Falstaff has grandly (and absurdly) declared that 'the laws of England are at my commandment' (V.iii.135). The fate of these women emphasizes the danger of having the laws at the commandment of any one person or tight little power group.

Before proceeding to *Measure for Measure*, which offers another intent look into the heart of darkness beneath authority's robe, it is worth considering the differently weighted picture of brothel life provided by *Pericles*. Crowding in here is the harsher side of Jacobean street life, where bawds lured and coerced girls into their houses; and where the trade's survival depended on a continuing supply of clients, undeterred by the hazards of pox. But it is only the first of the play's two brothel scenes which affects realism. The other required of Shakespeare's audiences a forgetfulness that the saint in the brothel, inviolate and shaming clients 'out of the road of rutting for ever' (xix.9), was sheer fantasy. The factual Marina would have been raped into submission, and used in the brothel until the pox made her unfit for service. Not that Shakespeare's romantic hagiography loses sight of the latter fate. Lysimachus, governor of Mytilene, comes looking for 'that a man may deal withal, and defy the surgeon' (xix.33); but Marina sends 'him away as cold as a snowball' (xix.164). It is a variant on the old romance situation of the lion (king of the forest) responding protectively to virtue – a convention ridiculed in Robert Anton's *Moriomachia* (1613), where the lion-dog responds favourably to a whore-heroine.[11] Nor is sordid reality far below the Shakespearean surface. It emerges in the bawd's reference to a sideline, 'bringing up of poor bastards – as I think I have brought up some eleven –' (xvi.13); whereupon Boult – his name both generic for a pimp and coital verb – quips: 'Ay, to eleven, and brought them down again'. So it is not altogether a joke when Lysimachus asks Marina: 'Were you a gamester / At five, or seven?' (xix.77). But now there is an embarrassing shortage of girls: the remaining three 'with continual action are even as good as rotten' (xvi.8). As the bawd admits,

'The stuff we have, a strong wind will blow it to pieces, they are so pitifully sodden' (xvi.17). They are lethal: one of them has 'pooped'[12] a 'poor Transylvanian', making 'him roast meat for worms' (xvi.20). So the arrival of Marina – fresh, virginal – is a boon. Boult is dispatched to sing her praises in the market, and reports how 'a Spaniard's mouth watered as he went to bed to her very description' (xvi.95). Another, 'Monsieur Veroles', a 'French knight that cowers i' the hams', has 'offered to cut a caper at the proclamation'; though the effort makes him 'groan', since he is as poxed as his name suggests. And her general impact is summed up in a bit of folklore with phallic toning: 'thunder shall not so awake the bed of eels as my giving out her beauty stirs up the lewdly inclined' (xvi.138). The latter verb has evoked the pleasure allegedly in store for Marina: 'men must comfort you, men must feed you, men stir you up' (xvi.87). This is yet another traditional slice of brothel life, advice to the novice: 'Mark me, you must seem to do that fearfully which you commit willingly, to despise profit where you have most gain. To weep that you live as ye do makes pity in your lovers' (xvi.112).

The ugly, coercive nature of brothel life is stressed here as part of the moral design. Boult, the most lively of the brothel team, has acquired Marina, 'bargained for the joint' (xvi.126), so will be permitted to 'cut a morsel off the spit'. But eventually Marina's virtue moves even him. This miracle in the whorehouse takes a traditional form, whereas the link between sanctity and sexuality in *Measure for Measure* follows a different pattern. It is apt that brothel and convent in this play seem as physically close as they often are in parts of Catholic Europe; for the novitiate heroine speaks in that Counter-Reformation imagery which gave a special place to the harlot:

> were I under the terms of death,
> Th'impression of keen whips I'd wear as rubies,
> And strip myself to death as to a bed
> That longing have been sick for, ere I'd yield
> My body up to shame.
>
> (II.iv.100)

David Craig is undoubtedly right to claim that 'The impression of this is erotic'. It is more debatable when he adds: 'some unfulfilled sensuality is seizing the chance offered by the threat of violation to flow out and satisfy itself by imaginary indulgence in the pangs of martyrdom'.[13] The actress may play this scene in terms of repressed sexual, even masochistic, desires. She may equally take it to be a stage on the *via mystica* towards spiritual espousal with Christ. Religious mysticism is seldom free of sexual imagery, and William James's classic account indicates why.[14] The mystic undergoes a private experience for which there is no public language, and is forced by this baffling ineffability to pillage from another area of intense experience which possesses an ample vocabulary.

The direct route towards union is by way of death; and that is the secret disclosed in Crashaw's 'St Teresa' hymn (1646): love of God is love of death. Isabella is no St Teresa; but although Crashaw's poem dates from some decades after the play, it is probably the most striking expression of the Counter-Reformation in English, amply demonstrating that Isabella's rhetoric stays well within the norms. Behind the poem lies that famous account of mystical transverberation in Teresa's autobiography.[15] Christ as phallic god – 'the immortall instrument / Vpon whose choice point shall be spent / A life so loved'[16] – conveys the painful impact of holiness upon unholiness, the dramatic and vivid pain of the Crucifixion which must be experienced by all believers. Crashaw's lines about 'a death in which who dyes / Loves his death, and dyes againe' could easily be transposed to a fornication song of the period. He knowingly embarks on this balancing act, teetering at the very edge with a still more startling picture:

> And that there bee
> Fit executioners for thee,
> The fairest and the first borne sons of fire,
> Blest Seraphims shall leave their quire,
> And turne Loves souldiers, upon thee,
> To exercise their Archerie.

And gang rape is an image which he requires us to retain for a more comprehensive understanding of divine love.

But St Teresa was only canonized in 1622. The supreme saint of the Counter-Reformation was Mary Magdalene, a reformed prostitute. Late medieval attitudes to whores were conflicting. By the fourteenth century, the requirement for whores to identify themselves by wearing special dress or sign was fairly common. This developed on the analogy of the Fourth Lateran Council's order (1215) for Jews so to proclaim their identity. Yellow became a colour associated with both, and in some parts of Italy prostitutes were still recognized by yellow dress decades after Shakespeare's death. The practice marks the whore as pariah; but the reclaimed whore became an increasingly important figure in Counter-Reformation Europe. Fynes Moryson (1617) describes how, of the eighteen nunneries in Padua, two were 'of repenting or illuminate women, so they call whores entring Cloysters'.[17]

The printing press ensured that Counter-Reformation influence spread well beyond Catholic Europe: witness how the responsibility laid on emperors, kings, and others in authority by the Council of Trent for the extirpation of duelling was accepted by James I, whose opposition to the practice follows the Tridentine argument.[18] The Magdalene phenomenon provides a less neat example; yet it would have been not only more accessible, but more consequential to the mass of people unaffected by honour codes. It was in the early fourteenth century that Giotto with paint, and Petrarch through a poem in Latin hexameters, personalized the Magdalene, making her a figure of human sympathy. Petrarch was the inspiration for countless poems of the Counter-Reformation when encouragements to repentance or returning to the fold had a special resonance.[19] Throughout this period his Magdalene poem was every bit as influential as his sonnets; and during the seventeenth century it touches Protestant poets from as far apart as Poland (Zbigniew Morsztyn) and Britain. Donne's 'To Mrs. Magdalen Herbert: On St. Mary Magdalen' (1607), reminds that the idea of the reconstructed Magdalene retained vitality into the early years of Elizabeth's reign, when Herbert was born. Indeed the poem, taking its form from the pictorial tradition of the portrait-Magdalene, testifies to a much longer survival.[20] Robert Southwell, who left behind several Magdalene poems and a draft sermon on the saint at his death in 1595, indicates her importance within the Elizabethan Catholic underground, where he was expecting to 'have sung Mass with all solemnity accompanied by choice instrumental and vocal music, on the feast of St. Mary Magdalen' (22 July 1586).[21]

The flood of vernacular poems released by the printing press inviting meditation on the career of a reformed prostitute must have produced some radical reshaping of contemporary perceptions in the sociological as well as the religious sphere. Greene is responding to this new cultural factor when he appends 'the Conuersion of an English Courtizan, reformed this present yeare, 1592' to his popular *Dispvtation, Betweene a Hee Conny-catcher, and a Shee Conny-catcher*. The woman tells her own story, from her lapse into whoredom following a too indulged childhood until she is persuaded back to virtue by a young clothier. The same eye to current trends is apparent in the theatrical debate conducted between Marston and Dekker, the former reacting against humanizing tendencies with his *Dutch Courtesan* (1603–4), though he never quite persuades that his whore lacks normal feelings. Dekker's *Honest Whore* (1604) evidently had the better of the argument since it spawned a sequel that same year or soon after. Of the same vintage is the anonymous *Faire Maide of Bristow*, including a whore indebted to Marston's Dutch courtesan. though judged with a significant Dekker bias: 'because we see, She sorrowes something for her follies past, Let her be had among the Conuertines' (ed. 1605, F2). Apparently the playhouse not only presented fictions of repenting whores but itself served as a reformatory for those coming there to ply their trade. According to Henry Harington in a commendatory poem prefacing the first collection of Beaumont and Fletcher's plays, many of the women coming to the theatre 'to be tane up' had been recalled to virtue by some of these plays 'and after left the game'.[22] Such was the climate in which Shakespeare was writing; Maudlin in *All's Well* is an off-stage shadow, but in *Measure for Measure* the saint is a spiritual presence. Whether or not Shakespeare was exposed directly to Magdalene print, his juxtaposing of brothel sub-culture and burgeoning conventual world of the Counter-Reformation tells its own story.

In the fifteenth century, according to Laura M. Ragg, to be cloistered under the rule of St Clare might involve 'considerable freedom of intercourse between the inmates of the convent and their relatives in the city'.[23] During the next century, the religious fervour produced by the Counter-Reformation filled the nunneries without closing the doors. Our first introduction to Isabella finds her 'wishing a more strict restraint / Upon the sisterhood' (I.iv.4). It is no accident that this scene follows immediately on the duke's admission that he has appointed the 'precise' Angelo to be his deputy as a test of the Puritan in office: 'Hence shall we see / If power change purpose, what our seemers be' (I.iii.53). This juxtaposition raises the question of whether Isabella too may be a 'seemer', since propagandists levelled the accusation at Catholics as well as Puritans: Spenser in *The Faerie Queene* says of the Romish priest Archimago, 'Sober he seemde' (I.i.29). Aldegrever, in 1530, copied a woodcut by Pencz showing a monk and nun confronted *in flagrante delicto* by a man with a sword. He also designed a cut showing the prelude to this scene, the pair still enjoying themselves while the swordsman watches from behind a tree.[24] An exactly similar slur is cast at a Puritan couple in a woodcut which, often with no regard for content, decorated numerous seventeenth-century ballads. This too includes a voyeur, and in the version used for *Loves Captivity and Liberty* it is a Cupid figure exhorting: 'Shove her home boy'.

While Isabella is no fornicating nun, Shakespeare certainly recalls the latter stereotype of the lapsed Puritan in portraying Angelo. Although sex is only incidental to the real issue of power, power (despite Harold Firsch)[25] is no more an idol of the Puritan than the non-Puritan; nor does the idea of power corrupting apply with any special force to the Puritan. Angelo's exercise of power may be ill-considered at times; it is only with his attempted rape of Isabella that he outrightly abuses it. So if Shakespeare offers a dramatized warning of how it might be if Puritanism held sway, the case is somewhat undermined by too heavy reliance on the stereotype of sexual hypocrisy. If the laws which Angelo seeks to implement are harsh and unjust, it is hardly to the duke's credit that they still remain on the statute books; and still less so that he now seeks to reactivate them through the agency of this Puritan scapegoat. But there is interesting sleight of hand here. We are persuaded that Angelo's use of the law is partial and arbitrary, though in one important respect his treatment of Claudio moves in a quite opposite direction. But this is where he would run foul of the bias of British sexual legislation. Thus, under Elizabeth, women producing chargeable bastards were customarily whipped, 'though in 1593 the Commons rejected a proposal that the men be whipped too, for fear the penalty might chance upon gentlemen or men of quality, whom it were not fit to put to such a shame'. A bill of 1628 sought unsuccessfully to meet this problem with 'a hundred marks' fine for gentlemen and a whipping for others'.[26] Angelo, as one of the new-style administrators, ignores such nice distinctions. Claudio, a young man of consequence, is caught in the legal trap, and Angelo is unmoved by Escalus's appeal to breeding: 'this gentleman / Whom I would save had a most noble father' (II.i.6). This is far from being a play where moral judgments are made clear, despite Angelo's unsympathetic treatment. But given that, it may be assumed that tradition is being upheld here against him. This would square with the way that Claudio's crime is softened from the rape usually found in this story-type (a felony, and therefore punishable by death) to a betrothed lover's frolic.

This downgrading of the offence follows the lead provided by Whetstone's *Promos and Cassandra* (1578), where the hero 'hath defilde no nuptial bed, nor forced rape hath mov'd' (II.iii). But Angelo's counterpart doggedly persists in refusing 'To pardon him that dyd commit a Rape' (IV.ii).[27] There is more involved here than local insensitivity. Lyndal Roper notes how the new mood of Reformation resulted in the closing of the brothel in Augsburg, with the consequence that 'The boundary between prostitute and non-prostitute became blurred'.[28] This is where Angelo, or the law he represents, seems unnecessarily crude in failing to articulate or even register differences in extramarital sexual behaviour. In fact, Claudio's offence is equated with murder:

> It were as good
> To pardon him that hath from nature stolen
> A man already made, as to remit
> Their saucy sweetness that do coin God's image
> In stamps that are forbid.
>
> (II.iv.42)

This blurring, one of language and perception, is parodied in the verbal dislocations of Elbow, another representative of the law, who leaves us uncertain whether his wife is 'respected' or 'suspected' (II.i.168). A further dimension is added by Pompey's commentary, awash with innuendo and artfully poised between the politic and the absurd. He finally exculpates Froth from a charge of rape by compelling Escalus's agreement that Froth has a harmless face; and since 'his face is the worst thing about him, . . . how could Master Froth do the constable's wife any harm' (II.i.149).

If meaning is eroded so far that Angelo can equate the taking of life with the producing of it outside marriage, this is part of a larger confusion which is endemic in his society. He has more than a little in common with Claudio, having abandoned a wife by pre-contract because her dowry was lost at sea (III.i.219). Claudio's misfortunes have arisen because, although 'Upon a true contract' he has 'got possession of Julietta's bed', they have kept the relationship secret 'for propagation of a dower' (I.ii.133): the sex–cash equation is underscored by his choice of image. Even Isabella, who could recommend the simplest of solutions to this predicament: 'O, let him marry her!' (I.iv.48), is later provoked by Claudio's desire to live at the expense of her chastity into declaring: 'Thy sin's not accidental, but a trade' (III.i.151). Both Angelo and Claudio, the one more rigidly than the other, seem to have absorbed the idea that to make the orgasmic transaction worthwhile, it must be priced accordingly: a legitimate prostitution. Tourneur's *Atheist's Tragedy* (1607–11) makes it clear why instinct must be constrained by the market:

> If Reason were
> Our counsellour, wee would neglect the worke
> Of generation, for the prodigall
> Expence it drawes vs too, of that which is
> The wealth of life.[29]

>   (I.iv.90)

Literal and metaphoric become drawn into an ethical tangle in which the bourgeois values of reason and self-command are identified with profitability against eroticism. The latter is dangerous not only for its overmastering urgencies but also insofar as it is a powerful manifestation of human love. Traditionally, it is at best suspect in seeming to offer a route to happiness independent of both God and Mammon, so irredeemably democratic: 'Ends love in this, that my man, / Can be as happy'as I can . . . ?'.[30]

'Sure it is no sin', protests Claudio, only to concede that his religion deems otherwise: 'Or of the deadly seven it is the least' (III.i.112). But these sins had always been subject to politic grading. Henry Kraus notes how, in the twelfth century, when 'clamorous burghers' overtook the aristocracy as the Church's 'chief opponents, Pride was replaced by Greed as man's basic error'.[31] Such expedient juggling, to some of the more critical amongst non-Calvinist contemporaries of Shakespeare, might well have made suspect the very idea of mortal sin. At any rate, the sexual scene, though subject to the constraints of family and community, law and faith, was more complex than N.W. Bawcutt allows. Observing the vehemence with which Puritan extremists denounced extramarital sex, he claims that 'very few even of the more moderate Elizabethans would have believed, and none would have had the audacity to put into print, the position increasingly popular in the twentieth century that sexuality is a purely private matter'.[32] But from 1477 onwards, numerous publishers brought out Chaucer's *Canterbury Tales*, placing before readers that most memorable Wife of Bath for whom empiricism excels authority as a guide to human behaviour. For her, there is nothing fortuitous about the way that male and female genitals match; and that is justification enough for her mode of conduct. She has no wish to impose her values on others, having no quarrel with chastity *per se*: 'Crist was a mayde'.[33] But her very choice of example pitches her insistence on the right to decide for herself at a more threatening level than the merely sexual.[34]

She echoes the Lollards in advocating liberty of conscience; and their spiritual descendants were the Familists and Brownists who unsuccessfully sought religious toleration following the accession of James I. These antinomian sects were under attack from high churchman and Puritan alike. Indeed, Keith Thomas makes it clear that efforts to close the gap between precept and practice in sexual matters were by no means confined to the Puritan. It was 1604, probably the year of *Measure for Measure*'s first appearance, which saw a bill 'for the better repressing of the detestable crime of adultery' reach 'a second reading in the Lords'.[35] Royalist interest in such legislation is noted from Cornwall in 1642, where it was that faction which clamoured to see 'penal laws enacted for punishing of adulteries and divers other offences not punishable by common law'.[36] Probably one motive behind the 1650 act for the suppression of sexual offences, with its notorious introduction of a death-penalty for adultery, was the need 'to woo the Presbyterians in order to avert the threatened alliance with the royalists';[37] but it was a royalist journal which criticized the act as toothless.[38] Indeed, the royalist Aphra Behn pointed to its most effective feature when joking, in *The Round-Heads* (1681) V.ii, that 'there are many Grievances in that Act; but there are many Conveniences too, for it ties up the villanous Tongues of Men from boasting our Favours'.[39]

In part, *Measure for Measure* anticipates those pamphlets appearing in the wake of the act to protest at the new restrictions threatening the livelihood of brothel functionaries.[40] The latter, as in the play, are caught between the risks of continuing in their trade and the difficulty of not continuing when they have no obvious earning capacity outside it. But in Shakespeare's day enforcement of the Church's sexual code was as patchy in the brothel sector as elsewhere. When Mary came to the throne in 1553, the first act of her government was to abrogate all the laws of Henry VIII, including his proclamation of Easter 1546 outlawing the London stews. Although Elizabeth reversed the procedure, no clean-up of the brothel areas took place during her reign. In short, the situation was much as it appears before Angelo's takeover in the play, when the business was illegal but tolerated.

The only real shift between Henry's time and the end of the century was that the houses had passed from the Church, which gave 'whores indulgences to sin',[41] into private hands. At least one theatre owner, Philip Henslowe, had acquired leases on brothel property,[42] a reminder that both theatres and brothels were kept across the river to prevent contamination of the city. The arbitrary way in which one of them was eventually lifted to respectability indicates how notions of what constitutes vice are culturally determined. Hence prostitution's causal link with social disintegration must be more problematic than the duke allows. Pompey is alert to this in his first brush with the law, perceiving that the bawd's trade is lawful 'If the law would allow it' (II.i.217), and adding sagely: 'If your worship will take order for the drabs and the knaves, you need not to fear the bawds'. Later, the constable chides that he 'will needs buy and sell men and women like beasts, we shall have all the world drink brown and white bastard' (III.i.271). The pun on Spanish wine of this name suggests that unwanted babies are the central problem, threatening the social and financial equilibrium. Pompey responds obliquely with a neat indictment of socio-legal values: ''Twas never merry world since, of two usuries, the merriest was put down, and the worser allowed by order of law, a furred gown to keep him warm'. He implicitly raises two issues: the brothel is only the seamy outward face of that venality marking sex in more discreet circles; and, in a society dedicated to moneymaking, only the overt commercializing of sex is banned. Ostensibly promiscuous fun is the enemy of bourgeois sobriety, the mystery and absurdity of sex an affront to the dignity of market operations. But Pompey has already shown how scruples vanish at the chance of profit, reassuring Mistress Overdone that the order for demolishing 'All houses in the suburbs' will mean only a change of 'place', not of 'trade' (I.ii.99). The city brothels have been spared because 'a wise burgher put in for them' (l.92).[43] But Pompey himself must submit to social pressures when he is threatened with severe punishment unless he changes from 'unlawful bawd' to 'lawful hangman' (IV.ii.14). The provost, knowing the one to be a weapon of the coercive state he himself serves, can still insist that there is not a feather's difference between the two.[44]

Authority figures appreciate the psychology of the confessional. This shows not only in the duke's pose as priestly confessor but also when Escalus anticipates the modern policeman's manner in inviting Pompey's confession that he is a bawd: 'Come, tell me true; it shall be the better for you' (II.i.212). The duke identifies the twin faces of his power as 'terror' and 'love' (I.i.19), and though the terminology may change, the techniques of control which it represents do not. Even under his benign rule, 'the gallows' is said to be one of the reasons why Mistress Overdone is 'custom-shrunk' at the brothel (I.ii.79), and Barnardine has been imprisoned for nine years on mere suspicion (that proof is finally obtained hardly disposes of the problem). 'It was a mad, fantastical trick of him to steal from the state', comments Lucio on the duke's absence, emphasizing that his joke about that 'old fantastical Duke of dark corners' has a political as well as a sexual edge (III.i.358; IV.iii.152). Such remarks almost prove fatal; for 'Slandering a prince' he is to be 'whipped and hanged' (V.i.512). But before that he must wed the whore Kate Keepdown, who has borne his child. It is the discovery that this fate appals him far more than hanging which brings the duke to remit the other penalties, causing Lucio to rehearse the grisly rituals of ducal law in protest: 'Marrying a punk, my lord, is pressing to death, whipping, and hanging' (l.521).

If we assume that a majority amongst Globe audiences would have been untroubled about the human rights of such as Barnardine and Lucio, there   remain other problems which have worried modern critics. While some will argue for a wise and benevolent duke, both his wisdom and benevolence have been challenged. Herbert C. Weil, Jr, discussing Peter Brook's influential Stratford production of 1950, with the duke as ideal ruler, stresses that it was generally applauded for its 'faithfulness to Shakespeare's conception and text'.[45] But Weil shows that numerous cuts were made in the

duke's speeches, eliminating passages apt to render him unpleasant
or absurd. Both Pompey and Lucio lost lines which assert their
role as part of the play's critical intelligence, making the latter
'seem only a malicious and selfish gossip'.[46] Weil prefers to believe
'that the dramatist was experimenting with divergent ideas of his
controlling figure than that he had left us a badly flawed or
careless text'.[47] That 'divergent ideas' are present in the folio
text seems beyond doubt; but whether, as Weil believes, the
folio provides us with a manageable theatrical script as it stands
is another matter. The ducal role – by far the most substantial –
is the nub of the problem. As Brook showed, judicious cutting
will allow a favourable presentation of the duke. But a different
pattern of trimming will highlight his meddlesome or even sinister
aspects. The text contains both possibilities, but it is difficult to see
how they could have coexisted on the Jacobean stage any more
than on the modern. Other characters will respond to emphasis
or interpretation to fit either view of the duke. Thus the social or
legal attitude to the visible signs of Juliet's pregnancy is implied in
Claudio's lines:

> The stealth of our most mutual entertainment
> With character too gross is writ on Juliet.
>
>   (I.ii.142)

But whether we hear it as acceptance of a rebuke or rejection of
a calumny will depend on the actor. Similarly, Juliet's echo of the
supposed friar's loaded question, 'Love you the man that wronged
you?', may convey contrition or irony: 'Yes, as I love the woman
that wronged him' (II.iii.26). Still more ambiguous is 'I do repent
me as it is an evil' (l.37). But for some of the duke's utterances,
control must come via the directorial scalpel rather than nuance;
and the way that it is wielded will determine the meaning of these
young lovers' speeches.

The Brook case reminds us that there is a lot of difference
between a printed, and thus stabilized, text and a theatrical
script. It is understandable that critics always view the folio
text of *Measure for Measure*, the only one with bibliographical
authority, as an integral whole. A mid-seventeenth-century critic,
Yorkshireman William Sankey, set the precedent when censoring
a copy of the folio at Valladolid for the Holy Office. Whereas he
confined himself to occasional deletions in the other plays, the

whole of *Measure for Measure* was hacked out of the volume.[48] Later critics have followed the approach in a more reverential spirit. In the study the folio text, or a version refined by the techniques of modern bibliography, satisfies the reader's need. But theatrical imperatives – not necessarily less respectful – are of a different kind. The scholar makes choices, but the director's choices must be more immediate and decisive. They must result in a script which plays intelligibly and pleasurably on stage. And in the present case, cuts are necessary not simply in an attempt to bridge an historical gap. The 'original' script would have been modified to suit varying conditions of performance; playing at court, for instance, might involve some re-angling of what took place before less exalted audiences. Bearing in mind that no Jacobean book-keeper would waste time transcribing a manuscript which could be modified instead, it is likely that the folio text's problem for modern directors results from its combining separate performance options.

It is idle to speculate about how different approaches to the duke might have affected the comic roles on the early stage. But it is noteworthy that Isabella is on an easier footing with Lucio than is the duke. His moral laxity offers no threat to her own integrity, and it is he who hides unease at entering a convent behind an ironic greeting: 'Hail, virgin, if you be' (I.iv.16). The duke devastates Lucio with a punitive marriage, the institution becoming his way of imposing orderly solutions on the problems thrown up by the play. If this has the capacity to disturb, so has his own matrimonial desire which conflicts with Isabella's vocation. That the Roman Catholic Church operated an extensive underground in this country with a policy of political subversion would have alienated many people. It may be that the play promotes a *via media* of Anglicanism against the recusancy on both sides, the duke's functioning as monk an echo of Henry VIII's arrogating to himself the title Defender of the Faith. The duke's testing activities recall those of Walter in Chaucer's *Clerk's Tale* in producing unnecessary mental anguish. But there is theological justification. When God tests the loyalty of his servants he is bestowing a sign of his interest and even his favour: 'Happy is the man whom God correcteth' (Job 5:17). Drawing Isabella from the arid confines of the nunnery to take her place in the procreative scheme might command approval.[49] But Isabella makes no response and the play's ending must be renegotiated at every reading. In the end, theatrical evidence reminds that this text requires little enough doctoring to produce either a benign duke or one whose relationship with Isabella is as coercive as Angelo's: 'Somewhere along the way, the Duke becomes attracted to her. In retrospect, his ruses, his testing – especially the cruel deception as to the death of her brother – looks alarmingly like a sado-masochistic game'.[50]

Conclusion

No artist can escape the constraints of his own time: all art is contemporary. But there has been a long-standing concern to interpret the word differently in the case of Shakespeare: he is *our* contemporary. This position, a dominant one until not so long ago, has its own interest. It has not, however, been endorsed in the foregoing: Shakespeare may speak *to* us; he manifestly does not speak *for* us. He is culturally too distant for that, though the point made in the last chapter about the text of *Measure for Measure* reminds that not everything is changed. It is still normal practice for theatre scripts to undergo modification both in rehearsal and for revivals. So if the version of the play preserved in the folio is a composite text, it means only that traces of customary change survived in the copy finding its way to the printer. In this sense, most play-texts are works of collaboration. And the claim that Shakespeare would have used his power as sharer in the theatre to maintain control over changes to his scripts is a guess prompted more by reverential than scholarly considerations. Charles Frey is aware of how tenuously based are 'methods of attribution that fail to take into account the many layers of managerial, scribal, and compositorial intermediaries that probably lie between authorial manuscript and Quarto print'.[1] He refers specifically to *The Two Noble Kinsmen*, but the point might be extended to other works in the Shakespeare canon. This is not to espouse a disintegrationist cause, but to emphasize the special nature of a play-text. And this is before we address the question of more formal collaboration.

Of 415 ascribed plays listed by Harbage for Shakespeare's 24 active years, more than a quarter are known works of collaboration. That Shakespeare was involved in collaboration both early in his career (*Sir Thomas More*) and at the end (*Henry VIII, Two Noble*

Kinsmen) is widely accepted. Frey has called in question the premises on which reassuring scientific proofs of Shakespearean authorship are based. But whether other works in the canon are the results of collaboration seems more a matter of political than of artistic moment, since as a theatrical writer Shakespeare was committed to a necessarily collaborative enterprise. The fierceness with which Shakespearean integrity is defended shows what is at stake. Brian Morris claims that theatrical collaborations 'were rough-and-ready affairs based on dividing responsibility for plot and sub-plot, or Act by Act, or scene by scene'.[2] But such divisions of responsibility had advanced well beyond the rough-and-ready stage in various artistic fields. They had achieved highly unified results in the manuscript *ateliers* of the previous century, and were still employed by mainstream painters. Some of Fletcher's collaborations, including those with Shakespeare, show a high degree of sophistication, and the authors of *Eastward Hoe* match their talents very skilfully. Jonson, one of the trio responsible for the latter play, may have joined forces with Chapman in *Sejanus* too. But in his preface he points out that the printed text 'is not the same with that which was acted on the publike Stage, wherein a second Pen had good share', preferring to substitute his own 'weaker (and no doubt lesse pleasing)' version for that of the collaborator.[3]

So once the playtext leaves the theatrical domain, different values come into play. As we have noted, the primacy of the scriptwriter was a cause behind which Jonson threw his full weight. Just how effectively this worked on Shakespeare's behalf needs no demonstration. But another dimension shows up in the recent acceptance of *The Two Noble Kinsmen* into the canon. Suddenly it has rated that special attention which only Shakespeare commands. And since it is hardly possible to give close attention to the Shakespearean half of the play, assuming that his share can be positively determined, and not to Fletcher's, the latter too comes under the microscope. 'We may not be used to discussing Fletcherian dialogue so subtly', say Madelon Lief and Nicholas Radel with a hint of embarrassment.[4] But the alternative threatens to be like marking an examination script according to expectation rather than performance: the discredited theory of post-Shakespearean decadence still leaves an afterglow.

Serious critical interest in Shakespeare's collaborations is one of two major developments in recent years. The other is the recognition that Shakespeare is not always giving expression to views of which we may approve. Peter Berek, contributing to a volume entitled *'Bad' Shakespeare*, comments on our 'problems with Shakespeare's portrayals of blacks and Jews', suggesting that 'We have few problems with Shakespeare's monarchist ideas only because there is no serious current debate in which those ideas matter'.[5] Alexander Leggatt, reviewing the collection, fastens on to the question: 'can bad values generate good art'. It is one, he suspects, which 'is going to confront us more and more as our values move farther from Shakespeare's'.[6] Probably the reality is that, until recently, the extent to which our values had shifted from those of Shakespeare's time – which he must inescapably represent – had been masked by that powerful coalition of forces which made him the only uncontested choice for the national curriculum in secondary school English studies.

All the same, the *Realpolitik* which he sets in motion before us is entirely familiar. And his representation of the Jew, enemy of Christendom, is more balanced than many a modern representation of the Communist, enemy of capitalism. What is deemed to be good art depends on a whole complexity of cultural assumptions. It is easy enough to forget what bad ideas underlie the good art of Raphael when he represents Pope Julius II, a Renaissance Mussolini, with his Swiss bully-boys. But the shadow of Auschwitz falls across Shylock, so that a recent director of the play persuades himself that a twentieth-century Shakespeare would have brought *The Merchant of Venice* into line with current liberal sensibilities. Such a reincarnation would be truer to original form if the latter continued to complicate his image of the Jew, victim of the vilest persecution certainly, but also innovator of modern terrorism in the shape of the Stern Gang.

For the post-moderns, Shakespeare has been in danger of succumbing to his own publicity. The idea that he speaks for all time has been around for so long that it is shed only with considerable discomfort. For the most part he is read in modernized texts which encourage the delusion that he is a modern. So when the reader encounters views which are manifestly of Shakespeare's own time and culture rather than ours, the result can be demoralizing. That the myth has not been more comprehensively discredited is due to two factors: cultural conditioning and Shakespeare's habitual slipperiness. Since he avoids the narrowly ideological, he has become all things to all men. But present tendencies suggest that some women are less impressed. Shakespeare's was a society which theorized extensively about the subordination of women, though the actual condition was the common lot of most people, men and women alike. But when the few have control over the many it is needful to have the latter collude in their own subjection. Dividing is the secret of such ruling, and to offer the powerless an illusion of power confuses them into believing they have a stake in the system of oppression. That they are permitted to wield the little stick under strictly controlled conditions seems to legitimize the wielding of the big stick across their own backs. The technique, though not unrecognized ('The working class can kiss my arse, I've got the foreman's job at last'), continues effective. Sexual demarcation is particularly useful in these power moves, since like skin pigment its physical effacement is nearly impossible. Hence the new feminists' project to dispense with conventional man–woman categories, and their hostile view of heterosexuality.

'Teacher bans Romeo and Juliet for being heterosexual' howls the headline of a front-page article by John O'Leary, education editor of *The Times* (20 January 1994). The teacher concerned, 'head of Kingsmead School in Hackney, explained that until books, films and the theatre reflected all forms of sexuality, she would not be involving her pupils in heterosexual culture'. Her position was attacked by the Education Secretary as 'creeping political correctness', though it is unclear whether this was before or after the egg-attack which an adjacent article reports that he himself sustained while speaking at the London School of Economics. One interesting feature is that, while the teacher's ban had been imposed on a trip to the ballet, the opposition took it as an affront to Shakespeare, a fellow teacher defiantly protesting that he would continue to teach 'this great play'. Even a colleague seeking to defend her against charges of 'trying to promote homosexuality' felt constrained to add: 'Shakespeare wrote brilliantly about gang fights, teenage sexuality and suicide. But we want the children to . . . see that you can be a boy and be gentle'.

Not least interesting in this pattern of changing social values is the challenge to the culture hero. The shift in social values giving rise to the controversy is reproduced on many fronts, including that of the prostitute discussed in the last chapter. At different periods the harlot's motivation has varied from religious devotion to hatred of men, with corresponding shifts in social valuation. In Jacobean London, the pressures of poverty were fully recognized: 'want will perjure / The ne'er-touched vestal' (*Antony and Cleopatra* III.xii.30). Shakespeare's attitudes towards the institution, which was as much a subject of debate as that of marriage, are firmly of his time.

One respect in which the prostitute of Shakespeare's day might resemble her modern rather than medieval counterpart is noted by Gervaise Markham, not Shakespeare. The protagonist of his *Famovs Whore* (1609) had read and imbibed Aretino,

> So that his book-rules I could well discouer
> To euery ignorant, yet wanton louer.
>
> (C4ᵛ)

Like practically everything else by this time, her activities were taking some of their definition from print. Aretino would provide more than a practical manual. To find one's attitudes or modes of behaviour represented in print would have been a great boost to confidence, helping to settle patterns in an unsettled world. Thus Shakespeare repeatedly uses the phrase 'in print' to mean 'with exactness or precision'.[7] But those Jack Cade scenes discussed earlier (p. 29) or Biron's prioritizing of experience over reading (pp. 149, 164) are signs that anxiety over print as a destabilizing force were well understood by Shakespeare. A couple of generations on, they are given expression by John Aubrey when noting that 'till a little before the Civil-warres, the ordinary sort of People were not taught to reade'. But now, 'the divine art of Printing and Gunpowder have frighted away Robin-good-fellow and the Fayries'.[8] That he has immediately in mind those civil wars and an antiquarian's regret at the passing of a slice of oral culture does not blunt the effect of his linking print with gunpowder – or the sense that the former had proved the more explosive.

Notes

Full details of works cited in abbreviated form may be found in the bibliography.

Journal abbreviations
MLN   *Modern Language Notes*
MLR   *Modern Language Review*
N&Q   *Notes and Queries*

Introduction
1   'The Soul of the Age: Towards a Historical Approach to Shakespeare', in *Shakespeare in a Changing World*, ed. A. Kettle (Lawrence & Wishart, 1964) 17–42 (p. 28).
2   'The Taming of the Scold: the Enforcement of Patriarchal Authority in Early Modern England' in *Order and Disorder in Early Modern England*, ed. A Fletcher and J. Stevenson (Cambridge University Press, 1987) 116–36 (p. 129).

Chapter 1   The Shakespearean Reputation
1   Kirschbaum, p. 32.
2   See Sonnets 19 and 81. This had become not only a commonplace of European poetry, but helps to explain the rise of portraiture in the sixteenth century. Licinio's painting of his brother's family (*c*.1535, Borghese Gallery, Rome: in Jane Martineau and Charles Hope, *The Genius of Venice 1500–1600* (London: Royal Academy of Arts, 1983, p. 174) has a Latin inscription, claiming that the artist prolonged life for the family with their image and for himself with his art.
3   *Sunday Times* and *Observer* (2 August 1964).
4   Lectures on Shakespeare, etc. (rept. London: Dent/New York: Dutton, 1951) p. 156.
5   *All's Well that Ends Well* (Cambridge University Press, 1955) p. xxiv.
6   *Rvbbe, and A great Cast* (1614) sig. K3 (II.92).

7 *The Amanda Group of Bagford Poems*, ed. J.W. Ebsworth (Hertford: Ballad Society, 1880) p. 531. Similarly, Thomas Robinson, *The Anatomy of the English Nvnnery at Lisbon* (1622) p. 17, describes how the nuns' confessor, who enjoyed a bawdy relationship with them, would 'reade a little of *Venus and Adonis*' or similar 'scurrilous booke'.

8 John Bossy, *Giordano Bruno and the Embassy Affair* (New Haven/London: Yale University Press, 1991) p. 176. Roesslin's *The Birth of Mankynde*, in Raynolde's 1545 translation the first printed treatise on midwifery in English, served a similar purpose. Midwives urged that the work was 'a slaunder to women, forsomuche as therein was descried and set foorth the secretes and priuities of woman, and that euerye boye and knaue hadde of these bookes, reading them as openly as the tales of Robin hood' (ed. 1565, Prologue sig.C1ᵛ). Following its translation in 1595, Aristotle's *Problems* is frequently found in lists of pornography.

9 Dodsley, X, p. 158.

10 *Roxburghe Ballads*, IV, p. 17.

11 D'Urfey, VI, p. 220.

12 Beaumont and Fletcher, VIII, p. 312.

13 Printed with William Wright's *The Oxford Alderman's Speech to the D. of M.* (Oxford? 1681).

14 *The Dramatic Works*, ed. A. H. Bullen (London, 1887) I, p. 111.

15 Dekker, ed. Bowers, I, pp. 372, 311.

16 'A Short View of Tragedy' (1693), in Spingarn, II, p. 219.

17 New York: Putnam, 1963, p. 20.

18 William Sampson, *The Vow-breaker*, ed. H. Wallrath (Louvain: Uystpruyst, 1914).

19 *Amusements*, p. 221.

20 See *DSL*, two-backed beast.

21 *Dramatic Works*, III, p. 67; II, pp. 50, 292, 275.

22 *Dramatic Works*, II, p. 277.

23 *OED*, quoting from Coles, *Latin Dictionary*, 1678.

24 *Dramatic Works*, V, p. 7.

25 *Pepys Ballads*, III, p. 118.

26 *Shakespeare's Bawdy* (London: Routledge and Kegan Paul, 1961) p. 50.

Chapter 2 Performance versus Text

1 'Royal Shakespeare: Theatre and the Making of Ideology' in *Political Shakespeare. New Essays in Cultural Materialism*, ed. Jonathan Dollimore and Alan Sinfield (Manchester University Press, 1985) 158–81 (p. 175).

2   *Shakespearean Tragedy*, p. 386.
3   *The Extra-Dramatic Moment in Elizabethan Plays before 1616* (University of Philadelphia, 1930) p. 8.
4   *Histrio-Mastix: The Players Scovrge* (1633) p. 930.
5   *Shakespeare's Clown* (Cambridge University Press, 1987) p. 164; Chambers, *The Elizabethan Stage*, IV, p. 340.
6   Chambers, II, p. 365.
7   *The Arte of English Poesie*, ed. Edward Arber (London: Constable, 1906) p. 42.
8   *The Works of John Lyly*, ed. R. Warwick Bond (Oxford: Clarendon, 1902) III, p. 115.
9   *Non-Dramatic Prose Works*, III, p. 340.
10 *Jonson*, ed. Herford and Simpson, VI, p. 16.
11 Translated in *The Times* (20 Nov. 1839) from *La France Musicale*.
12 *Complete Method of Singing* (Boston: Oliver Ditson, 1851?) p. 94: he is reacting against the way that the practice 'for the past 60 years has been carried to an extreme, even to abuse'. Percy A. Scholes, *The Mirror of Music 1844–1944* (London: Novello/Oxford University Press, 1947) I, p. 282.
13 See Louis B. Wright, 'Will Kemp and the *Commedia dell' arte*', *MLN*, XLI, 8 (Dec. 1926) 516–20.
14 'What is a Text?', *Research Opportunities in Renaissance Drama*, 24 (1981) 3–6 (pp. 6, 3).
15 Alfred Hart, *Stolne and Surreptitious Copies* (Melbourne/London: Melbourne University Press, 1942) pp. 290, 119–49.
16 *The Bad Quarto of 'Romeo and Juliet'* (Ithaca, New York: Cornell University Press, 1948) p. 93.
17 *Romeo and Juliet: Parallel Texts of the First Two Quartos*, ed. P.A. Daniel (London: New Shakspere Soc., 1874) p. 70.
18 Cf. Middleton's quibble in *The Family of Love* (*c*.1602: *Works*, III, p. 98) V.i.123, where a physician muses on his would-be cuckolders: 'I know you ha' the horn of plenty for me, which you would derive unto me from the liberality of your bawdies, not your minds'.
19 This proverbial expression (Tilley H522) similarly indicates a suspected whore in Middleton's *Fair Quarrel* (*c*.1617; *Works*, IV, p. 263) V.i.133. For the anatomical implications, see *DSL*, hole in one's coat.
20 *Cupid's Whirligig* (1607) I.ii.146: *Works*, p. 445.
21 *Popular Appeal in English Drama to 1850* (Totowa, New Jersey: Barnes & Noble, 1982) p. 41.
22 *The Poems of Sir John Oldham*, ed. Harold F. Brooks and Raman Selden (Oxford: Clarendon, 1987) p. 69.

23 *Shakespearean Tragedy*, p. 259.
24 See *DSL*, stick 2.
25 Schultze-Gallera, p. 7; Paul Sartori 'Der Schuh im Volksglauben', *Zeitschrift des Vereins für Volkskunde*, IV (Berlin 1894) p. 49.
26 Michael Ratcliffe, *Observer* (8 Nov. 1987).

Chapter 3   Censorship and Evasion
 1 When Charles V banned it in 1521, the year after he had become Holy Roman Emperor, that too was politically motivated. See Sidney L. Jackson, 'Printed Books and the Mass Mind', *Libri: International Library Review*, 18 (1968) 35–50 (p. 39).
 2 *The Statutes of the Realm* (London: Dawson, 1810–28) III, p. 896.
 3 Hirsch, p. 87.
 4 Chambers, IV, p. 265.
 5 Sir Philip Sidney, *An Apology for Poetry*, ed. Geoffrey Shepherd (London: Nelson, 1965) p. 117.
 6 Chambers, IV, p. 263.
 7 Ibid., p. 270.
 8 Ibid., p. 316.
 9 J.Q. Adams (ed.) *The Dramatic Records of Sir Henry Herbert Master of the Revels, 1623–1673* (New Haven: Yale University Press; London: Oxford University Press, 1917) p. 6.
10 Ibid., p. 23.
11 Ibid., pp. 20–1; 53.
12 *Dramatic Works*, III, p. 155.
13 Ibid., p. 149, though Gifford retains the 1637 compositor's misreading 'slicke'. Shirley clearly borrows the German *stichfrei* (*DSL*, stick free).
14 Despite his hostility to Cade, Hall in his *Chronicle* records that the rebel leader prohibited 'Murder, Rape, or Robbery' (appended to the Arden *2 Henry VI*, ed. Andrew S. Cairncross (London: Methuen rept, 1969, p. 170).
15 Henri Stein, 'La Papeterie d'Essones', *Annales de la Société Historique et Archéologique du Gatinais*, XII (1894) pp. 335–64 (p. 354).
16 See *DSL*, kiss.
17 W.W. Greg, *Two Elizabethan Stage Abridgements: The Battle of Alcazar and Orlando Furioso* (Malone Soc., 1922) p. 141.
18 *Hengist, King of Kent; or The Mayor of Queenborough*, ed. R.C. Bald (New York/London: Scribner's, 1938).
19 Ed. George B. Ferguson (The Hague/London/Paris: Mouton, 1966).
20 Ibid., Introduction, p. 34.
21 *A Critical Edition of MS Dyce 9 (1625)*, ed. John Gerritsen (Groningen, Djakarta: J.B. Wolters, 1952).

22 It perhaps indicates late Elizabethan anxiety about such disclosure that 'Dr. Rainolds cites a remarkable instance of stage nudity in a Jesuit play' by way of warning: J.W. Binns, 'Women or Transvestites on the Elizabethan Stage?: An Oxford Controversy', *Sixteenth Century Journal*, II (1974) 95–120 (p. 113).

23 Spingarn, II, p. 288.

24 Chambers, IV, p. 209.

25 Jonson, ed. Herford and Simpson, V, p. 338; Dekker, ed. Bowers, II, p. 428.

26 Middleton, *Works*, III, p. 169.

27 John Feather, 'Robert Armin and the Chamberlain's Men', *N&Q*, 217 (1972) 448–50, suggests that he joined in 1598, requiring a date after that to which *Two Maids* is assigned. This is because the play subsequently belonged to the Children of the Revels, and he cannot conceive of the Chamberlain's Men releasing it to a rival company. But someone evidently did, since the boy company seems only to have operated in 1607–8; and a parallel would be provided by its acquisition of Middleton's *Family of Love*, a newer play, from the Admiral's (or by that date Prince Henry's) Men. Gary Taylor, 'The Date and Auspices of the Additions to *Sir Thomas More*' in *Shakespeare and 'Sir Thomas More'*, ed. T.H. Howard-Hill (Cambridge, etc.: Cambridge University Press, 1989) 101–29 (p. 104), mentions similar changes of ownership.

28 Straightforward argument for the folio text as representing a later version of the play than the 1602 quarto has properly been rejected. The folio apparently includes occasional material from a 1597 première already replaced in 1602. But it would be equally rash to assume that the entire folio text has a pre-1602 provenance.

29 *Works*, V, p. 323.

30 *Arundel Harington MS*, I, p. 219.

31 Cf. Downes, *Roscius Anglicanus* (1708), ed. Judith Milhous and Robert D. Hume (London: Soc. for Theatre Research, 1987) p. 53, on a Restoration performance of *Romeo and Juliet*: 'Mrs. *Holden* . . . enter'd in a *Hurry*, Crying, O my Dear *Count*! She Inadvertently left out, O, in the pronuntiation of the Word *Count*', which reduced the audience to hysterics.

32 See *DSL*, cock 1.

33 Bullough, II, p. 483.

34 Daniel Turner, *Syphillis* (1727) p. 342, mocks a translation by Willoughby: 'prick forth *(for Goodness sake, what Term is that?)* in burnish'd Steel'.

35 *Works*, I, p. 20. He uses it again in *More Dissemblers Besides Women*

Notes

237

(c.1615) III.ii.108 (VI, p. 432); and cf. Marston's *Plays*, III, p. 28 where, in *The Insatiate Countesse* (c.1610) II.i, the writer of a love-letter is said not to have 'left out a pricke'.
36 Dodsley, IX, p. 288.
37 See *DSL*, club, codpiece.
38 *Arundel Harington MS*, II, p. 80.
39 See *DSL*, inch.
40 Montaigne, II.xvii (II, p. 442); Tilley M553.
41 Chambers, IV, pp. 199, 216.
42 *Shepheards Garland* (1593): *Works*, ed. J.W. Hebel (Oxford: Shakespeare Head, 1951) I, p. 55.
43 *Observer* (16 Dec. 1962).
44 *The Common Muse*, ed. V. de Sola Pinto and A.E. Rodway (London: Chatto & Windus, 1957) p. 37.
45 *The Theme of the Three Caskets*, in *The Complete Psychological Works*, XII (London: Hogarth Press and Institute of Psycho-Analysis, 1958) p. 295.

Chapter 4   The First Print Era: Reader-Spectator as Voyeur
1 The title of Humfre Lloyd's 1550 translation: see ed. 1558, sig. O6ᵛ.
2 *The Poems*, I, p. 121.
3 *The Cambridge History of the Bible 2: The West from the Fathers to the Reformation*, ed. G.W.H. Lampe (Cambridge University Press, 1969) p. 441.
4 Formerly in the Contini Bonacossi Collection, Florence: T. Pignatti, *Veronese* (Venice, 1976) II, fig. 813.
5 *Arcadia*, p. 285.
6 Contemporaries delighted to show that they penetrated Sidney's code, and were therefore in the literary-social swim; see Hoyt H. Hudson, 'Penelope Devereux as Sidney's Stella', *Huntington Library Bulletin*, 7 (1935) 89–129.
7 'Disclosures in Print: The "Violent Enlargement" of the Renaissance Voyeuristic Text', *Studies in English Literature*, 29 (1989) 35–59.
8 Ned Ward, *Writings* (3rd edn, 1706) II, p. 364.
9 Taylor, *Workes*, II, p. 112.
10 *Works: Poems*, p. 255.
11 *Dramatic Works*, V, p. 336.
12 *Ovids Metamorphosis* (Oxford, 1632) p. 100.
13 Dunbar, p. 43; Chaucer, l. 2353.
14 Nath. Hodges, *Loimologia. Or an Historical Account of the Plague in London in 1665* (3rd edn, 1721) p. 77 refers to 'that Expence of Spirit' which coition entails.

15 'The Waste Land', *Collected Poems 1909–1935* (London: Faber, 1958) p. 70.
16 A commonplace (*DSL*, cunt 2).
17 Nashe, *Works*, III, p. 276; Marston, *Plays*, II, p. 201; *King Lear*, xx.122 (*DSL*, hell).
18 *An Elizabethan in 1582: The Diary of Richard Madox, Fellow of All Souls*, ed. E.S. Donno (London: Hakluyt Soc., 1976) p. 108.
19 Dodsley, XII, p. 246. Cf. *Merchant of Venice* I.ii.41, on the prince who shoes his own horses: 'I am much afeard my lady his mother played false with a smith'; *Henry V* V.ii.223, where Henry's father 'thinking of civil wars when he got me', fitted him for the battlefield rather than the boudoir; and *Measure for Measure* III.i.369, where cold Angelo is supposed 'not made by man and woman, after this downright way of creation. . . . Some report a sea-maid spawned him, some that he was begot between two stockfishes'.
20 *The Works*, ed. Thomas Keynes (London: Faber, 2nd edn, 1964) II, p. 466.

Chapter 5   Roman Rapes
1   *The Scholemaster* (1570): *English Works*, ed. W.A. Wright (Cambridge University Press, 1904) p. 275.
2   *Elegy on Randolph's Finger*, ed. G.C. Moore Smith (Oxford: Blackwell, 1923) p. 13.
3   Ovid, tr. Golding, pp. 8, 18.
4   Cited by Louis B. Wright, *Middle Class Culture in Elizabethan England* (rept. London: Methuen, 1964) pp. 133, 112.
5   *Works*, II, p. 55. Cf. *Hæc-Vir* (1620) sig. C^v: 'Goodnesse leaue mee, if I haue not heard a Man court his Mistris with the same words that *Venus* did *Adonis*, or as neere as the Booke could instruct him'.
6   *I Ragionamenti*, II.i, pp.123, 152.
7   Georgina Masson, *Courtesans of the Italian Renaissance* (London: Secker & Warburg, 1975) pp. 115–21, 156–61.
8   *Works and Life: Poems*, p. 61.
9   G.B. Pezzini, S. Massari, and S.P.V. Rodinò, *Raphael Invenit. Stampe da Raffaello nelle Collezione dell'Istituto Nazionale per la Grafica* (Rome: Quasar, 1985) p. 793.
10 F.W.H. Hollstein, *German Engravings, Etchings and Woodcuts ca.1400–1700*, II (Amsterdam: Hertzberger, 1954) pp. 38–9.
11 *Vita di Gian Lorenzo Bernini*, ed. Sergio S. Ludovici (Milan: Edizioni del Milione, 1948) p. 151.
12 *Imagines*, tr. Arthur Fairbanks (London: Heinemann/Cambridge, Mass.: Harvard University Press, 1960) p. 17 (I.4).
13 Reproduced in *Old Master Paintings* (London: Thos. Agnew, 1978)

pl. 34; another version appears in Noemi Gabrielli, *Galleria Sabauda Maestri Italiani* (Turin: Ilte, 1971) fig. 160.

14 See *DSL*, do reason.

15 He has spliced it with a term borrowed from *Henry VIII* I.iv.12, where Sandys, coarsely eyeing Wolsey's women guests, would evidently exchange the cardinal's dinner for 'a running banquet' (quick fornication) with one of them.

16 *Works*, II, p. 57. For other notable Shakespearean uses see *DSL*, trim.

17 Cf. D'Urfey on old plays in his Prologue to *The Injured Princess* (1682), which borrows extensively from *Cymbeline*, including the scene in Imogen's bedroom. He is anxious to persuade that '*Old Plays like Mistresses*, . . . *Long after please, whom they before had cloy'd*'. But he hedges his bets with the suggestion that this is a new play, for it is they which draw audiences '*Like Bride-grooms, hot to go to Bed ere noon*'.

Chapter 6 Sexual Temptresses

1 Tomasso Garzoni, *The Hospitall of Incurable Fooles* (1600) p. 83. Cleopatra's continuing reputation in this way shows in Fletcher and Massinger's *The False One* (*c*.1620; Beaumont and Fletcher, VIII, p. 160) III.ii.32 which renders her as 'a witch' full of 'damn'd inchantment', as does May's *Cleopatra* (1626).

2 *The Florida of the Inca*, p. 299.

3 Taylor, *Workes*, II, p. 108.

4 Besides Marlowe's *Massacre at Paris* (1593), Henslowe bought from Dekker and Drayton on 30 December 1598 'A Booke called the 3 pte of the syvell wares of france' (*Diary*, ed. R.A. Foakes and R.T. Rickert, Cambridge University Press, 1961 p. 103). In Fletcher's *Woman's Prize* (1604 or later) III.iii.58 (Beaumont and Fletcher, IV, p. 67), an order is placed for hangings 'of the civill wars of *France*, / Let 'em be large and lively, and all silke work'.

5 *List and Analysis of State Papers. Foreign Series Elizabeth I*, vol.I (August 1589 – June 1590), ed. Richard Bruce Wernham (London: HMSO, 1964) pp. 400, 415.

6 *Deutsche Illustrierte Flugblätter des 16. und 17. Jahrhunderts, vol.I, pt.1: Die Sammlung der Herzog August Bibliothek in Wolfenbüttel*, ed. Wolfgang Harms (Tübingen: Max Niemeyer, 1985) p. 203.

7 Dunbar, p. 57; Aretino, *Ragionamenti*, I.ii.56; *The Plays of Nathan Field*, ed. William Peery (Austin: University of Texas, 1950) p. 164.

8 Roy Strong, *Gloriana: The Portraits of Queen Elizabeth I* (Thames & Hudson, 1987) p. 34.

9 As late as 1585 interest was expressed in a match between Elizabeth

and the Duke of Lorraine, represented as heir to the Danish throne: *Calendar of State Papers, Foreign Series*, XIX (Aug. 1584–Aug. 1585), ed. Sophie Crawford Lomas (London: HMSO, 1916) p. 434.

10 *List and Analysis of State Papers*, ed. Wernham, II (1969) pp. 112, 173, 185, 189.

11 Introduction to his Oxford Shakespeare edn, p. 10.

12 Bullen, *Collection*, III, p. 286.

13 Mary Harron, *Observer* (17 May 1987).

14 *Astraea: The Imperial Theme in the Sixteenth Century* (London/Boston: Routledge, 1975) p. 75.

15 Thomas Lake, in this letter (1 Oct. 1591) to Sir Robert Sydney, also reports that 'French matters go waywardly. The Queen has fallen out with the King': *Historical Manuscripts Commission. Report on the Manuscripts of Lord De L'Isle & Dudley Preserved at Penshurst Place*, vol.II, ed. C.L. Kingsford (London: HMSO, 1934) p. 123.

16 *The Poems*, ed. Phyllis Brooks Bartlett (New York: Russell, rept. 1969) p. 33.

17 *The Odes and Epodes*, tr. C.E. Bennett (London: Heinemann/Cambridge, Mass.: Harvard University Press, 1946) p. 377.

18 *Westward Ho*, III.iv.56 (Dekker, III, p. 358).

19 *Anatomy* (tr. John Streater, 1668) p. 74.

20 *Ar't Asleepe Husband?* (1640) Appx.

21 Bullough, V, p. 251.

22 Bullen, *Collection*, IV, p. 262.

23 *Plutarch's Lives of the Noble Grecians and Romans*, tr. Sir Thomas North, 1579 (London: David Nutt, 1895–6) VI, pp. 23, 25.

24 J.D. Mylius, *Opus medico-chymicum* (1618), illustrates 'Cleopatra Ægypti Regina' in this way; reproduced in Stanislas Klossowski de Rola, *The Golden Game: Alchemical Engravings of the Seventeenth Century* (New York: George Braziller, 1988) p. 140.

25 Max J. Friedländer and Jakob Rosenberg, *The Paintings of Lucas Cranach* (New York: Tabard, 1978) pl. 272–5.

26 Reproductions appear in Edward Hodnett, *English Woodcuts 1480–1535* (Oxford University Press, 1973) fig. 230; E. Major and E. Gradmann, *Vrs Graf* (London: Home and Van Thal, 1947) pl. 39; Geisberg I, p. 376. In a version by Peter Flötner, in Eduard Fuchs, *Geschichte der erotischen Kunst* (Munich: A. Langen nd) fig. 157, the fool blows a horn and prods the woman's genitals with a phallic blossom.

27 *Complete Works*, ed A.B. Grosart (Blackburn: Chertsey Worthies' Library, 1878) II, p. 9

28 Shakespeare is one of many writers who uses 'the rot' (*Timon*, IV.iii.64) as pox synonym (*DSL*, rot).

29 Parker's translation of *Forty-six Lives* does not include that of Cleopatra. Lydgate, in his *Fall of Princes*, based on Boccaccio's *De Casibus Illustrium Virorum*, ed. Henry Bergen, 4 vols (London: EETS, 1924–27), VI.3620, skips over the tragedy of Antony and Cleopatra because he has been anticipated by Chaucer.

30 Adam Fox, 'Ballads, Libels and Popular Ridicule in Jacobean London', *Past and Present*, 145 (Nov. 1994) 47–83 (p. 52).

31 Jacquart and Thomasset, p. 79.

32 Andrew Stephen, Washington, 'When the going got tough, women GIs wouldn't go', *Observer*, 21 Jan. 1990.

33 *Arcadia*, p. 121 (I.11).

34 Quoted by G.G. Gervinus, *Shakespeare Commentaries*, tr. F.E. Bunnett (rept. London: Smith, Elder, 1892) p. 724.

35 John Cleland, *Memoirs of a Woman of Pleasure* (New York: Putnam's, 1963) p. 186

36 See *DSL*, garland.

37 See *DSL*, stride, port.

38 *Plays*, I, p. 199; Rabelais, *Gargantua and Pantagruel*, II.1. Cf. the current gesture, bequeathed by Italy, of an upwardly jerked forearm with clenched fist.

39 William Buttes, *Dyets Dry Dinner* (1599, sig. B2) mentions the Eden tradition. The fig tree as passion-queller is noted by both Pliny, *Natural History*, 23.64.130, and Plutarch, *Quaestiones conviviales*, 2.7 and 6.10; G. Rogers, *The Horn Exalted* (1661, p. 59) recalls it.

40 For a contemporary use see Edward Sharpham, *Cupid's Whirligig* (1607) V.vii.42 (*Works*, p. 515).

Chapter 7   Trojan Whores

 1 C.S. Lewis, *English Literature in the Sixteenth Century Excluding Drama* (Oxford: Clarendon, 1954) p. 84.

 2 *Ars Poetica*: *Works*, XI (1946), pp. 147–52.

 3 A.P. Rossiter, *Angel with Horns*, ed. Graham Storey (London: Longman, rept. 1970) p.130.

 4 *On Romances*, p. 6.

 5 *Chapman's Homer*, ed. Allardyce Nicoll (London: Routledge and Kegan Paul, 1957) I, p. 546.

 6 Ibid., p. 545.

 7 Cinthio, *On Romances*, p. 55.

 8 Ibid., pp. 19, 20.

 9 *Acts and Monuments of Matters most speciall and memorable, happening in the Church*, 8th edn (London, 1641) II, p. 362.

10 Una Ellis-Fermor, *Shakespeare's Drama*, ed. Kenneth Muir (London/New York: Methuen, 1980) pp. 123, 126.

11 John Donne, 'An Anatomie of the World' (1611): *Poems*, I, p. 237.

12 Wind, *Pagan Mysteries*, pp. 85–94.

13 Conventionally, sexual ardour either inspires the martialist or distracts him, as Sidney shows respectively in *Astrophil and Stella* 41 and 53. Chrétien de Troyes's Lancelot provides the *locus classicus*, in *Le Chevalier de la Charrete*, ed. M. Roques (Paris: Champion, 1958) 3675 ff. The thirteenth-century *Aucassin et Nicolette*, ed. M. Roques, 2nd edn (Paris: Champion, 1936) p. 10, playfully represents the hero so full of thoughts of his lady that he is captured without striking a blow. But the prospect of being put to death, and thus separated from Nicolette permanently, prompts a killing spree in which he despatches the enemy leader and thus ends the war.

14 Cf. Heywood's *Iron Age, Part II* (1612–13 V.i (*Works*, III, p. 415), where Synon recalls how Achilles would return to Briseis after carving holes in the Trojan ranks, and 'tumble with her on a soft day bed', shaking 'a Lance that had no print of steele'.

15 *Works*, I.iv.393.

16 J. Cock's character of '*A common Player*, Chambers IV, p. 256.

17 *The Arte of English Poesie* (1589), ed. Edward Arber (London: Constable, 1906) 58: *Works*, III, p. 302.

18 See *DSL*, quail.

19 Ashwell, *Modern Troubadours* (London: Gyldendal, 1922) p. 128.

20 Parker, *Forty-Six Lives*, p. 117.

21 Wind, *Pagan Mysteries*, p. 270.

22 *Two Maids of More-clacke* (1607–8) sig. A4ᵛ.

23 For analogues see *DSL*, needle 1, brains between legs.

24 Beaumont and Fletcher, V, p. 556; Jonson IV, p. 127. See Ch. 13, n.12.

25 For this joke pattern see *DSL*, fall 3.

26 *Progress of a Rake* (1732) p. 43; Beaumont and Fletcher, IX, p. 600; D'Urfey, *Wit and Mirth*, IV, p. 66.

27 'Limblifter' was a well-established term for fornicator (*DSL*, limb).

28 'A Cake-making Image in *Troilus and Cressida*', *Shakespeare Quarterly*, XXI (1970) 191–4.

29 Brown, *Amusements*, p. 192. Shakespeare makes similar use of plum (*DSL*).

30 See *DSL* for the (phallic) monster and undertake.

31 Adriano Politi, *Dittionario Toscano* (Rome, 1613); Florio, *A Worlde of Wordes* (London, 1598) gives it as 'the foreskin or prepuce of a mans priuie member'. Marlowe's *Jew of Malta* (*c*.1589) provides the first use of 'cazzo' in English print, as well as an offshoot, 'catzerie', meaning phallic activity (*Works*, IV.i.20; IV.v.12).

32 Perhaps secularizing a religious figure: St Augustine, *Confessions*,

IV.12, expands the Vulgate 'sponsus procedens de thalamo' (Ps. 19:5) into Christ emerging from the Virgin's womb like a spouse from the bridal chamber. Cf. Chaucer's Wife of Bath (*Prologue*, 618) on her 'chambre of Venus'.

33 At IV.vii.93 he recalls his warlike days – 'I have seen the time' – as Shallow recalls his sexual conquests in *2 Henry IV*. These *Henry IV* plays had already exposed honour to critical scrutiny; it is surely no accident that three of the four Falstaff plays are steeped in allusions to the Troy legend.

34 See *DSL*, pop.

35 *Arcadia*, p. 474.

36 *Dramatic Works*, IV, p. 277.

37 The ancient equation of finger and penis is discussed by Schultze-Gallera, p. 40. There is innuendo in *Taming of the Shrew* IV.iii.145, when a servant challenges a tailor's order, saying he will prove the error 'upon thee though thy little finger be armed in a thimble'.

38 In his translation of Raoul Lefevre, *The Recuyell of the Historyes of Troye*, ed. H. Oskar Sommer (London: David Nutt, 1894) p. 590.

39 *Comicall Satyre and Shakespeare's* Troilus and Cressida (San Marino, California: Huntington Library, 1938) pp. 197, 227.

40 St Augustine, *Of the Citie of God*, tr. John Healey 'with the learned comments of Io. Lod. Vives' (1610) IV.4, p.159, where reference to international thievery is glossed by Vives: 'The world (saith *Cyprian* very elegantly to *Donatus*) is bathed in flouds of mutuall bloud: when one alone kills a man, it is called a crime, but when a many together doe it, it is called a vertue'. On sixteenth-century anti-war sentiment see my 'Humanist Responses to War: Sidney's Contribution', *Trivium*, 16 (1981) 45–61.

41 *The Complaint of Peace*, tr. Thomas Paynell (1559) sigs. C7, E3.

42 Lydgate's *Troy Book*, ed. Henry Bergen (London: EETS, 1906–35) II, p. 548.

43 William Caxton, *The Recuyell of the Historyes of Troye*, ed. cit., p. 613.

44 R.A. Yoder, '"Sons and Daughters of the Game": An Essay on Shakespeare's "Troilus and Cressida"' *Shakespeare Survey*, 25 (1972) 11–25 (p. 14).

45 Keen, *The Laws of War in the Late Middle Ages* (University of Toronto Press/London: Routledge and Kegan Paul, 1965) p. 154; Castiglione, *The Courtier*, p. 70.

46 See *DSL*, Cressida.

47 See *DSL*, gear.

48 Muir, in his Oxford edition (1984), blunders in glossing these as whores (*DSL* door-keeping). Shakespeare, anticipated by the author

of *The Cobler of Caunterburie* (1590; Mish, *Short Fiction*, p. 150), makes the meaning clear in *Henry V* IV.v.14, where Bourbon would have the man unwilling to follow him in battle act the 'base leno hold the chamber door Whilst by a slave no gentler than my dog His fairest daughter is contaminated'.

49 See *DSL*, bone-ache, rheum.

Chapter 8   Cupid-Adonis: 'Prettie Boyes' and 'Unlawfull Joyes'

1 *On Romances*, p. 121. Some of this discussion has appeared as 'The Coming of Age of Shakespeare's Adonis', *Modern Language Notes*, 78 (1983) 769–76.

2 *Palladis Tamia* (1598) fo. 281ᵛ.

3 *The Metamorphoses*, tr. Mary M. Innes (Harmondsworth, Middlesex: Penguin, 1955) p. 260; Panofsky, *Studies in Iconology*, p. 87.

4 Lorenzo Lotto's *Master Marsilio and his Wife* (1523: Prado, Madrid) shows the child Cupid linking the couple with his bow.

5 The topicality of this figure is attested by a ballad on the Wife preserved in the Roxburghe collection. H.E. Rollins, *An Analytical Index to the Ballad-Entries (1557–1709) in the Registers of the Company of Stationers of London* (rept. Hatboro, Pennsylvania: Tradition Press, 1967) 2962, notes that it was entered 25 June 1600, and that it caused the printers and a ballad-seller to be fined.

6 See Wind, *Pagan Mysteries*, pp. 85–91.

7 This is echoed by Chapman, *The Shadow of the Night* (1594: *Poems*, ed. P.B. Bartlett [New York: Russell, 1962] p. 28), for whom Shakespeare's Adonis seems to suggest chaste Diana: 'Musicke, and moode, she loues, but loue she hates'. But in the second hymn, Adonis may be thought to have joined 'The huntsmen . . . Mounted on Lyons, Vnicorns, and Bores', who 'saw their hounds lye licking of their sores' (like Adonis's in Shakespeare's poem, l.915).

8 Bullough, II, p. 166.

9 For instance, the comparison of 'shrill-tongu'd tapsters answering every call' (l.849), used during her lonely night, hints at the sexual satisfaction which is open to her as well as indicating her desire for something less easily attainable.

10 *Faerie Queene* III.2.39; see *The Structure of Allegory in* The Faerie Queene (Oxford: Clarendon, 1961) p. 142.

11 'Paradise and Utopia: Human Interest in *Paradise Lost*', *Études Anglaises* 27 (1974) 461–70 (p. 466).

12 This pattern is recalled in *Faerie Queene* III.7.26–31, when Florimell's flight from the Foster brings her up against lust in various other guises. Notably, she is likened both to Myrrha and to Daphne fleeing

from Apollo. The predictability of the second comparison scarcely smooths over the unexpectedness of the first.

13 See *DSL*, root.

14 W.R. Streitberger, 'Ideal Conduct in *Venus and Adonis*', *Shakespeare Quarterly*, 26 (1975) 285–91 (p. 285).

15 'On Venus and Adonis', in *Elizabethan and Jacobean Studies in Honour of F.P. Wilson*, ed. H. Davis and H. Gardner (Oxford: Clarendon Press, 1959) 100–11 (p. 110).

16 The only reappearance of the phallic tooth in Shakespeare is in *Henry VIII* I.iii.48, quibbling on 'colt's tooth' and 'stump'.

17 Continual attention is drawn to the breath of Adonis. At one point, as he pants beneath her, Venus feeds on his steamy breath which, to her heated imagination, becomes a sexual distillation, a 'heavenly moisture' (1.62). The phrase recurs at 1.542, and at 1.552 we hear how 'she will draw his lips' rich treasure dry' – moving into Faustian fantasy where lips suck forth souls. Finally (1.1171), Venus compares the anemone's fragrance 'to her Adonis' breath', prompting her to pluck it.

18 For instance, those dissolving palms (1.143) which, along with 'Witness this primrose bank whereon I lie' (1.151), may well have inspired lines in Donne's 'The Extasie'. Or again commonplaces of the wax impression (1.565), the plucked rose (1.574, given a special resonance at the end of the poem), and the picking of locks (1.575), where the reversed roles continue to be a notable feature.

19 'Venus and Adonis and the Boar', MLR, 41 (1946) 353–61 (p. 356).

Chapter 9   *Pox and Gold: Timon's New World Heritage*

1 Ed. Henry Walter (Cambridge: Parker Society, 1850) p. 171.

2 His *Medusa* (*c*.1597) is in the Uffizi Gallery, Florence.

3 Antoine Oudin and Laurens Feretti, *Dittionario Italiano, e Francese* (Venice, 1693); Dekker, *Dramatic Works*, II, p. 54. It is of moment that in the anonymous *Buggbears* (*c*.1564) IV.v.44, *Early Plays from the Italian*, ed. R. Warwick Bond (London: Oxford University Press, 1911) p. 133, 'She is stung wth a lizart' indicates pregnancy. Since colloquial expressions are often used indifferently for pregnancy and poxing, it may be that this one is no exception. It is not found in the sources, but seeming lack of English currency suggests that it comes from Italian. A parallel would be 'to send hym in to Corne wayle', for which the play provides the first English use (III.i.29: Tilley, C666). This again does not derive from the sources, though it was already proverbial in Italian.

4 *Fayre Warning* (*c*.1635): *Roxburghe Ballads* I, p. 125; and *The*

Married-womans Case (*c*.1625): *Pepys Ballads*, I, p. 410. J.T., *The Hvnting of the Pox* (1619) sig. B, observes that 'The Scots', when suffering from pox, 'vse in iest to say that they are bit with *Spanish Fleas*'. But in 1554, John Bale, *A Declaration of Edmonde Bonner* (1561), fo. 69, alludes to a cleric 'sore bytten wyth a Wynchester gose'.

5   See *DSL*, sting 3.

6   Later (IV.iii.427) it is said that bandits are not content with ordinary fare, but 'must eat men'. Timon himself would have 'the whole life of Athens' in a root: 'Thus would I eat it' (l.285).

7   *A Caveat for Common Cursitors* (1566), in A.V. Judges, *The Elizabethan Underworld* (London: Routledge, 1930) p. 102.

8   *Pagan Mysteries*, p. 160.

9   *Poems*, ed. E. Arber (Westminster: Constable, 1896) p. 6. On this theme see Carlo Dionisotti, 'Amore e Morte', *Italia Medioevale e Umanistica*, I (1958) 419–26.

10   Jean Lemaire, *Oeuvres*, ed. J. Stecher (Louvain: J. Lefever, 1882–91) III, p. 53; *Recueil de Poésies Françoises des XVe et XVIe Siécles*, ed. Anatole de Montaiglon (Paris: Jannet, 1856) IV, p. 267.

11   Cf. Jonson, *Bartholomew Fair* (1614) I.iii.78 (VI, p. 25), adapting Martial's Epigram III.93: 'A sweet course for a man to use the brand of life for, to be still raking himselfe a fortune in an old womans embers'. Alexander Radcliffe, *Ovid Travestie* (1681), in *Works* (1696) p. 109, makes Paris present himself to Hellen as a 'Fagot-stick, I burn apace, / Oh quench me Madam in your wat'ring-place': no innuendo of pox here, but two pages on Cassandra warns her brother against 'a Fireship'.

12   See *DSL* , boil, pickle, stew.

13   *The Medical Knowledge of Shakespeare* (London: Longman, 1860) p. 256; Hutten fo. 16^v.

14   Paul von Middelburg's *Prenostica ad viginti annos duratura* (Antwerp, 1484) foretold that a conjunction in the sign of Scorpio in November of that year would result in an outbreak of genital disease ten years on. This is recalled in Dürer's woodcut of a syphilitic man adorning the broadside of Ulsenius's dream (Nuremburg, 1496). The dream concerned both disease and cure, but unfortunately Ulsenius had forgotten the cure when he awoke. See Karl Sudhoff, *Graphische und Typographische Erstlinge der Syphilisliteratur aus den Jahren 1495 und 1496*, ed. G. Klein (Alte Meister der Medizin 4, Munich 1912) p. 168. Sudhoff reprinted the broadside as pl. 5 of *Zehn Syphilis-Drucke aus den Jahren 1495–1498* (Milan: R. Lier, 1924).

15   Andrea Caesalpino, *Praxis Vniversae Artis Medicae* (Treviso, 1606)

p. 249; Gabriele Falloppio, *De Morbo Gallico*, in Luisinus, I, p. 663. James J. Abraham, in his intro. to Fracastoro's *Syphilis*, p. 4, offers circumstantial evidence that the French king, Charles VIII, succumbed to the disease.

16 Ed. J.C. Bulman and J.M. Nosworthy (Malone Soc., 1980).

17 James C. Bulman, Jr. discusses 'Shakespeare's Use of the "Timon" Comedy', *Shakespeare Survey*, 29 (1976) 103–16.

18 *Poems*, ed. E. Arber (Westminster: Constable, 1896) p. 30.

19 Beaumont and Fletcher, III, p. 403.

20 Cf. *Henry VIII* II.iii.88, where the bawdy old lady, who has long sought favour at court, marvels that the newly arrived Anne Boleyn can 'have your mouth filled up / Before you open it'.

21 Tom Brown, *Letters from the Dead* (1702): *Amusements*, p. 412.

22 Rabelais, V.21; the expression had been gathered by Ray in *A Compleat Collection of English Proverbs* (1678).

23 *Diary*, ed. Robert Latham and William Matthews (London: Bell & Hyman, 1970-83) VIII, p. 337. Cf. *Lear* IV.vi.190 on the poisonous, vaginal hell, 'the sulphurous pit – burning, scalding / Stench, consumption'.

24 *A Profitable and Necessarie Booke of Obseruations, for all those that are burned with the flame of Gun Powder..With..a short treatise, for the cure of lues venerea* (1596), p. 172.

25 *Works*, III, p. 145.

26 Charles Cotton, Ἐρωτόπολις. *The Present State of Betty–Land* (1684) p. 169 describes sufferers who, 'having lost the Organs of Speech . . . curse . . . the Artist for not having made their new Noses according to Directions, for having a new Pallat more like the Roof of an Oven than to be put into the Mouth of a Gentleman'. Early poetic reference occurs in Skelton's 'Elynour Rummynge' (?1517), *The Complete English Poems*, ed. John Scattergood (New Haven/London: Yale University Press, 1983) p. 223, where Elynour 'spake thus in her snout, Snevelyng in her nose, As though she had the pose'.

27 *On Generation and Corruption*, II.10, 337a. Averroës's gloss, denying personal immortality, was condemned by the Bull *Apostolici Regiminis*, issued in the eighth session of the Fifth Lateran Council (19 Dec. 1513).

28 *Frontier: American Literature and the American West* (Princeton, New Jersey: Princeton University Press, 1965) p. 166.

29 Luisinus, I, p. 332; Hutten (ch. 6) fo. 10ᵛ. Rafael Larco Hoyle, *Chacan* (Geneva/Paris/Munich: Nagel, 1965) p.122, describes ancient Peruvian pottery representing men with syphilitic sores and hypertrophy of nose or phallus.

30 Fracastoro, *Syphilis*, p. 6.
31 *European Americana: A Chronological Guide to Works Printed in Europe Relating to the Americas, 1493–1776*, I, ed. J. Alden, assisted by Dennis C. Landis (New York: Readex Books 1980) p. xviii; and cf. Earl J. Hamilton, 'What the New World Gave the Economy of the Old', *First Images of America*, ed. Fredi Chiappelli (Berkeley/Los Angeles/London: University of California Press 1976) II, pp. 679–80. Mirko D. Grmek, *Diseases in the Ancient Greek World*, tr. M. and L. Muellner (Baltimore, Maryland: John Hopkins University Press 1989) p. 140, notes that bones from pre-1500 showing syphilitic lesions have been found nowhere but the Americas and Oceania. But the quest continues. An attempt to establish a pre-1493 date for skeletons found at Waterford and Gloucester was reported in the *Observer* (14 March 1993).
32 *Storia d'Italia*, ed. Lucio Felici (Rome: Avanzini and Torraca, 1967) p. 245. He concludes his second book with an account of the disease brought back from the New World by Columbus, and spread throughout Italy by Charles VIII's forces as they returned to France from Naples.
33 *Essayes of Certain Paradoxes* (1617) sig. F^v. Gideon Harvey, *Venus Unmasked* (1665) p. 2, furnishes among the learned terms for syphilis '*Malum Indicum*, the *Indian* Evil; *Serpico Indica*, the *Indian* Tetter', while Spaniards call it '*las Buas*, and *Patursa*, from the *Indians*'.
34 *Works*, II, p. 280.
35 In Dekker's *Strange Horse-Race* (1613), in *Prose Works*, III, p. 352, the devil bequeaths to the 'Puncks of the Cittie..Carbuncles a peece'. 'John Dando' and 'Harrie Runt', *Maroccus Extaticus* (1595), ed. E.F. Rimbault (London: Percy Soc., 1843) p. 15, portray a 'lecherous landlord' who wears 'his mistres favors, viz. rubies and precious stones on his nose, &c. And this *et cetera*, shall . . . bee the perfectest poxe that ever grewe in Shordich or Southwarke'.
36 Letter dated 28 November 1577, tr. S.A. Pears, *The Correspondence of Sir Philip Sidney and Hubert Languet* (London: Pickering, 1845) p. 124.
37 R.H. Tawney, *Religion and the Rise of Capitalism* (West Drayton: Penguin, rept. 1948) p. 21.
38 Jean Descolo, *The Conquistadors*, tr. Malcolm Barnes (London: Allen & Unwin, 1957) p. 377.
39 Mendel Peterson, *The Funnel of Gold* (Boston/Toronto: Little, Brown, 1975) p. 32.
40 Gideon Harvey, *Venus Unmasked* (1665) p. 21.
41 In his narrative of the third voyage, *The Four Voyages of Christopher Columbus*, tr. J.M. Cohen (Harmondsworth: Penguin, 1969) p. 221.

42 Columbus's letter to the sovereigns of Spain (1503): Cohen, *The Four Voyages*, p. 300.

43 *Essayes*, III.vi (III, p. 180); *Tempest*, IV.i.223.

44 John Ford, *'Tis Pity She's a Whore* (*c*.1632) III.vi: *Works*, I, p. 164.

45 See *DSL*, scald.

46 *Works*, VI, p. 45.

47 Ibid., p. 49.

48 Ibid., p. 48.

49 Ibid., p. 49.

50 Ibid., p. 40.

51 *European Encounters with the New World* (New Haven/London: Yale University Press, 1993) p. 4.

52 Elizabeth repealed the statute outlawing interest in 1571 (13 Eliz. c.8), imposing a limit of 10 per cent.

53 *Politics*, I.10,1258b. Ironically, Aristotle's geographical conceptions had stimulated New World adventure.

54 *Palladis Tamia* (1598) fo. 322. The same idiom is apparent in the ballad peddled by Autolycus (*Winter's Tale* IV.iv.260) telling 'how a usurer's wife was brought to bed of twenty money-bags at a burden'.

55 Tawney, *Religion and the Rise of Capitalism*, p. 140.

56 Ed. Stephen Orgel (New York/London: Garland, 1979) III.iii.40.

57 *Aristotle and the American Indians*, p. 8.

58 Book VI, chapter 9 (p. 560).

Part III Introduction

1 *Monk's Prologue*, l. 1947.

2 Castiglione, *Book of the Courtier*, III, p. 234.

3 *The Munich Gallery, Alte Pinakothek* (London: Thames and Hudson, 1970) p. 138.

4 'A sociological interpretation of the early Renaissance in Florence', *South Atlantic Quarterly*, 38 (1939) 427–48 (p. 437).

5 Erwin Panofsky, *Hercules am Scheidewege und andere antike Bildstoffe in der neueren Kunst* (Leipzig/Berlin: Teubner, 1930) p. 155.

Chapter 10   The Education of Women: Textual Authority or Sexual Licence

1 *The Surfeit. To ABC* (1656) p. 58; *CCXI. Sociable Letters* (1664) p. 246 (Letter CXXIII).

2 Donne's 'Elegie XIX: Going to Bed' (*Poems*, I, p. 121); *Two Noble Kinsmen* V.ii.9.

3 Cohn, p. 227. Henry Boguet, *Discours des Sorciers*, tr. E. Allen Ashwin as *An Examen of Witches* (rept. London: Muller 1971)

p. 88, has a chapter on 'How Midwives, if they are Witches, Kill the Children they Deliver'; and Nicolas Remy, *Demonolatry* (1595), tr. Ashwin (rept. London: Muller, 1970) p. 100, relates Renaissance practice to Pliny's account of midwives and harlots dislimbing abortions as ingredient for poisons.

4 *Meteorologica*, tr. E.W. Webster, I.14, 353a. See p. 136.

5 *Meteorologica*, II.5, 362b. See Anthony Pagden, *European Encounters with the New World* (New Haven/London: Yale University Press, 1993) p. 90.

6 Lewis Hanke, *Aristotle and the American Indians* (London: Hollis & Carter, 1959) p. 17.

7 *Historia Animalium*, IX.1, 608b; *Politics*, I.13, 1260a.

8 'A Woman's Place was in the Home: Women's Work in Renaissance Tuscany' in *Rewriting the Renaissance*, ed. M.W. Ferguson, M. Quilligan and N.J. Vickers (Chicago: University of Chicago Press, 1986) 207–24 (p. 215).

9 Beaumont and Fletcher, IV, p. 36. Women's claims to superiority may have been common; certainly William Gouge, *Of Domesticall Duties* (1622) p. 271, complains that many wives 'thinke themselues euery way as good as their husbands', though he is obliged to concede that there is but 'small inequalitie' between them.

10 *Complete Works*, VII, p. 79.

11 *Instruction*, sig. Eiv (I.5).

12 Gertrud Schiller, *Iconography of Christian Art*, tr. Janet Seligman (London: Lund Humphries, 1970) I, p. 42. Her reading comes to be identified as Isaiah 9:6, 'For unto us a child is born'.

13 This is wholly distinct from that Romanesque type of the *sedes sapientiae*, where it is the Christ child who frequently holds a book as sign of his priestly authority. For a striking example, see *Sculpture Romane de Haute-Auvergne*, ed. André Muzac (Aurillac: USHA, 1966) p. 55.

14 *Works*, I, p. 30.

15 Beaumont and Fletcher, IX, p. 487.

16 *Elizabethan Melancholy* (East Lansing: Michigan State College Press, 1951) p. 166.

17 Alan Brien's review of the first National Theatre production, *Sunday Telegraph* (27 Oct. 1963).

18 *The Christen State of Matrimonye*, tr. Miles Coverdale (1541) sig. A6ᵛ.

19 N.M. Kay, *Martial Book XI: A Commentary* (London: Duckworth, 1985) p. 222; Jacquart and Thomasset, pp. 174–6; Laurentius, *A Discovrse of the Preservation of the Sight: of Melancholike Diseases; of Rheumes, and of Old Age*, tr. Richard Surphlet (1599) p. 122.

20 *Plays*, I, p. 105.
21 In *Jyl of Brayntfords Testament*, ed. F.J. Furnivall (London: n.p., 1871) pp. 29–33.
22 *Works*, I, sig. A3ᵛ. It is genially dedicated 'To all the pleasant conceited London *Gentlewomen, that are friendes to mirth*, and enemies to dull Melancholy'.
23 Sir Anthony Weldon, *The Court and Character of King James* (1651), p. 99.
24 John Dickenson, *Greene in Conceipt* (1598), pp. 17–21; Thomas Deloney, *Jack of Newbery* (1597), ch. 8.
25 B.H. Cowper, *Apocryphal Gospels and other Documents relating to the History of Christ* (London/Edinburgh: Williams & Norgate, 1867) ch. 6.
26 A fine example occurs in an English MS. of *c.*1410: Bodleian Library, Oxford, Lat. liturg. f.2, fo. 104ᵛ.
27 *Gent Duizend Jaar Kunst en Cultuur* (Ghent: Museum voor Schone Kunsten, 1975), pl. 30.
28 Cowper, *Apocryphal Gospels*, ch. 6.
29 *An die Radherrn* (1524), tr. A.T.W. Steinhaeuser, in *Luther's Works*, gen. ed. H.T. Lehmann, vol. 45: *The Christian in Society II*, ed. W.I. Brandt (Philadelphia: Fortress Press, 1962) p. 368.
30 Arden edition (London/New York: Methuen, 1981) p. 129.
31 *The Taming of a Shrew*, ed. Graham Holderness and Bryan Loughrey (Hemel Hempstead, Hertfordshire: Harvester Wheatsheaf, 1992) p. 21.
32 'Fears of Flying: Representations of Witchcraft and Sexuality in Early Sixteenth-Century Germany', *Australian Journal of Art*, 8 (1989–90) 19–47 (pp. 32, 34).
33 Cf. D.E. Underdown, 'The Taming of the Scold: the Enforcement of Patriarchal Authority in Early Modern England' in *Order and Disorder in Early Modern England*, ed. Fletcher and Stevenson, 117–36 (p. 120): 'The scold who cursed her more fortunate neighbour and the witch who cast a spell on him (or her) were both rebelling against the place assigned them in the social and gender hierarchies'.
34 *Europe's Inner Demons*, p. 230.
35 Hirsch, *Printing, Selling and Reading 1450–1550*, p. 129.
36 Beaumont and Fletcher, VII, p. 573 (III.iv.8).
37 Heinrich Heine, *Sämtliche Schriften*, ed. Kraus Briegleb (Frankfurt/Berlin/Vienna: Ullstein, 1981) I, p. 284, l.243.
38 *Malleus Maleficarum*, tr. Montague Summers (rept. London: Pushkin, 1948) p. 47.
39 Oxford Shakespeare (Oxford/New York: Oxford University Press, 1990) p. 170.

40 *News from Scotland* (1591), ed. G.B. Harrison (Bodley Head Quartos; London: John Lane, 1924) p. 13.

41 See *DSL*, assignation resorts.

42 *The Crown of Life* (rept London: Methuen, 1964), p. 218.

43 See *DSL*, cap.

44 *Works*, V, p. 101.

45 Shakespeare has loaded him with various linguistic eccentricities, some of which are clearly Welsh importations. Examples from the first scene include instability between 'p' and 'b' sounds, deriving from Welsh mutation; 'is . . . give' and 'is make' (ll.47, 55) for 'has given' and 'has made', since past participles in Welsh cling to the infinitive form of the verb; 'a Christians' (l.94), where the problem is either the absence of indefinite article in Welsh or (more probably) unfamiliarity with final 's' to signify a plural; use of 'it' for 'he' in 'if it is a pickpurse' (l.146), since Welsh fails to distinguish gendered from neuter.

46 Cf. his Latin ablative construction: 'ask of Doctor Caius' house which is the way' (I.ii.1).

47 See *DSL*, hackster.

48 *The Merry Wives of Windsor* (Oxford/New York: Oxford University Press, 1990), p. 34.

49 *Tell-Trothes New-Yeares Gift* (1593), ed. F.J. Furnivall (New Shakspere Society, London: Trübner, 1876) p. 5, speaks of parents 'more regardinge the linkinge of wealth and money together, then of loue with honesty', so that 'they marry their children in their infancy, when they are not able to know what loue is'. In the same volume, Thomas Powell, *Tom of All Trades* (1631), p. 144, cynically advises: 'bee sure to match your eldest sonne' while he 'will bend to your will, before his blood begin to feele the heate of any affections kindling about him'.

50 *Wily Beguiled* (1596–1606), Dodsley IX, p. 244.

Chapter 11   Othello, Cuckoldry and the Doctrine of Generality

1 *Two Renaissance Book Hunters. The Letters of Poggius Bracciolini to Nicolaus de Niccolis*, tr. Phyllis W.G. Gordan (New York/London: Columbia University Press, 1974) pp. 24–30.

2 Geisberg, G263.

3 K. Sudhoff, *Aus der Frühgeschichte der Syphilis. Studien zur Geschichte der Medizin*, 9 (Leipzig: Johann Barth 1912) pp. 28, 33, 37, quotes a warning issued by the Nuremberg council on 16 Nov. 1496 against admitting to public bath-houses those 'marked by the new disease of the French sickness', and similar official statements from Freiburg im Breisgau dated 26 Sept. 1496 and 14 March 1498.

4 Cf. *Il Decamerone* III.i, where a gardener seduces a convent of nuns, brides of Christ who thereby has horns set on his hat ('poneva le corna sopra il cappello').

5 See Arthur M. Hind, *Early Italian Engraving. Part I: Florentine Engravings* (London: Quaritch, 1938) pl. 108.

6 B.J. Whiting, *Proverbs, Sentences, and Proverbial Phrases from Early English Writings* (Cambridge, Mass.: Harvard University Press/London: Oxford University Press, 1968) H483, supplies an unpersuasive fourteenth-century example. It is likewise impossible to credit those oblique allusions perceived by Thomas W. Ross, *Chaucer's Bawdy* (New York: Dutton, 1972), *s.v. horn*, without evidence of common currency.

7 Chapman, *All Fools* (1599–1604) V.ii.241, ed. Parrott, p. 159. Tilley H628 cites *Comedy of Errors*, II.i.57.

8 *I Honest Whore*, I.iv.16 (*Dramatic Works*, II, p. 33).

9 *The Brazen Age* (1610–13): *Works*, III, p. 238.

10 Herford and Simpson, III, p. 288. Cf. *Westward Ho* IV.ii.111 (*Dramatic Works of Thomas Dekker*, II, p. 370): 'Hornes feard, plague worse, than sticking on the head'.

11 *Instruction*, sig. fi^v (II.vii).

12 *Works*, III, p. 82. For a parallel see *DSL*, wind as fructifier.

13 Ed. Montague Summers (London: John Rodker, 1930) III.ix (p. 30).

14 *The Town-Misses Declaration and Apology* (1675) p. 5. Tilley N235 cites 'To make one's nose swell' from Ray (1678), meaning 'To make one jealous or envious'.

15 Ed. J.O. Halliwell (London: Percy Soc., 1848) p. 36.

16 The anecdote is first collected in Poggio's *Facetiae* 223 and recurs frequently. The year before Sharpham's play was published, it appeared in a reprint of L. Guicciardini, *Detti, et Fatti Piacevoli, et Gravi* (Venice) p. 34.

17 *Ram Alley* (1607–8), ed. Claude E. Jones (Louvain: Librairie Universitaire Uystpruyst, 1952) V.i.2586; 1 Cor. 11:3.

18 *An Apologie for Women* (1609) p. 45.

19 *Instruction*, sig. fii (II.5).

20 According to Andrew Willet, *A Treatise of Salomons Mariage* (1612) p. 15.

21 William Gouge, *Of Domesticall Dvties* (1620) p. 219.

22 See *DSL*, adultery for earlier advocacy of the death penalty.

23 If, as Varchi thought, 'the Southern Nations, and such as dwell in hot Regions are very Jealous', whereas northerners continue to be much less prone, the translation would have been uncommercial. But even prior to the cultural impact of southern Europe on the north during

the Renaissance, Russia provided a stumbling-block to the idea that degrees of sexual jealousy reflect hot or cold climatic conditions. Earlier, oriental influence was the common factor between Russia and southern Europe.

24 *The Art of Courtly Love*, tr. John Jay Parry (New York: Norton, 1969) p. 184.

25 'Sexual Anxiety and the Male Order of Things in *Othello*', *English Literary Renaissance*, 10 (1980) 384–412 (p. 396).

26 IV.ii.31. Whores commonly used a throat-clearing 'hem' as a way of attracting a potential client's attention, while bawds used it as a cautionary signal. The sound was used to mock those engaged in prostitution (*DSL*, hem).

27 Similar psychological promptings lie behind Belforest's questioning of his wife's pander in Tourneur's *Atheist's Tragedy* (1607–11) IV.iv.30: *Works*, p. 239. Proust has them sharply in focus in *A la Recherche du Temps Perdu: Du Côté de Chez Swann* (Gallimard, 1958) II, pp. 186–90.

28 'Unproper Beds: Race, Adultery, and the Hideous in *Othello*', *Shakespeare Quarterly*, 40 (1989) 383–412 (pp. 384, 394).

29 '*Othello* and the Dignity of Man', ed. Arnold Kettle 123–145 (p. 127).

30 V.ii.356. There is no necessary problem about identifying Desdemona with a pearl, a substance traditionally invested with profound spiritual meaning. Its sexual-spiritual implications blur with those of the marguerite: see James I. Wimsatt, *The Marguerite Poetry of Guillaume de Machaut* (Chapel Hill: Univ. of N. Carolina Press 1970) pp. 9, 31, 38. Folio replaces quarto's 'Indian' with 'Iudean'; though the first half of the seventeenth century provides no corroboration for a Jewish allusion, racial insults have a strong migratory habit (see p. 180).

31 In a note to the Arden *Othello* (London: Methuen 1958).

32 G.M. Matthews, '*Othello* and the Dignity of Man', p. 143.

33 *Shakespeare's Tragic Justice* (London: Methuen, 1961) p. 37; *Tudor Royal Proclamations*, III, p. 221.

34 B. Harris, 'A Portrait of a Moor', *Shakespeare Survey*, 11 (1958) 89–97 (p. 94).

35 Collected in his *Miscellanies*, I (1717) p. 142.

36 *A Selection of his Writings*, tr. George Sanderlin (New York: Knopf, 1971) p. 100. In fact, European diseases outstripped European brutality in decimating the Indians.

37 *The Florida of the Inca*, II.i (p. 113).

38 *The Shakespeare Apocrypha*, ed. C.F. Tucker Brooke (Oxford: Clarendon Press, 1918) p. 398.

39 Myths of black sexuality are noted by Eldred Jones, *Othello's*

Countrymen: The African in English Renaissance Drama (London: Oxford University Press, 1965) pp. 8, 11; E.H. Tokson, *Popular Images of Black Men in English Drama 1550–1688* (Boston: Hall, 1982) p. 17, and Karen Newman "'And Wash the Ethiop White'", in *Shakespeare Reproduced*, Howard and O'Connor, 141–62 (pp. 147–9). The latter finds that accounts tend to reflect classical authors on the subject rather than actuality.

40 *The Cosmographical Glasse* (1559) fo. 200. Vespucci's *Letters*, tr. Clements R. Markham (London: Hakluyt Soc., 1894) p. 8.

41 Vespucci's *Letters*, p. 46.

42 *The Conquest of New Spain*, tr. J.M. Cohen (Harmondsworth: Penguin, 1963) p. 19. Paul H. Gebhard, 'Sexual Motifs in Prehistoric Peruvian Ceramics', *Studies in Erotic Art*, ed. Theodore Bowie and Cornelia V. Christenson (New York/London: Basic Books, 1970) 109–69 (p. 126), notes of coitus depictions on Mochica pottery that at least '21 percent is anal rather than vaginal'. Gonzalo Fernandez de Oviedo, *Historia General y Natural de las Indias*, ed. Juan Perez de Tudela Bueso (Madrid: Atlas, 1959) Bk V, ch. 3 (I, p. 118), says it is common knowledge that 'many of the Indian men and women were sodomites. . . . In some parts they wear jewels in the form of one man on another in the diabolic and abominable act of Sodom, wrought in gold relief'. One obtained in the port of Santa Marta and sent to Darien for smelting he took pleasure in smashing himself.

43 Díaz, *The Conquest of New Spain*, p. 225.

44 *Arcadia*, p. 159; perhaps recalled by Fletcher, *Island Princess* (c.1620) I.i.45: 'She is a Princesse, and she must be faire, / That's the prerogative of being royall' (Beaumont and Fletcher, V, p. 554).

45 Reprinted in Spingarn, *Critical Essays*, II, pp. 195, 223.

46 Suetonius, *The Twelve Caesars*, I.51 (on the relationship between baldness and virility see Aristotle *Historia Animalium* III.11.518a; *Problems*, IV.18, 878b; X.57, 897b). Massinger, *Bashful Lover* (1636) IV.i.96, (*Plays and Poems*, ed. Philip Edwards and Colin Gibson. Oxford: Clarendon, 1976, IV, p. 351) suggests 'All armor, and no smock' is 'Abominable'; and every general 'desir'd to have his sweat wash'd off / By a juicie Bedfellow'.

47 In Spingarn, *Critical Essays*, II, p. 223.

48 Ibid., p. 224.

49 Ibid., p. 222.

50 Ibid., p. 221.

51 *Magic in the Web. Action and Language in Othello* (rept. Westport, Connecticut: Greenwood Press, 1977) pp. 202–7.

52 For 'guinea-hen' as a slang term for prostitute, see *DSL*, turkey. In Davenant's *Albovine* (1606–9) III (*The Dramatic Works*, ed. J.

Maidment and W.H. Logan, 1872–4) I, p. 53, 'some old land-carrack' is sought by a man who would live as a gigolo. *Mercurius Fumigosus*, 6 (5–12 July 1654) p. 44 announces the arrival of foreign whores as '*a Fleet of* Venice Land-Friggots, *bound for* Blackwall'. *Land* often serves as dubious prefix; so Ford, *Lady's Trial* (1638) I (*Dramatic Works* III, p. 10) uses 'Land-pirates' for roués and 'land-rats' (III; III, p. 48) for cheats; cf. *Merchant of Venice* I.iii.22.

53   '*Othello* and the Dignity of Man', p. 135.

54   I.i.133; ed. Parrott, p. 370.

55   *Magic in the Web*, p. 204.

56   *The Historie of Italie* (1549) fo. 84ᵛ. Thomas Coryat's *Crudities* (1611; rept. Glasgow: MacLehose, 1905) I, p. 402, accounts for the plethora of courtesans in the city in the same terms: 'For they thinke that the chastity of their wives would be the sooner assaulted, and so consequently they should be capricornified, (which of all the indignities in the world the Venetian cannot patiently endure) were it not for these places of evacuation'. Cf. *Much Ado* I.i.253, where Don Pedro suggests that Cupid may have 'spent all his quiver in Venice'.

57   *Broken Nuptials in Shakespeare's Plays*, pp. 122–3.

58   He is scorning that mistrust which follows the menstrual pattern noted by Beaumont, *Knight of the Burning Pestle* (1607) III.59 (Beaumont and Fletcher, I, p. 47): 'the sea and women / Are govern'd by the Moone, both ebbe and flow'.

59   *Magic in the Web*, p. 173. Cf. Claudio's 'Time goes on crutches till love have all his rites' (*Much Ado* II.i.334).

60   Neely, *Broken Nuptials in Shakespeare's Plays*, p. 112.

61   Newman '"And Wash the Ethoiop White"' in Howard and O'Connor, p. 152.

62   *The Passions of the Minde in Generall* (1604), p. 174.

63   Howard and O'Connor, p. 152.

64   Spingarn, II, p. 221.

65   'The Alienated City. Reflections on "*Othello*"', *Encounter*, 17 (1961) 3–14 (p. 13).

66   Spingarn, p. 248.

67   *Prefaces to Shakespeare*, 4th Series (London: Sidgwick and Jackson, 1945) p. 18.

68   Wells-Taylor's change of 'housewives' to 'hussies' disturbs the quibbling symmetry. The proverb is found in Tilley W702. Italian and French examples occur respectively in John Florio, *Florios Second Frutes* (1591) p. 175, and Béroalde de Verville, *Le Moyen de Parvenir*, ed. Hélène Moreau and André Tournon (Aix en Provence: Provence University Press, 1984) p. 63.

69 See *DSL*, black.

70 *Courtier*, p. 191.

71 II.12 (p. 295).

72 Bianca's name is ironic comment on the association of blackness with moral corruption. But Neely, *Broken Nuptials* p. 114 properly shows that in describing her as a whore we indicate what she does, not what she is.

Chapter 12   Class and Courtship Ritual in Much Ado

1 Bullough, II, p. 73.

2 *The Partiall Law*, ed. Bertram Dobell (London: Dobell, 1908) pp. 4–5.

3 Ibid., pp. 13–15.

4 Ibid., p. 23.

5 Ibid., pp. 90–7.

6 Ibid., p. 82.

7 Ibid., p. 64.

8 *Complete Works*, XII, p. 138.

9 *Much Ado About Nothing*, ed. A.R. Humphreys (London/New York: Methuen, 1981) p. 50.

10 Cf. Curtis Breight, 'Branagh and the Prince, or a "royal fellowship of death"', *Critical Quarterly*, 33.iv (1991) 95–111 (p. 98), where he argues that Branagh's film version fails to 'grasp Shakespearean irony and ignores Shakespeare's engagement with late Elizabethan culture, especially the murderous Elizabethan wars that had wasted tens of thousands of Englishmen, not to mention a huge number of Irish'.

11 See Panofsky, *Studies in Iconology*, ch. 4, and *DSL*, brothel signs.

12 Cf. Sidney's *Arcadia*, II, 18 (p. 335), where women's assault on their seducer with bodkins is to climax when they 'put out his eyes'. In one of Cornelisz van Haarlem's extraordinary versions of *The Massacre of the Innocents* (Rijksmuseum, Amsterdam, 1590), which he loads with his feelings about the Spanish sack of Haarlem in 1573, he conveys the idea of wholesale rape by painting the soldiers naked, one of them being held by two women while a third claws out his eyes. English law made the connection prior to 1375, demanding that the rapist 'should lose his eyes and his privy members, unlesse she that was ravished before judgement demaunded him for her husband' (Sir Edward Coke, *The Second Part of the Institutes of the Lawes of England*, 1642 p. 180).

13 *Plays and Poems*, ed. R.H. Shepherd (London: Pearson, 1874) I, p. 172.

14 Sir Philip Sidney, *The Poems*, ed. William A. Ringler, Jr (Oxford: Clarendon, 1962) p. 191.

15   See *DSL*, orange.

16   *The Humorous Lieutenant* (1619?) II.iv.88 (Beaumont and Fletcher, V, p. 336). Shakespeare had used the figure in *1 Henry VI* IV.vi.16, of Talbot junior and Orléans who 'drew blood' and 'had the maidenhood / Of thy first fight'.

17   'Those "soft and delicate desires". *Much Ado* and the Distrust of Women' in *The Woman's Part*, ed. Lenz *et al.* 79–99 (p. 88).

18   Glapthorne, *Plays and Poems*, vol.I, p. 215.

19   I, p. 210. Notably too, Shakespeare's George Seacoal is translated into social comment: 'tis likely we shall have frost, / That will make Sea-coales deare; heaven helpe poore people' (I, p. 225).

20   *Microcosmography*, ed. Dr Bliss (rept. Bristol: Hemmons/London: Simpkin, Marshall, Hamilton, Kent, 1897) p. 135.

21   For a note on the most popular of these, *The Academy of Complements* (1639), and its imitators, see my 'Gascoigne's *Master F.J.* and the Development of the Novel', *Trivium*, X (1975) 137–50 (p. 149).

22   Beaumont and Fletcher, VII, p. 560.

23   *Some of Shakespeare's Female Characters*, 5th edn (Edinburgh/London: Blackwood, 1893) p. 293.

24   See *DSL*, devil.

25   See this entry in *DSL*.

26   George Cameron Stone, *A Glossary of the Construction, Decoration and Use of Arms and Armour* (rept. New York: Jack Brussel, 1961) p. 605.

27   *Works*, II, p. 394. See the respective entries in *DSL*.

28   *Works*, II, p. 301; III, p. 148.

29   With this 'will' pun cf. p. 51.

30   C.C. Park, 'As We Like It. How a Girl Can Be Smart and Still Popular', in *The Woman's Part*, ed. Lenz *et al.*, 100–16 (p. 106).

31   *Some of Shakespeare's Female Characters*, p. 306.

32   Ibid., p. 325.

33   See *DSL*, nothing.

34   *Some of Shakespeare's Female Characters*, p. 313.

35   Cf. *Musarum Deliciae* (1656), *Facetiae* II, p. 86: 'A *woman* is a book, and often found / To prove far better in the Sheets then bound'.

36   The earlier genital sense of 'stuff' occurs in *Timon* IV.iii.273, where Apemantus is told that his father 'in spite put stuff / To some she-beggar and compounded thee'.

37   *The Poems English and Latin*, ed. G.C. Moore Smith (Oxford: Clarendon, 1923), p. 4.

Chapter 13   Honest Whores, or the State as Brothel

 1   *Poems*, ed. Robert Krueger (Oxford: Clarendon, 1975) p. 143.

2   Henry Thomas Riley, *Memorials of London and London Life . . . A.D. 1276–1419* (London: Longmans, Green, 1868) p. 535.

3   Laura Gowing, 'Gender and the Language of Insult in Early Modern London', *History Workshop*, 35 (Spring 1993) 1–21 (p. 16).

4   The phrase derives from *Ten Pleasures of Marriage* (1683) p. 105, but variations are found through most of the seventeenth century (*DSL*, pie).

5   See *DSL*, brothel-signs, stewed prunes, diet.

6   In Sassoon's 'The Kiss' (published in the *Cambridge Magazine*, 27 May 1916), it is 'Sweet Sister'; and a French postcard of the same period pictures an assertive blade fondled by a nubile young woman, with the legend: 'La piquante Rosalie – L'amie du poilu' (cf. Henri Lavedan, 'Rosalie', *Messidor*, V [5 March 1915] 142–3).

7   Both quarto and folio texts read 'calme', and the quibble that follows is varied in *Antony and Cleopatra* I.iii.53, with the commonplace of the body politic 'grown sick of rest'.

8   See *DSL*, pearl 2, gem 4.

9   Cf. *Troilus* IV.ii.39 (p. 111 above).

10   New Cambridge edn (1989) p. 19.

11   Mish, *Short Fiction*, p. 55.

12   For details of this bawdy vocabulary, see *DSL*, boult, rot, pox decay, sodden (also p. 107 above), and poop. Cf. *All's Well* IV.iii.170, where an army, 'rotten and sound, upon my life amounts not to fifteen thousand poll, half of the which dare not shake the snow from off their cassocks lest they shake themselves to pieces'.

13   'Love and Society: *Measure for Measure* and Our Own Time' in *Shakespeare in a Changing World*, ed. Kettle, 195–216 (p. 206).

14   *The Varieties of Religious Experience* (London/New York/Bombay: Longmans, Green, 1902) pp. 380, 405.

15   Translated (by Sir Toby Matthew?) as *The Flaming Hart or the Life of the Gloriovs S. Teresa* (1623; Antwerp edn 1642, ch. 29) p. 420.

16   *The Poems*, ed. L.C. Martin (Oxford: Clarendon, 2nd edn, 1957) p. 133.

17   *An Itinerary* (Glasgow: James MacLehose, 1907–8) I, p. 154.

18   *Sacros Concilii Tridentini Canones et Decreta item declarationes cardinalivm concilii interpretum* (Paris, 1627), Session 25, ch. 19 (p. 779); James's 1613 ban with annexed articles appears as *STC* entries 8497–8.

19   See Joseph Gibaldi, 'Petrarch and the Baroque Tradition', *Hebrew University Studies in Literature*, III, pt. 1 (1975) 1–19.

20   The model for these half-length portraits seems to be the right wing of Roger van der Weyden's *Braque Triptych* (Louvre). Although this probably dates from the 1450s, it was the Counter-Reformation which gave impetus to the fashion for society women to be painted

with 'Magdalen's loose hair and lifted eye' (Alexander Pope, *Moral Essays*, II: *The Poems* ed. F.W. Bateson (London: Methuen/New Haven: Yale U.P., 1961) III, ii, p. 49.).

21   *The Poems*, ed. J.H. McDonald and N.P. Brown (Oxford: Clarendon, 1967) pp. xxi, xxiv, 32, 45; *William Weston: The Autobiography of an Elizabethan*, tr. from the Latin by Philip Caraman (London/New York/Toronto: Longmans, Green, 1955) p. 77. Celebration of the Feast of the Magdalen had been reinstated by Henry VIII in 1541 after being discontinued because it clashed with harvesting (*Tudor Royal Proclamations*, I, p. 301).

22   *Comedies and Tragedies* (1647) sig. F4ᵛ

23   *The Women Artists of Bologna* (London: Methuen, 1907) p. 100.

24   F.W.H. Hollstein, *German Engravings, Etchings and Woodcuts ca. 1400–1700*, (Amsterdam: Hertzberger, 1954), I, pp. 76–7.

25   'Shakespeare and the Puritan Dynamic', *Shakespeare Survey*, 27 (1974) 81–92.

26   Keith Thomas, 'The Puritans and Adultery: The Act of 1650 Reconsidered', *Puritans and Revolutionaries: Essays in Seventeenth-Century History Presented to Christopher Hill*, ed. Donald Pennington and Keith Thomas (Oxford: Clarendon, 1978) 257–82 (pp. 267, 273).

27   Bullough, II, pp. 452, 468.

28   Lyndal Roper, 'Discipline and Respectability: Prostitution and the Reformation in Augsburg', *History Workshop Journal*, 19 (1985) 3–28 (p. 21).

29   *Works*, p. 189.

30   Donne, 'Loves Alchymie', *Poems*, I, p. 39.

31   *The Living Theatre of Medieval Art* (Philadelphia: University of Pennsylvania, 1967) p. 67.

32   In his edition of *Measure for Measure* (Oxford: Clarendon, 1991) p. 8.

33   Chaucer, l.139.

34   Chaucer, l. 107. The Wife's popularity is shown by her appearance in a 1600 broadside ballad (H.E. Rollins, *Analytical Index to the Ballad-Entries . . . in the Registers of the Company of Stationers of London*, rept. Hatboro, Pennsylvania: Tradition, 1967, 2962). Sir John Harington, in his Preface to *Orlando Furioso* (1591), alludes to 'flat scurrilitie . . . in the good wife of Bathes tale'; and Samuel Rowlands, borrowing elsewhere from *The Miller's Tale*, places her amongst the 'blithe Wenches' in *Tis Merrie when Gossips meete* (1602) sig. A2.

35   Thomas, 'The Puritans and Adultery', p. 273.

36   Ibid., p. 275.

37 Ibid., p. 276.

38 Ibid., p. 279.

39 *The Works*, ed. Montague Summers (London: Heinemann, 1915) I, p. 414. Even so, it took only a fortnight for the act to take effect as far away as north Monmouthshire, Walter Powell of Llantilio Crossenny noting in his *Diary*, ed. Joseph A. Bradney (Bristol: Wright 1907) p. 41: 'Bridgett Vaughan & the 2 others sent to the house of correcc'on'. Diary jottings run from 1603 without anything of this kind appearing earlier.

40 A particularly good example is *A Dialogue between Mistris Maquerella, a Suburb Bawd, Ms Scolopendra, a noted Curtezan, and Mr Pimpinello an Usher* (1650).

41 *1 Henry VI* I.iv.35.

42 William Rendle and Philip Norman, *The Inns of Old Southwark* (London: Longmans, Green, 1888) pp. 333–4, 337.

43 Bishop Latimer, preaching before Edward VI in March 1549, claims that it had turned the whole city into a brothel: 'Ye have but changed the place, and not taken the whoredom away . . . . there is nowe more whoredom in London than ever there was on the Bank' (*Sermons*, ed. G.E. Corrie. Cambridge: Parker Soc., 1844, p. 134). That moment in Richard Brome's *Covent Garden Weeded* (1632): *Dramatic Works*, ed. R.H. Shepherd (London: Pearson, 1873) II, p. 13, when a 'parboil'd Bawd' is asked: 'Art thou travel'd cross the Seas from the Bankside hither, old Countess of Codpiece-row?', suggests that the pattern was repeated after royal proclamations of 1629 finally ended Southwark's dominance as a centre of entertainment.

44 Roper (pp. 8–9) notes the way that hangman and whore, both following tainted professions at the margins of society, had been linked in Augsburg legislation from 1276, while 'In Vienna, hangman and beadle were paid from the revenues of the brothel'. In *Pericles* (xix.201), Marina urges that Boult become indentured 'to the public hangman' rather than continue as bawd.

45 'The Options of the Audience: Theory and Practice in Peter Brook's "Measure for Measure"', *Shakespeare Survey*, 25 (1972) 27–35 (p. 28).

46 Ibid., p. 32.

47 Ibid., p. 30.

48 Roland Mushat Frye, *Shakespeare and Christian Doctrine* (Princeton, New Jersey: Princeton University Press/London: Oxford University Press, 1963) p. 291.

49 Though this would offend not only supporters of the conventual life but the New Feminist, for whom Isabella's vows would align her

with the lesbian, leading the struggle against traditional categories of male and female.

50   Frank Marcus on John Barton's Stratford production (*Sunday Telegraph*, 5 April 1970). Carolyn E. Brown, 'Erotic Religious Flagellation and Shakespeare's *Measure for Measure*', *English Literary Review*, 16 (1986) 139–65, is one of those who place Isabella too amongst the sado-masochists. But, the question of her devoutness apart, yielding to her brother's needs is calculated to destroy her socially besides making her own life forfeit to the law.

Conclusion

1   *Shakespeare, Fletcher and 'The Two Noble Kinsmen'*, ed. Charles H. Frey (Columbia: University of Missouri Press, 1989) p. 2.

2   Arden edition of *The Taming of the Shrew* (London/New York: Methuen, 1981) p. 67.

3   Herford and Simpson, IV, p. 351.

4   'Linguistic Subversion and the Artifice of Rhetoric in *The Two Noble Kinsmen*', *Shakespeare Quarterly*, 38 (1987) 403–25 (p. 421).

5   'Text, Gender, and Genre in *The Taming of the Shrew*', *'Bad' Shakespeare: Revaluations of the Shakespeare Canon*, ed. Maurice Charney (London/Toronto: Fairleigh Dickinson University Press, 1988) 91–104 (p. 92).

6   *Shakespeare Quarterly*, 40 (1989) p. 353.

7   *Two Gentlemen of Verona*, II.i.159; *Love's Labour's Lost*, III.i.167; *As You Like It*, V.iv.88.

8   *Three Prose Works*, ed. John Buchanan-Brown (Fontwell, Sussex: Centaur, 1972) p. 290.

Select Bibliography

Apocryphal Gospels, Acts, and Revelations, tr. Alexander Walker, Ante-Nicene Christian Library, Edinburgh: Clark, 1870.

Aristotle, *The Works*, English translation ed. J.A. Smith and W.D. Ross. Oxford: Clarendon, 1908–52, 12 vols.

Armin, Robert, *The Collected Works*, New York/London: Johnson, 1972, 2 vols.

Arundel Harington MS. of Tudor Poetry, ed. Ruth Hughey, Columbus: Ohio State University Press, 1971.

Beaumont, Francis, and John Fletcher, *The Dramatic Works in the Beaumont and Fletcher Canon*, ed. Fredson Bowers, Cambridge University Press, 1966–94, 9 vols.

Bradley, A.C., *Shakespearean Tragedy*, London: Macmillan, 1957.

Brown, Tom, *Amusements Serious and Comical*, ed. Arthur L. Hayward, London: Routledge, 1927.

Bullen, A.H. (ed.) *A Collection of Old English Plays*, London: Wyman, 1882–5.

Bullough, Geoffrey (ed.) *Narrative and Dramatic Sources of Shakespeare*, London: Routledge and Kegan Paul/New York: Columbia University Press, 1957–75, 8 vols.

Castiglione, Baldassare, *The Book of the Courtier*, tr. Sir Thomas Hoby, London: Dent/New York: Dutton, 1956.

Chambers, E.K., *The Elizabethan Stage*, Oxford: Clarendon, 1923 4 vols.

Chapman, George, *The Plays*, ed. T.M. Parrott, London: Routledge, 1910–14.

Chaucer, Geoffrey, *The Riverside Chaucer*, ed. Larry D. Benson, Oxford University Press, 1988.

Cinthio, Giraldi, *On Romances*, tr. Henry L. Snuggs, Lexington: University of Kentucky Press, 1968.

Cohn, Norman, *Europe's Inner Demons: The Demonization of Christians in Medieval Christendom*, London: Pimlico, 1993.

Cotgrave, Randle, *A Dictionarie of the French and English Tongues*, London, 1611.

Dekker, Thomas, *The Dramatic Works*, ed. Fredson Bowers, Cambridge University Press, 1953–61, 4 vols.
Dekker, Thomas, *The Non-Dramatic Prose Works*, ed. A.B. Grosart, New York: Russell, 1963, 5 vols.
Dodsley, Robert (ed.) *A Collection of Old English Plays*, revd. W.C. Hazlitt, London: Reeves & Turner, 1874–6, 15 vols.
Donne, John, *The Poems*, ed. H.J.C. Grierson, Oxford University Press, 1912, 2 vols.
DSL: Gordon Williams, *A Dictionary of Sexual Language and Imagery in Shakespearean and Stuart Literature*, London/Atlantic Highlands, NJ: Athlone, 1994 3 vols.
Dunbar: *Poems of William Dunbar*, ed. James Kinsley, Oxford: Clarendon, 1979.
D'Urfey, Thomas (ed.) *Wit and Mirth; or Pills to Purge Melancholy*, London: Pearson, 1876, 6 vols.

Facetiae, Rept. London: John Camden Hotten, 1874, 2 vols.
Fletcher, Anthony, and John Stevenson (eds.) *Order and Disorder in Early Modern England*, Cambridge University Press, 1987.
Ford, John, *Dramatic Works*, ed. William Gifford and Alexander Dyce, New York: Russell, 1965, 3 vols.
Fracastoro, Girolamo, *Syphilis or the French Disease*, tr. H. Wynne-Finch, London: Heinemann, 1935.

Garcilaso de la Vega, *The Florida of the Inca*, tr. John Grier Varner and Jeannette Johnson Varner, London/Edinburgh/Paris/Melbourne/Toronto: Nelson, 1951.
Geisberg, Max, *The German Single-Leaf Woodcut 1500–1550*, ed. W. L. Strauss, New York: Hacker, 1974, 4 vols.
Greene, Robert, *Life and Complete Works*, ed. A.B. Grosart, Huth Library, p.p 1881–6, 15 vols.

Hanke, Lewis, *Aristotle and the American Indians*, London: Hollis & Carter, 1959.
Harbage, Alfred, *Annals of English Drama 975–1700*, revd. S. Schoenbaum, London: Methuen, 1964.
Heywood, Thomas, *The Dramatic Works*, ed. R.H. Shepherd, London: Pearson, 1874, 6 vols.
Hirsch, Rudolf, *Printing, Selling and Reading 1450–1550*, Wiesbaden: Otto Harrassowitz, 1967.

Howard, Jean E., and Marion F. O'Connor (eds), *Shakespeare Reproduced*, New York/London: Methuen, 1987.

Hutten, Ulrich von, *De Morbo Gallico*, tr. Thomas Paynel, London, 1533.

Jacquart, Danielle and Claude Thomasset, *Sexuality and Medicine in the Middle Ages*, tr. Matthew Adamson, Cambridge: Polity, 1985.

Jonson, *Ben Jonson*, ed. C.H. Herford and Percy Simpson, Oxford: Clarendon, 1925–52, 11 vols.

Kettle, Arnold (ed.) *Shakespeare in a Changing World*, London: Lawrence & Wishart, 1964.

Kirschbaum, Leo, *Shakespeare and the Stationers*, Columbus: Ohio State University Press, 1955.

Lenz, C.R.S., G. Greene and C.T. Neely (eds) *The Woman's Part*, Urbana/Chicago/London: University of Illinois Press, 1980.

Luisinus, L., *De Morbo Gallico*, Venice, 1566–7.

Marlowe, Christopher, *Works and Life*, gen. ed. R.H. Case, London: Methuen, 1930–3, 6 vols.

Marston, John, *The Plays*, ed. H. Harvey Wood, London: Oliver & Boyd, 1934–9, 3 vols.

Middleton, Thomas, *The Works*, ed. A.H. Bullen, London: Nimmo, 1885–6, 8 vols.

Mish, Charles C. (ed.) *Short Fiction of the Seventeenth Century*, New York University Press, 1963.

Montaigne, Michael, Lord of, *The Essayes*, tr. John Florio, London: Grant Richards, 1908, 3 vols.

Nashe, Thomas, *Works*, ed. R.B. McKerrow and revised by F.P. Wilson, Oxford: Blackwell, 1966, 5 vols.

Neely, Carol Thomas, *Broken Nuptials in Shakespeare's Plays*, New Haven/London: Yale University Press, 1985.

OED: *The Oxford English Dictionary*, prepared by J.A. Simpson and E.S.C. Weiner, 2nd edn, Oxford: Clarendon, 1989, 20 vols.

Ovid: *Shakespeare's Ovid: Being Arthur Golding's translation of the Metamorphoses*, ed. W.H.D. Rouse, London: De La More, 1904.

Panofsky, Erwin, *Studies in Iconology*, New York/Evanston: Harper & Row, 1962.

Parker, Henry, Lord Morley, *Forty-Six Lives*, tr. from Boccaccio's *De Claris Mulieribus*, ed. Herbert G. Wright, EETS, 1943.

Pepys Ballads, ed. W.G. Day, Cambridge: Brewer, 1987, 5 vols.

Rabelais, François, *Gargantua and Pantagruel*, tr. Sir Thomas Urquhart and Peter Le Motteux, London: Navarre Soc., 1931.
Rowlands, Samuel, *The Complete Works*, Glasgow: Hunterian Club, 1880, 3 vols.
Roxburghe Ballads, ed. W. Chappell and J.W. Ebsworth, Hertford: Ballad Soc., 1869–99.

Schultze-Gallera, S. (pseud. Dr Aigremont) *Fuss- und Schuh-Symbolik und Erotik*, Leipzig: Deutsche Verlags-Aktien Gesellschaft, 1909.
Shakespeare, William, *The Complete Works*, ed. Stanley Wells and Gary Taylor, Oxford: Clarendon, 1986.
—— *The Merry Wives of Windsor*, London: Johnson, 1602 (quarto 1).
—— *Romeo and Juliet*, London: Danter, 1597 (quarto 1).
Sharpham, Edward, *The Works*, ed. C.G. Petter, New York/London: Garland, 1986.
Shirley, James, *The Dramatic Works and Poems*, ed. William Gifford and Alexander Dyce, London: John Murray, 1833, 6 vols.
Sidney, Sir Philip, *The Countess of Pembroke's Arcadia*, ed. Maurice Evans, Harmondsworth: Penguin, 1977.
Spingarn, J.E. (ed.) *Critical Essays of the Seventeenth Century*, London: Oxford University Press, 1908, 3 vols.
STC A Short-Title Catalogue of Books Printed in England, Scotland, & Ireland and of English Books Printed Abroad 1475–1640, compiled by A.W. Pollard and G.R. Redgrave; 2nd edn revd. by W.A. Jackson, F.S. Ferguson and Katharine F. Pantzer, London: Bibliographical Soc., 1976–91, 3 vols.

Taylor, John, *All the Workes*, London, 1630.
Tilley, M.P., *A Dictionary of the Proverbs in England in the Sixteenth and Seventeenth Centuries*, Ann Arbor: University of Michigan Press, 1950.
Tourneur, Cyril, *Works*, ed. Allardyce Nicoll, London: Fanfrolico, 1929.
Tudor Royal Proclamations, ed. Paul L. Hughes and James F. Larkin, New Haven/London: Yale University Press, 1964–9, 3 vols.

Vives, Joannes, *The Instruction of a Christen Woman*, tr. Richard Hyrde, London, 1529?

Webster, John, *Complete Works*, ed. F.L. Lucas, London: Chatto & Windus, 1927, 4 vols.
Wind, Edgar, *Pagan Mysteries in the Renaissance*, London: Faber, 1968.

Index